The New MINI Performance Handbook

Jeffrey Zurschmeide

CarTech®

CarTech®
CarTech®, Inc.
39966 Grand Avenue
North Branch, MN 55056
Phone: 651-277-1200 or 800-551-4754
Fax: 651-277-1203
www.cartechbooks.com

© 2010 by Jeffrey Zurschmeide

All rights reserved. No part of this publication may be reproduced or utilized in any form or by any means, electronic or mechanical, including photocopying, recording, or by any information storage and retrieval system, without prior permission from the Author. All text, photographs, and artwork are the property of the Author unless otherwise noted or credited.

The information in this work is true and complete to the best of our knowledge. However, all information is presented without any guarantee on the part of the Author or Publisher, who also disclaim any liability incurred in connection with the use of the information.

All trademarks, trade names, model names and numbers, and other product designations referred to herein are the property of their respective owners and are used solely for identification purposes. This work is a publication of CarTech, Inc., and has not been licensed, approved, sponsored, or endorsed by any other person or entity.

Edit by Josh Brown
Layout by Sue Luehring

ISBN 978-1-61325-022-8
Item No. SA182P

Library of Congress Cataloging-in-Publication Data

Zurschmeide, Jeffrey.
 The new MINI performance handbook / by Jeffrey Zurschmeide.
  p. cm
 ISBN 978-1-934709-14-6
1. MINI-Cooper automobiles–Performance–Amateurs' manuals.
2. MINI-Cooper automobiles–Maintenance and repair–Amateurs' manuals. I. Title.

TL215.M465Z87 2009
629.28'722–dc22

2009040948

Printed in USA

Front Cover:
Pete Taylor drives his MINI Cooper S to victory in the SCCA National Championship Runoffs.

Title Page:
Anthony Savini and his MINI finished second at the SCCA Solo Nationals but first in the 2008 SCCA Pro-Solo series. (Photo courtesy Craig Wilcox)

Back Cover Photos

Top Left:
Autocrossers are perhaps the best suspension tuners in the world. Because their sport depends on razor-sharp car placement and precise handling, they know how to get the most out of their suspension. (Photo courtesy Craig Wilcox)

Top Right:
This well-dressed engine in Stephan McKeown's R53 includes an MSD coil pack, Dinan cold air intake, larger intercooler, and more that you can't see. And, of course, it's squeaky clean! (Photo courtesy Stephan McKeown)

Middle Left:
Dynamometers are a tremendous tool for performance tuning, but don't put too much stock in big numbers on the dyno. It's the incremental difference between changes that you care about.

Middle Right:
As on its predecessor, the R57 convertible top can be used open, closed, or just partially opened like a sunroof. It's rare to see one closed unless it's raining. (Photo courtesy Northwest Automotive Press Association)

Bottom Left:
The stock flywheel is held on with eight bolts. It installs in only one orientation, so pay attention when you fit up the new one. All eight bolts must line up.

Bottom Right:
Here is how the factory tool works on the rear brake caliper. The correct tool costs a couple hundred dollars, or you can buy a similar generic disc brake caliper tool set at your favorite discount tool store for about $20.

CONTENTS

Acknowledgments 4

Introduction 4

Chapter 1: A Brief History of the MINI 5
    Introducing Our Project Cars 6
    MINI Spotter's Guide 7
    Building Your MINI Right 19

Chapter 2: Increasing Engine Power 23
    How an Engine Does its Work 24
    The MINI Engine 25
    Engine Air Intake Upgrades 27
    Exhaust Component Upgrades 32
    Supercharger Upgrades 39
    Intercooler Upgrades 42
    Turbocharger Upgrades 43
    Related Turbo and Supercharger Upgrades 47
    Radiator and Oil Cooler Upgrades 48
    Naturally Aspirated Engine Upgrade 49
    Controlling the Engine: ECU Upgrades 50

Chapter 3: Improving Handling 54
    Suspension Terms and Concepts 55
    MINI Suspension Design 59
    Shock and Spring Upgrades 60
    Sway Bar Upgrades 67
    Suspension Brace and Bushings Upgrades 69
    Other Suspension Parts Upgrades 72
    Wheel and Tire Upgrades 74
    Alignment 78

Chapter 4: Improving Braking 81
    MINI Stock Brake System 81
    Upgrading Your Brakes 83

Chapter 5: Upgrading Transmission and Driveline 100
    Electronic Traction Control 100
    Manual Transmissions 102
    Limited Slip Differentials 103
    Clutch and Flywheel 112
    Agitronic Automatic Transmission 115

Chapter 6: Interior and Exterior Upgrades 116
    Adding Lights 116
    Gauges and Indicators 117
    Steering Wheels 120
    Short Shifters, Shift Knobs and Brake Handles 120
    Seats 124
    Safety Equipment 124
    Sound-Deadening Materials 125
    Roll Bars and Roll Cages 126
    Aerodynamic Devices 126

Chapter 7: MINIs in Competition 129
    Autocross 130
    Track Days 132
    Time Attack 133
    Hill Climb 136
    Amateur Racing 136
    Road Rally 139
    Rallycross 141
    Stage Rally 142
    Car Show Competition 142

Final Build Sheets 144
    Project R53 144
    Project R56 144

Source Guide 144

ACKNOWLEDGMENTS

This book would not have been possible without the cheerful assistance of George Mehallick at MINI-Madness; Jeff Perrin, Adam Taft, John Herring, John Leitl, and Jarid Perry at Alta Performance; Warren Gilliland and Cory Lamarra at The Brake Man; Al Hafner at ProMINI.com; Kellen Russell at Craven Speed; Barry Brazier and Peter DuPre at *MC2 Magazine;* Don Racine at MINI Mania and Gary Anderson, authors of *Motoring: Getting the Maximum From Your New MINI;* and expert MINI Mechanic Brandon Vlaew.

Special mention goes to Paul Aragon for the use of his R56 Cooper S as a test mule for R56 projects.

Most of all, I thank my daughter Kate for her good humor and my wife Jill for her patience, even when I stole her Cooper and modified it without her permission.

INTRODUCTION

As an automotive journalist, people often ask me for my favorite car of all those I've driven. I usually answer them by saying: "The Ferrari 612 Scaglietti is hands-down the best car I've ever driven. But if you mean cars that mere mortals can afford, my favorite is the car I bought to be my own daily driver—the MINI Cooper S."

Since its introduction in the 2002 model year, the "New MINI" has become a daily sight in every American city and town. The combination of sporty fun and practical, with a heavy helping of economical and reliable on the side, make the MINI a consistently popular choice. Now with a convertible option, the longer-wheelbase Clubman variant, and a John Cooper Works hot rod package, the adaptable little MINI can be customized to almost anyone's needs.

I believe a variety of opinions and experiences make a better guide. In the course of my work on this book I've talked with folks who know MINIs down to the last nut and bolt. This book is the result of extensive consultation with a great many of those subject matter experts. The experts I interviewed are quoted in this book and the project would have been impossible without them. Most of them sell, install, and maintain the products they talk about, and their contact information appears in the Source Guide.

This book is designed to give you necessary information as you consider various performance modifications and products available for your car. I have included some step-by-step projects for common performance enhancements that can be performed in a standard garage, but this is not a comprehensive repair or maintenance manual. If that's what you need, I recommend you get an official MINI factory shop manual for your car. In fact, I recommend that you get one of them no matter what. Also, most aftermarket parts come with installation instructions, and you should always follow those instructions.

This book contains snapshot overviews of a variety of successful, custom, high-performance MINIs, built for a wide range of purposes. These profiles show how all aspects of the car come together to enhance performance for a particular purpose, and to provide a model for you to consider as you plan and build your own ride.

In general I've avoided endorsing any particular brand of parts or any particular setup for a car. If your

The new MINI is one of the most popular cars on the road today because of it's performance, size, fuel economy, and good design. With a few easy projects, you can bump your MINI's performance to the next level and enjoy it even more. (Photo courtesy Northwest Automotive Press Association)

favorite manufacturer or a product is not mentioned by name, it's only because it would be impossible to mention everything available for the MINI today. Also, I have not personally tested every kind of brake, every kind of shock, or every kind of turbo. In each area, I simply chose a few representative products to show what's widely available on the market, and I personally installed or observed the installation of those parts to create the project procedures. All the products installed in this book are quality parts that I would use on my own car.

CHAPTER 1

A BRIEF HISTORY OF THE MINI

Few cars in the history of the world carry such a storied background as the original Mini. In the late 1950s, the British Motor Corporation (BMC) wanted a new, small, fuel-efficient car. The existing Morris Minor was outdated, and BMC needed something that could be produced inexpensively and sold in large numbers to Europeans.

Alexander "Alec" Issigonis was chief engineer for BMC, and the man who designed the Morris Minor in the 1940s. He accepted a challenge to design the next-generation small car for the company. He famously said, "Never copy the opposition," and then produced the revolutionary Mini design.

What made the Mini unique was not its transverse engine and front-wheel drive—SAAB had been producing cars that way for ten years. But the Mini design moved the wheels to the extreme corners of the vehicle, leaving more space in the passenger compartment and adding to the car's stability and handling. The Mini was also box-shaped, which offered more passenger and cargo space than prior designs. The Mini's 10-inch wheels and rubber cone suspension also helped save weight and space.

Virtually every front-wheel-drive hatchback since the original Mini was designed using those same principles. The Honda Civic, Volkswagen Rabbit, and numerous other small cars are all descendants of Issigonis' original design.

During its production run (and continuing to this day) the original Mini has been a huge success in racing, rallying, autocross, and any other motorsport in which it has been entered. The cars are iconic representations of Britain and have appeared in dozens of movies and TV shows. More recently, both old and new Minis are competitive in SCCA Club Racing, winning national

The original Mini was made from 1959 until 2000, but only a few were sold in the United States through the 1960s. Still, that was enough to create a fan base that has lasted to today.

The original Mini has had a legendary racing career that continues to this day. Old Minis and new Minis continue to be competitive in SCCA racing.

THE NEW MINI PERFORMANCE HANDBOOK

championships as recently as 2007. In autocross competition, the new MINI is dominant in both H stock and G Stock classes.

The original Mini was made in many countries and in many variations until 2000. The original Mini's 40-year production run with only minimal design changes is unique in the automotive industry. But starting in 1995, plans were started for a new Mini. Through the 1970s and 1980s, the British automobile industry went through tremendous turmoil, and by the mid-1990s, the Mini was being made by Rover Group, which was owned by BMW. The new company and its car was named MINI. The MINI was introduced at the Paris Auto Show in September of 2000 as a 2001-model-year car, and the last of the original Minis rolled off the line in October 2000.

Introducing Our Project Cars

Throughout this book you can see example MINIs that illustrate the range of possibilities for performance enhancement, but most of the step-by-step procedures for performance modification and parts installation were performed on just two cars: a 2005 R53 Cooper S and a 2008 R56 Cooper S. In the course of each project, we've enhanced the performance of these cars by at least 20 hp and improved handling, braking, and interior utility as well.

Jeff's 2005 R53 Cooper S

Jeff's MINI is a 2005 Cooper S in Hyper Blue with the Sport Package and Cold Weather Package. Dealer options include the iPod support adapter and white bonnet stripes. If it had a limited slip differential, it would be perfect.

The original Mini has been built in many countries. Some of the most collectible Minis are the cars built by Innocenti in Italy. This one was parked on the street in Padua in 2008.

Aftermarket modifications include:
- Alta cold-air intake
- Magnaflow cat-back exhaust
- MSD ignition upgrade
- Madness 15-percent-reduction supercharger pulley
- Texas Speedwerks springs
- Madness polyurethane engine and suspension bushings
- Madness strut tower reinforcements
- MINI Mania precision steering amplifiers
- PROMINI 15-mm wheel spacers
- Alta 19-mm rear sway bar
- Brake Man big-brake kit
- Craven Speed short shifter
- Stubby antenna
- E-brake handle
- PROMINI boost and oil pressure gauges
- Non-run-flat Kumho Ecsta tires
- Madness rally lights across the front grille
- PROMINI Wheel Stud Kit

Paul's 2008 R56 Cooper S

Paul's MINI was ordered in Chili Red with black roof and bonnet stripes, Premium Package, Sport Package, and Cold Weather Package.

Aftermarket modifications include:
- DDM Works cold-air intake system

This 2005 R53 Cooper S was factory stock when this book was started. It's definitely not stock now, and makes about 200 hp at the drive wheels. Most of the projects in this book were performed on this car.

This R56 was the test subject for projects related to the 2007-and-newer cars in this book. With just a few modifications, this car delivers performance well beyond the general run of the factory.

This is my wife's R50 Cooper. I stole it and modified it a couple times. She forgave me when she found out how much better it drives with a PROMINI strut tower bar and SuperSprint cat-back exhaust.

- Borla cat-back exhaust
- John Cooper Works Challenge turbocharger
- PIAA 17-inch wheels
- 3/4-inch lowering springs
- 22-mm rear sway bar

Jill's 2004 R50 Cooper

Among all the upgrades available for the Cooper S models, we chose to perform two key upgrades to this plain-Jane Cooper:

- PROMINI front strut tower bar, which greatly improved the car's steering response
- Supersprint cat-back exhaust, which gained well over 10 hp and a corresponding improvement in torque throughout the RPM range

With just these two simple modifications, the basic MINI can be transformed into a much more sporty package. (These two projects are described in detail in Chapter 2 and Chapter 3.)

MINI Spotter's Guide

There are only a few variations on the new MINI, but there are substantial differences you need to understand between the early (2002–2006) and later (2007-and-later) cars, as well as technical details on the differences between hardtop and convertible and Clubman models, and of course between the Cooper and Cooper S variants.

Anyone looking into MINIs soon hears people talking about their cars using the company's internal model designations—R50, R53, R56, and so on. These terms are used for two reasons: They sound cool and they are specific. If you say you've got a Cooper S, do you have the supercharged R53 or the turbocharged R56 version?

To help you understand the range of model options available, here's a rundown on the various models of MINI that have been sold in North America since 2002.

R50 MINI Cooper (2002-2006)

This is the basic MINI Cooper sold for the first five years MINI in America. This model has a 1.6-liter, single overhead cam (SOHC), 16-valve, fuel-injected engine that operates at a compression ratio of 10.6:1 and produces about 114 hp and 110 ft-lbs of torque. The engine allows the Cooper to turn a 0–60 time of about 8.5 seconds, and the car is governed to a top speed of 126 mph. Whether or not anyone has ever actually achieved that speed in an unmodified Cooper is an unanswered question.

The R50 Cooper uses front-wheel drive and a choice of 5-speed manual transmission or Continuously Variable Transmission (CVT). The CVT is very weak, and the early 5-speed "Midlands" transmissions sometimes wear out their bearings at 60,000 to 100,000 miles. In 2005, MINI updated the base Cooper 5-speed with a different transmission from Getrag.

The R50 Cooper weighs about 2,513 pounds ready to drive, and uses four-wheel disc brakes. The base Cooper was delivered with 15-inch alloy wheels. The R50 Cooper gets about 35 mpg on the highway and 28 in city driving. Combined real-world fuel economy is usually about 30 mpg.

Options may vary a bit from year to year, but three option packages were available on the R50 Cooper: The Premium Package included a glass sunroof, upgraded steering wheel, automatic climate control, and a trip computer. The Sport Package included Dynamic Stability Control (DSC), sport wheels, sport seats, fog lamps, and a rear spoiler. The Cold Weather Package included heated seats, heated mirrors, and heated windshield-washer fluid.

There were a number of individual options available, and you could assemble your Cooper to your own specifications. Coopers were offered with an expensive Navigation Package that displaced the large central speedometer, which was reduced in size and moved to the steering column.

If you're shopping for an R50 Cooper, look for sport seats. Based on

One of the first ways you can tell the R53 from the R56 at a glance is to look for the "'bustle"' bulge under the rear window of the R56. The older R50 and R53 cars have a smoother line down the back.

The base seats in the MINI are not very comfortable and don't hold you in place around corners. The optional sport seats (shown) are well worth the money whether you get them in cloth or in leather.

CHAPTER 1

unscientific observations, the base seats were not delivered on many cars because they were not very comfortable. The sport seats option cost about $270, so it was an inexpensive and obvious upgrade, and often led to the purchase of the Sport Package for the Cooper.

MINI did a good job on the heated seats, and if you live in the 90 percent of North America that sees cold winter mornings, you'll be glad to have those heaters. The Cold Weather Package was also a good deal at about $300, so many used Coopers on the market are so equipped.

Many Coopers were also sold with the Premium Package and its big glass sunroof. Be aware that this feature adds at least 100 pounds to the total vehicle weight. If you're running the air conditioning with a fully loaded car, you'll notice the performance difference.

R53 MINI Cooper S (2002-2006)

The R53 is the performance MINI Cooper S sold through the 2006 model year in North America. This model has a 1.6-liter, SOHC, 16-valve, fuel-injected, supercharged engine that produced about 161 hp through the 2004 model year, and 168 beginning in 2005. The early 2002–2004 models produced 155 ft-lbs of torque and 162 ft-lbs in 2005 and thereafter. The supercharger induction system included a top-mounted intercooler. Cooper S 0–60 time is about 6.9 seconds and the car is governed to 135 mph, which is still pretty optimistic. The base compression ratio of the S engine is reduced in the head design, which allows the boost from the supercharger to increase effective compression without endangering the engine.

The R53 MINI Cooper S uses front-wheel drive and a rugged 6-speed manual transmission. Starting in 2005, the automatic option on the Cooper S was introduced with a traditional 6-speed automatic with steering-mounted paddle shifters.

In 2005, several updates improved the Cooper S. All cars received the enhanced supercharger from the 2004 John Cooper Works (JCW) kit, a revised exhaust, and a new closer-ratio 6-speed manual transmission. Also beginning mid-year in 2005, a factory limited slip differential was available as an option.

The Cooper S is rated at 33 mpg on the highway and 24 mpg in the city, but real-world experience indicates that an average combined fuel economy is about 27 mpg.

The R53 weighs about 2,678 pounds ready to drive, and uses 4-wheel disc brakes. The Cooper S was delivered with 16-inch alloy wheels, but many received the 17-inch sport wheels instead. All Cooper S models received factory run-flat tires because there's no room to carry a spare.

The Cooper S option packages were fundamentally the same as the Cooper's. The Sport Package included 17-inch wheels, DSC, fog lamps, HID Xenon headlights, and headlight washers. The Cooper S came stock with sport seats, so the Xenon headlights were included in this Sport Package.

The Premium Package was the same as the Cooper's, with multi-function wheel, sunroof, and automatic climate control. The Cold Weather Package was also the same, including heated seats, mirrors, and washer jets.

The R53 Cooper S also had an available Gauge Package that included ammeter, water-temperature gauge and oil-temperature gauge in the center speedometer area. This reduced and displaced the speedometer to the steering column. The Navigation Package and Gauge Package were mutually exclusive.

Desirable packages and options on the R53 Cooper S included the Sport Package, Cold Weather Package, and of course, the limited slip differential in 2005 and 2006. For the ultimate

The 2002–2006 supercharged R53 Cooper S is the competition car of choice for hundreds of racers across the country. Out of the box, this car has the potential to win races in the hands of a competent driver. (Photo courtesy Dan Bryant)

A BRIEF HISTORY OF THE MINI

The MC40 was the first special-edition Cooper S to make an appearance in America. This was primarily a stickers-and-appearance package, but also included HID Xenon headlights and fog lights.

Adding a few aftermarket upgrades won't materially affect the market value of this car in the near term, but in 30 years you'll want this one to be bone stock for maximum collectability.

All of the MC40 cars carry the license number of the original Monte Carlo Rally winner.

R53 hot rod that's not a John Cooper Works edition, look for a 2005–2006 car with the Sport Package, no sunroof, and limited slip differential.

R53 Cooper S MC40 Special Edition (2004)

In 2004, the Monte Carlo Commemorative Package (MC40) was available, which included Chili Red paint and a white roof, replica stickers, and magnetic number plates matching the "37" car of Paddy Hopkirk in the Monte Carlo Rally. The Monte Carlo cars also came with a laundry list of other options, including DSC, carbon fiber dash, HID Xenon headlights, fog lights, rally lights, custom red and black leather sport seats, and of course a special plaque signed by Paddy Hopkirk himself.

R53 John Cooper Works Editions (2004–2006)

Beginning in 2004, MINI offered the JCW edition as a dealer-installed kit of upgrades to the R53 Cooper S. The kit included a lightly modified head, replacement supercharger with coated vanes, cat-back exhaust system, modified intake system, larger fuel injectors, 11-percent-reduction supercharger pulley, and a reflash on

One of the only reliable ways to identify a John Cooper Works car is by the special badges on the front grille and back of the car.

the engine management software. The JCW kit raised the R53 Cooper S power output to 197 hp in 2004, and cost about $5,000 installed.

For 2005, JCW kit power was boosted to 207 hp and the Cooper S received the same upgraded supercharger as the JCW.

In 2006, the JCW edition became a factory option, and included a limited slip differential and upgraded brakes with fixed calipers. The price rose to $6,300 for the package.

In Europe, a JCW package was available for the naturally aspirated Cooper. The kit included a ported head, cat-back exhaust, replacement air filter, and computer reflash. The kit raised the Cooper's horsepower to 126 and torque to 114 ft-lbs. This kit was available in North America starting in 2004, but few were ever sold.

R53 JCW GP Edition (2006)

To wind up the R53 MINI Cooper S line with a flourish, the automaker created 2,000 lightweight MINI Cooper S JCW GP cars custom-built by Italy's famous Bertone coachworks. These R53 Cooper S variants were bumped to 215 hp and 180 ft-lbs of torque. The GP version shaved about 85 pounds off the regular

The factory lightweight GP edition is the ultimate R53, made only in 2006. They made this one as light as possible—even pulling the rear seats.

CHAPTER 1

All JCW GP cars have the same paint scheme. Look for the GP on the back of the car, in the hood scoop, and the car's individual serial number over the driver's door.

The R56 Cooper uses the same body and chassis as the R56 Cooper S. Both have the same "bustle" under the rear window.

The R56 Cooper was introduced in 2007 and features a naturally aspirated version of the Peugeot/BMW collaboration engine also used in the R56 Cooper S.

The GP edition is the only Cooper ever to receive these wheels. You can easily see the red JCW brake calipers through the spokes.

Cooper S by deleting the air conditioner and eliminating the rear seat. The cars were also made without some of the sound-deadening insulation and included cast-aluminum rear trailing arms to save weight.

This edition also included a larger intercooler, strut tower bar, limited slip differential, custom Recaro sport seats, and the entire 2006 JCW package of upgrades. All GP cars were individually numbered, and painted in a custom color called "Thunder Blue," with a silver roof and red mirrors. They received unique wheels and an aggressive aerodynamics package including a special rear spoiler, air dam, underbody trays, and side cladding.

R56 MINI Cooper (2007+)

The most comprehensive model-year change for the MINI came in 2007 with the introduction of the R56 chassis. This model year saw tremendous changes in both the MINI Cooper and Cooper S, and both models received the same chassis designation.

Every body panel was changed at least a little bit on the R56, but the most noticeable change is the "bustle" where the hatchback bulges out beneath the rear window. The new car is more than 2 inches longer than the R50/R53 chassis.

The R56 Cooper still uses a naturally aspirated 1.6-liter, 16-valve engine, but it's a double overhead cam (DOHC) design atop an entirely different engine than the R50 used. The new engine features BMW's Valvetronic infinitely variable valve timing and produces 118 hp and 114 ft-lbs of torque. Factory 0–60 time on the R56 Cooper has been reduced to 8.5 seconds and the top speed governed to 126 mph with the manual transmission, and 118 mph with the automatic. The car's weight has been boosted to 2,546 with the manual transmission and a hefty 2,634 for the automatic. Fuel economy is rated at 37 highway and 24 city, and 32 mpg in combined driving.

One of the most notable changes is that the R56 Cooper now features a close-ratio 6-speed manual transmission or 6-speed automatic similar to the R56 Cooper S, but with different gear ratios and a 4.3:1 final drive ratio. A limited slip differential is still a factory option, as is a set of steering wheel paddle shifters for the automatic transmission.

The suspension of the R56 was also changed, and includes the aluminum components first seen on the JCW GP cars in 2006.

Inside, the R56 offers a telescoping steering wheel and a more stylized dash treatment. The signature MINI toggle switches changed their shape and the display for the stereo

A BRIEF HISTORY OF THE MINI

For a more rakish look, consider adding the factory Aero kit. This body kit provides you with a more aggressive-looking front bumper and under-bumper treatment plus different side skirts from the bottom of the front wheel wells to the rear wheels.

The 2007-and-later R56 Cooper S is a technologically sophisticated, yet easily modified car. It's less edgy than the R53, but delivers more power and features.

was moved to the central speedometer. MINI enthusiasts either love or hate the R56 interior compared to the R50. The key is also different; a lenticular device that fits into a slot in the dash, as compared to the traditional key in the R50.

Driving the R56 Cooper is much like its predecessor, but there's a "Sport" button that sharpens the electronic power steering and the electronic throttle response. One amusing feature is that you can change the color of the ambient glow-lights for evening driving.

Option packages for the R56 Cooper are substantially the same as for the previous generation. The Premium Package includes sunroof, automatic climate control, and a leather or wood steering wheel. The Sport Package includes Dynamic Traction Control, sport seats, bonnet stripes, front fog lights, rear spoiler, and 16-inch wheels. The Cold Weather Package is unchanged, featuring heated front seats, heated powerfold mirrors, and heated washer jets.

New for the R56 models is the Convenience Package, including Bluetooth hands-free phone support, an iPod/USB adapter for the stereo, rain-sensing wipers, a convenience key, auto-dimming mirror, and a universal garage door opener.

The R56 Cooper can also be purchased with several individual JCW options, including sway bars, springs and shocks, strut brace, aero kit, and a JCW brake package.

R56 MINI Cooper S (2007+)

The 2007 R56 Cooper S is the most changed model from the previous year. Instead of a belt-driven supercharger, the R56 Cooper S makes its power from a twin-scroll turbocharger. (More information on turbo design is provided in Chapter 2.)

The twin-scroll turbo sits atop the new DOHC, 16-valve, 1.6-liter engine. The Valvetronic variable valve timing used in the Cooper is incompatible with a turbocharged engine, so it has been omitted. The new engine uses direct injection,

There's absolutely nothing you can't do with a MINI Cooper.

THE NEW MINI PERFORMANCE HANDBOOK 11

like many of the latest-generation turbocharged gasoline engines from a variety of manufacturers. In this design, fuel is sprayed directly into the combustion chamber, rather than somewhere in the intake path. Direct injection allows for finer control of mixture and timing, which aids in fuel economy, emissions, and power output.

The R56 Cooper S engine delivers 172 hp and 177 ft-lbs of torque. The twin-scroll turbo and direct injection deliver that level of torque from about 1,600 to 5,000 rpm. Additionally, when you push the accelerator to the floor, the R56 engine computer allows the turbo to boost the engine to 192 ft-lbs of torque for up to 15 seconds.

The R56 Cooper S goes from 0–60 mph in 6.7 seconds, and is governed to a top speed of 139 mph. The R56 S weighs in at 2,634 pounds with manual transmission and 2,688 with the optional 6-speed automatic. Fuel economy is 34 on the highway, 26 in the city, with an average of about 29 mpg. The automatic transmission costs you 2 mpg.

Option packages for the R56 Cooper S are slightly different from the R56 Cooper. Sport seats are standard equipment. The Sport Package includes HID Xenon headlights, 17-inch wheels, and white turn signal indicators in addition to the usual bonnet stripes, traction control, and front fog lights. The Convenience Package on the S adds auto-dimming headlights. The Cold Weather and Premium packages are the same as delivered on the R56 Cooper.

Among the desirable options on the R56 Cooper S is a 17-inch (denoting required wheel size) brake package that features fixed calipers and drilled and slotted rotors. This is

The new factory R56 JCW cars feature a high-performance fixed front brake caliper. Smooth-faced vented rotors are the choice of serious racers everywhere.

comparable to an aftermarket "big-brake kit," but comes with a factory warranty from MINI. A factory warranty is always a good thing.

You can also get various JCW suspension components and sway bars, wheels up to 18 inches, extra gauges on the steering column, and a shift light as factory options.

R56 John Cooper Works (2007+)

The JCW special performance edition followed the 2007 change from R53 to R56 in the Cooper S hardtop. However, the R52 Convertible Cooper S retained the older supercharged engine through the 2008 model year.

R56 Cooper S buyers can purchase a dealer-installed JCW kit that boosts performance to 189 hp and 184 ft-lbs of torque. The R56 overboost feature is not affected by this kit and temporarily raises torque to 199 ft-lbs. The JCW kit includes a replacement intake, exhaust, and ECU reflash.

The factory-produced R56 JCW cars arrived in 2008, producing 208 hp and 192 ft-lbs of torque. The R56 overboost feature is included and temporarily raises engine torque to 207 ft-lbs. Top speed is governed to

The R52 MINI Cooper convertible took the MINI community by storm in 2005, and remains a popular option. Just be sure that you try backing up with the top closed before you buy one!

147 mph and accelerates from 0–60 in 6.2 seconds. Even with the higher output engine and the increased weight at 2,701 pounds, JCW fuel economy is identical to the R56 Cooper S at 34 highway, 26 city, and 29 average.

The JCW edition is available only with a manual transmission, and includes upgraded 12.4-inch front brakes with Brembo fixed calipers and 11.0-inch rear brakes. The JCW comes with traction control, limited slip differential, electronic differential locking, upgraded shock absorbers and springs, and an aero kit.

For an extra $500, you can buy a set of larger, stiffer sway bars, but these are not included as standard in the JCW edition.

For the 2009 model year, celebrating 50 years since the first MINI hit the road, the factory produced the JCW World Championship 50 edition. Just 250 of these cars were made, based on a 2009 R56 JCW. Power is raised to 211 hp, but torque stays at 192 ft-lbs. As with previous commemorative editions, most of the modifications are in the bodywork and interior. The car is painted in a unique shade of green, with

The R52 chassis can accommodate a Cooper and a Cooper S (even JCW) variation. A convertible Cooper S is the best summer car seen around, because you can carry a little bit of stuff in the back seat.

stripes and roof in MINI's popular Pepper White. Custom wheels are also part of the package, along with numerous carbon fiber components. Good luck finding one.

R52 MINI Cooper Convertible (2005–2008)

The R52 MINI Cooper Convertible was introduced for the 2005 model year. Like the R50 Cooper of the same year, the convertible had a 1.6-liter, SOHC, 16-valve, fuel-injected engine that operated at a compression ratio of 10.6:1 and produced 115 hp and 110 ft-lbs of torque. This engine package was continued through the end of the 2008 model year. The R52 Convertible offered a choice of 5-speed manual transmission or the CVT.

The R52 Convertible got about 35 mpg on the highway and 28 in city driving. Combined real-world fuel economy was usually about 30 mpg.

Option packages on the R52 Convertible are necessarily slightly different from the hardtop version. The Premium Package on the hardtop is built around the glass sunroof, but on the convertible it adds the Chrome Line option in addition to the upgraded steering wheel, automatic climate control, and a trip computer. The Sport and Cold Weather packages were unchanged.

If you're shopping for an R52 Cooper Convertible, look for heated sport seats and the upgraded Harmon-Kardon stereo. Both of these features are a godsend in a convertible.

Before you buy any MINI convertible, be sure to test-drive it with the top up, as you would use the car in wet weather. Rearward visibility in any R52 is extremely limited, especially in the lane-changing blind spot. That's why MINI put backup radar on all of these cars!

R52 MINI Cooper S Convertible (2005–2008)

The R52 Cooper S Convertible was introduced at the same time as the R52 Cooper, and tracks the development of the R53 hardtop Cooper S. But while the hardtop Cooper S changed to the R56 body style and turbocharged engine for the 2007 model year, the R52 Cooper S convertible was delivered with the supercharged engine through the 2008 model year.

The R52 Convertible Cooper S weighed in at 2,877 pounds and offered the same 1.6-liter, SOHC, 16-valve, fuel-injected, supercharged engine that produced 168 hp and 162 ft-lbs of torque. R52 Cooper S buyers had their choice of 6-speed manual transmission or 6-speed automatic with steering-mounted paddle shifters.

The R52 Cooper S Convertible was rated at 34 mpg on the highway and 26 mpg in the city, and 29 mpg on average.

The R52 Cooper S convertible option packages were fundamentally the same as the R52 Cooper's. The Premium Package was the same as the Cooper's, substituting chrome for the sunroof, and offering a multi-function wheel and automatic climate control.

Desirable packages and options on the R52 Cooper S convertible included the Sport Package, Cold Weather Package, and limited slip differential.

The R52 Cooper S was also available with the JCW edition modifications as a dealer-installed option in 2005 and a factory option in 2006.

R57 MINI Cooper Convertible (2009+)

Beginning in the 2009 model year, the convertible MINI Cooper was updated to second-generation R56 specifications, including the updated engine. The new Convertible

CHAPTER 1

The R57 is the convertible version of the R56. It is available as a Cooper or Cooper S, and continues the tradition of convertible MINI fun.

As on its predecessor, the R57 convertible top can be used open, closed, or just partially opened like a sunroof. It's rare to see one closed unless it's raining. (Photo courtesy Northwest Automotive Press Association)

and includes sport seats and electronic traction control, among other features.

The poor rearward visibility of the R52 was improved for the R57 convertibles, including a larger rear window and smaller cloth section in the rear corners, but if you're test-driving on a sunny day, you should still drive a while and try backing up with the top completely raised.

R57 MINI Cooper S Convertible (2009+)

For the 2009 model year, the R52 Cooper S was upgraded to the R56 engine and chassis package and the result was the R57 Cooper S. The engine is the same as the R56 Cooper S, delivering 172 hp and 177 ft-lbs of torque. The twin-scroll turbo and direct injection deliver that level of torque from about 1,600 to 5,000 rpm. Additionally, when you push the accelerator to the floor, the R56 engine computer allows the turbo to boost the engine torque to 192 ft-lbs for up to 15 seconds.

The R57 S weighs in at 2,855 pounds and turns in a 0–60 time of 7.0 seconds, with a governed top speed of 138 mph. Fuel economy on the R57 is 34 highway, 26 city, and 29 average with the manual transmission. Automatic drivers sacrifice 2 mpg.

Option packages for the R57 Cooper S are slightly different from the R56 Cooper S hardtop. Sport seats are standard equipment. The Sport Package includes HID Xenon headlights, 17-inch wheels, and white turn-signal indicators in addition to the usual bonnet stripes, traction control, and front fog lights. The Convenience Package adds auto-dimming headlights to the basic list from the R57 Cooper. The Cold Weather and Premium

designation is R57. The car weighs 2,745 pounds, or 2,822 with the automatic transmission, and offers the same 118 hp and 114 ft-lbs of torque as the R56 Cooper. Performance is also comparable, with 0–60 time of 8.9 seconds and a 124 mph top speed (119 mph with the automatic transmission).

Fuel economy on the R57 Cooper Convertible is 36 highway, 28 city, and 32 average, and 2 mpg less for the automatic transmission cars.

As with all the convertible models, the Premium option package for the R57 substitutes the chrome package for the sunroof. The Sport Package upgrades the wheels to 16 inches packages are the same as delivered on the R56 Cooper S hardtop, except that the sunroof is replaced with chrome line trim.

Among the desirable options on the R57 Cooper S is a 17-inch (denoting required wheel size) brake package that features fixed calipers and drilled and slotted rotors. A limited slip differential is still a $500 option.

You can also obtain a variety of optional JCW suspension components and sway bars, wheels up to 18 inches, extra gauges on the steering column, and a shift light as factory options.

R55 MINI Cooper Clubman (2008+)

To answer the demand for a MINI with a little more legroom in the back, MINI developed the Clubman extended-wheelbase car. The Clubman name had previously been given to an extended variant of the original MINI, so the name was in keeping with MINI traditions.

The Clubman offers a number of changes from the standard R56 MINI Cooper. The rear hatchback is replaced with a pair of "barn doors" that hinge on the outer edges of the car. This places a central vertical bar in the driver's rearview field of vision, but the obstruction is not critical. The Clubman also includes a third side door on the passenger side, which opens facing the existing side door to create a large space for access to the rear seat.

The Clubman is 9.6 inches longer than the R56 MINI Cooper and Cooper S. The wheelbase is 3.2 inches longer, and 2.5 inches is given over to legroom for the rear-seat passengers. The rest of the space is used to provide a more spacious cargo area behind the rear seats.

As with all normally aspirated MINI Coopers, there's not a lot of power under 4,000 rpm on the basic Clubman. The turbocharged Cooper S engine is much better suited to the Clubman body because of its greater torque and higher horsepower throughout its range. The Clubman is several hundred pounds heavier than the smaller Coopers, and you can really feel it. The Clubman with a manual transmission weighs 2,723 pounds, or 2,800 pounds with the automatic. The basic Clubman offers 118 hp and 114 ft-lbs of torque. You will do a lot of shifting, especially if you need to pass someone on the freeway.

Yet for all its weight, the Cooper Clubman pulls from 0–60 in 8.9 seconds, and MINI claims a top speed of 125 mph, or 120 with the automatic transmission.

Fuel economy on the Clubman is 28 in the city and 36 on the highway (2 mpg lower with the automatic), so a Clubman makes a great replacement for a larger crossover SUV or any other bigger car that guzzles the gas without providing a whole lot more utility. In real-world combination driving, I have seen a solid 35 mpg average from a Cooper Clubman with a manual transmission, which is better than a lot of hybrids can get.

The Clubman has a full slate of option packages, including the Convenience Package, which includes a leather multi-function steering wheel, universal garage door opener, keyless entry, auto-dimming rearview mirror, and automatic wipers and headlights. The Premium Package includes the glass sunroof, but also includes a better stereo and automatic climate control on the Clubman. The Sport Package and Cold Weather Package are the same as in all R56-based Coopers.

The Aero kit is available for all R56-based cars, and it looks better than any aftermarket body kit on this R57 Cooper S.

For the 2008 model year, MINI brought out the extended-wheelbase Clubman. For families with growing kids, this car was a godsend. Be aware that a Clubman is heavier than a standard MINI, though. You may want to upgrade to the S or JCW.

Another Clubman feature is this third door to provide better access to the back seat. This car can carry four adults in reasonable comfort.

R55 MINI Cooper S Clubman (2008+)

The Cooper S Clubman was introduced for the 2008 model year, and it's not a stretch to say that this is the Clubman you must test-drive before you buy. The extra power of the turbocharged R56 engine makes the Clubman S a joy to drive.

The R56 engine offers 172 hp and 177 ft-lbs of torque. Additionally, the temporary overboost feature raises the engine torque output to 192 ft-lbs for up to 15 seconds. That's handy, because the Clubman S is the heaviest of all the MINI Coopers—tipping the scales at a hefty 2,855 pounds with the manual transmission, or 2,900 pounds with the automatic transmission.

The Clubman S goes from 0–60 mph in 7.0 seconds (7.2 seconds with the automatic), and is governed to a top speed of 139 mph (137 with the automatic). Fuel economy comes in at 34 on the highway, 26 in the city, with an average of about 29 mpg. The automatic transmission costs you 2 mpg.

The driving experience on the Clubman S is very good, yet different from its standard-length siblings. A standard-size MINI is a very lively car; with its wide stance and short wheelbase, it loves to turn but has a tendency to get pulled along in the studded-tire troughs on the freeway. The Clubman S feels more solid on the road, but sacrifices some of the lively handling in the turns. Yet this is only in comparison to a regular MINI—compared to just about any other car on the road, the Clubman S is an absolute giggle to drive.

Like the Cooper Clubman, the Clubman S comes with a barn-door rear access, more rear legroom, a reverse third door on the passenger side for rear-seat area access, and a larger cargo area. Also, as with the naturally aspirated Clubman, the long wheelbase on the Clubman S makes for a quick, yet stable platform. If you're shopping Clubman, you really need the S version to keep the "sport" in the world's best sport utility vehicle.

Option packages for the Clubman S are on par with other 2008+ models. The Convenience Package includes a leather multi-function steering wheel, universal garage door opener, keyless entry, auto-dimming rearview mirror, and automatic wipers and headlights. The Premium Package includes the glass sunroof, upgraded stereo, and automatic climate control. The Sport Package on the Clubman S includes 17-inch wheels and HID Xenon headlights.

R55 Clubman S John Cooper Works Edition (2008+)

One of the advantages of a common platform for the entire MINI line is that performance parts fit as well on the Clubman as they do on the hardtop or convertible. So it was a no-brainer for MINI to offer the JCW options on the Clubman S.

The JCW edition of the Clubman S weighs 2,888 pounds—almost the heaviest new MINI ever made—so it makes good use of the 208 hp and 192 ft-lbs of torque from the turbocharged engine in the JCW configuration. The overboost feature on the engine still works, boosting torque to 207 ft-lbs briefly on acceleration. Similarly, the 12.4-inch front brakes with fixed calipers and 11-inch rear brakes come in handy.

The JCW Clubman does 0–60 in 6.5 seconds and is governed to a top speed of 147 mph. Fuel economy is still a thrifty 34 highway, 26 city, and combined average of 29 mpg.

Like all JCW cars in the modern era, the JCW Clubman S comes with traction control, limited slip

The Clubman you want is the Cooper S version. The turbocharged engine has enough power to move the Clubman the way you want your MINI to move, and the longer wheelbase makes the Clubman more stable on the road.

Of course, the factory also produced a John Cooper Works edition of the Clubman. With the same fixed front brake calipers as the hardtop, this is a great family car that wins races.

Look for the little JCW logo on the back of the Clubman, just like on the hardtops.

The MINI Cooper E was one of the first all-electric vehicles on the road in America. The pilot program leased cars in Los Angeles and New York.

differential, electronic differential locking, upgraded shock absorbers and springs, and an aero kit. Heavier sway bars are available as an option.

All option packages for the 2008+ Clubman JCW are the same as those offered for the Clubman S of the same year.

MINI Cooper E

The MINI Cooper E is a battery/electric version of the MINI. Currently it is available under a lease evaluation program exclusively in New York and Los Angeles, but it is likely to become more widely available in years to come.

The Cooper E is based on the basic R56 Cooper chassis, but incorporates several significant differences in addition to the obvious lack of an internal-combustion engine. The Cooper E lost the back seat to hold the sizable battery packs, and the brakes are made to regenerate electricity for the batteries as you slow down.

The transmission in the Cooper E is a direct-drive unit without gears. This is distinct from a continuously variable design as used by the original two-pedal Coopers—the direct drive is simply a reduction gear mated directly to the electric motor.

Other notable differences in the Cooper E include the charge indicator, which lives on top of the steering column where the tachometer generally sits. There's also the plug interface, predictably located under the "gas cap." Finally, there's the exhaust pipe, which isn't there. It's no surprise that there's no exhaust, but it's still something of a mind bender when you notice that the MINI's signature little chrome tip that looks like the bottom of a beer can isn't there. MINI used the rear bumper cover from the R56 Cooper S and put a plastic cover over the exhaust area.

Another critical difference between the Cooper E and a gas-engined car is that an electric car is very nearly silent in its operation. But apart from the lack of engine noise and exhaust tips, someone driving next to you would never know you're not driving a regular MINI.

Driving the Cooper E is a different experience than piloting a hybrid. Where a hybrid takes off and then kicks in the gasoline engine, all of the power runs through a traditional transmission. With its direct drive, the Cooper E simply takes off—and takes off fast! Electric motors are renowned for offering maximum torque at 0 rpm, so the off-the-line performance of the Cooper E is comparable to the Cooper S.

The electric engine in the Cooper E is rated at 204 hp and 162 ft-lbs of torque, but the Cooper E also weighs more, with a curb weight of 3,230 pounds. Still, the company says it'll do 0–60 in 8.4 seconds and has a top speed of 95 mph.

But as you drive the Cooper E, the first thing you notice is that the "gas pedal" feels different—it's a speed selector. That distinction is easy to feel, but difficult to describe. In a gasoline-powered car, stepping on the throttle increases the fuel and air fed to the engine, generally returning more horsepower and torque, which causes the engine to run faster; or the additional fuel keeps the engine from losing speed under greater load, such as when you're climbing a hill. But in the electric Cooper, changing the accelerator position does not vary the torque of the engine, it simply changes how fast the engine runs. So when you hit cruising speed, if you back off the throttle as you would with a conventional engine, the Cooper E slows down immediately. There's no "cruising throttle" position, so you just have to learn to hold the accelerator at the speed you want.

In addition to the accelerator, the brakes on the Cooper E feel different. As you transition from the accelerator to the brake, the car's already slowing down more than a gas-engined car just by virtue of withdrawing the accelerator input. But when you step on the brake, you're not initiating any friction from the brakes at first. What you feel when you apply the brakes is a smooth slowing based on the car kicking in a set of generators attached to each wheel. Then, at the last moment, the friction brakes kick in and there's a noticeable change in pedal feel. Hybrids such as the Toyota Prius also use this technique to regenerate electricity. It's a bit unnerving until you get used to it.

As you accelerate and brake, you can watch the new gauge mounted on your steering column (where the tachometer would be on a normal MINI). This gauge shows you the state of battery charge and the trip computer tells you how far you can go before you need to charge up. If you lay into the throttle, you can watch the gauge drop, but then it comes back a bit when you apply the brakes.

Recharging the MINI Cooper E from 0 to 100 percent takes about 24 hours on 110-volt house current, or about 3 to 4 hours if you can allocate a 220-volt stove or clothes-dryer circuit. With a full charge you can drive the Cooper E about 150 miles.

Foreign Market Cars—MINI Cooper One and MINI Cooper D

From time to time, people talk about the MINI Cooper D, especially if they've been to Europe recently. Over there, the Cooper D is equipped with a 1.6-liter, turbocharged diesel engine, and they are everywhere. The diesel MINI makes a respectable 108 hp, but its torque is 191, about the same as the Cooper S. The interesting thing about the Cooper D is that it gets about 64 mpg from that little turbo-diesel engine, while still achieving a 0–60 time of about 10 seconds flat. Europeans also have the option of the MINI One with a 1.4-liter or 1.6-liter gasoline engine, making about 95 hp. For 2009, Europeans can also get a MINI One D as a low-budget diesel option, and the One and D are available in the Clubman body as well.

In Europe, one of the most popular MINI models is the diesel-engined Cooper D. They're everywhere you look, and with European fuel prices, the 60-mpg Cooper D delivers. Performance is on par with the MINI Cooper.

Instead of a tachometer, the Cooper E gives you a charge meter on the steering column.

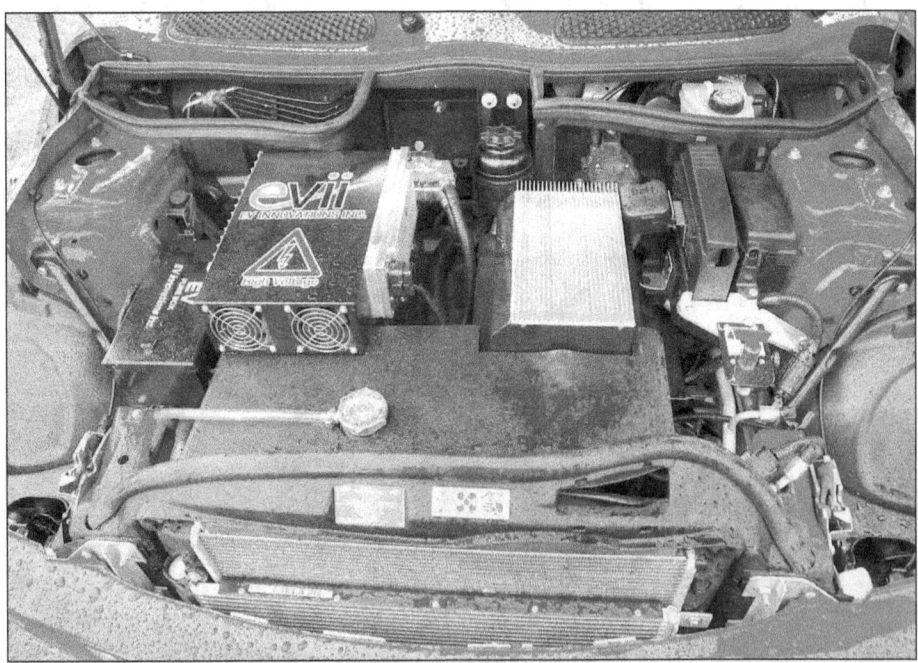

This Cooper has been converted to electric operation. It uses a water-cooled system to keep the electric motor from overheating. You can plug it into house current to recharge the lithium-ion batteries.

The Next MINIs

As this book goes to press, rumors and photos are circulating about a two-seat MINI speedster convertible; a sleek, rounded MINI coupe; and a larger, taller, MINI SAV (sports activity vehicle). The artist renderings of the new cars look great for concept cars, but whether we'll see any of these on the road is an open question. The SAV version is a full four-door with a raised stance and all-wheel drive (AWD), based on the concept shown at the 2008 Paris Auto Show. The Coupe and Speedster concepts were unveiled at the 2009 Frankfurt Auto Show, and MINI announced its intention to build at least the Coupe for public purchase.

Whether any or all of these prototypes comes to market, one thing seems clear: If MINI can put an AWD transmission and drivetrain into a crossover concept, it can put AWD into every model. And wouldn't that be fun?

Building Your MINI Right

MINIs have always been a car that owners would personalize. From painting a flag on the rectangular roof to all-out performance modification, MINIs have been customized since the beginning. But the notion of building and personalizing your ride is a tradition that goes back to the very first vehicle. I have no doubt that some ancient Egyptian once looked at his neighbor's chariot and said, "You know, if I used lighter wood and narrower spokes, I bet my ride could go faster and turn better than his." The rest, as they say, is history.

Throughout that history, we've learned a few things about going fast, staying in control, and the need to stop. We've also learned a few things about the dangers of fiddling with the design that the manufacturer decided was good, after a lot of testing. Stepping out of the safety zone and modifying your car means taking responsibility for the changes you make and the effect those changes have on performance, safety, and longevity.

There's an old saying in racing: "Speed, low cost, and longevity—pick any two." I've never seen that saying disproved, but a modern MINI comes as close as any car ever built to having all three. Still, stories of blown motors, broken transmissions, and cooked brakes are common, and you have to understand that possibility before you start. When you exceed the power and the stress tolerance that the engineers designed into the car, you're going to break things from time to time. Only a chump tries to blame the manufacturer when his customized hot rod breaks.

Here are some tried-and-true steps you can take to have fun and get a good outcome when modifying your car. Give them careful consideration before you start.

Step One: Play Safe

Safety must always be a primary concern when you're working on your car. I knew a guy who died when his car fell on him. He owned a set of jack stands but didn't use them that day, probably because it was just a quick little job. His ten-year-old daughter was the one who found him. Get yourself a set of good jack stands and a quality large-size floor jack and use them every time.

Similarly, be smart when you're making changes to your car. Don't go out and drive hard on brand-new parts or brand-new work. Have other people check your work whenever possible. Even professionals make mistakes from time to time—people leave nuts untightened, forget to

If you start changing the performance characteristics of your MINI, you have to be ready to take responsibility when things break. Racers understand this, but street-performance enthusiasts break parts just as often. (Photo courtesy Craig Wilcox)

adjust new parts, and leave fluids unfilled. Any of these mistakes may happen to you, and if you play with cars long enough something will happen to you, probably multiple times. At best these mistakes are embarrassing, usually they are expensive; at worst they can be dangerous or lethal.

The lesson is to be smart and play safe, and you'll have a good time.

Step Two: Learn About Your Car

You need to read and learn before you whip out your wrench or whip out your checkbook. The world is full of people who have spent a lot of money on their cars only to find that they've got a ride that is slower and uglier than when they started. The final tragedy is that they've cut up so much of the original car that they can never get it back to stock.

It pays to do your homework. Learn what's available for your car today and what fits on your particular model, because this book started getting stale the minute it went to the printer, and new products come out every day. Also, learn from what others have done before you. You can get a full shop manual for your year and model from Bentley for under $100. Your local MINI specialty shop will have valuable information and expertise for you. Enthusiast publications such as *MC2 Magazine* keep you up to date on new products and developments. Finally, public Internet forums such as North American Motoring and others are a great resource.

Step Three: Understand What You're Doing and Why

Once you know what's available, sit down and go over what you want your car to do for you. If you're looking at competition, make sure you've got the current rules in front of you. The worst thing you can do is show up to race with some minor modification that just put you in the "unlimited" class in an otherwise-stock vehicle.

Do you want to design your MINI for supreme handling for autocross competition? Do you want to enter hill climbs or drive on a race track? Or do you just want to look great, sound hot, and hit some car shows this summer? When you know what you really want to do, you can make a plan to get there.

The Japanese have a concept called *"Jinba Ittai,"* which translates as "horse and rider are one." What that means is that your car should be built so that it functions smoothly and comfortably, in harmony with you as the driver. If you overdo one aspect of a car and neglect another, you'll have problems. Ask anyone who ever built a

Racers spend a great deal of time and effort to make their cars as safe as possible. Make sure your work habits are also as safe as possible.

If you want an edge on the race track or on the street, the best way to start is by doing your homework. (Photo courtesy Dan Bryant)

These brakes look great, but they cost real money to buy and install. Take your time and make good use of your budget and you'll get a car that's a joy to drive.

really fast car, and never thought about his brakes! As you consider, plan, and build your car, think about balance and *Jinba Ittai*.

One of the most common mistakes people make when building a performance car is they try to make a car that's excellent for two (or more) very different purposes. Trust me, a performance rally car isn't going to be any good at an autocross, and a really pumped racing car makes a terrible daily driver. If you try to split the difference between two radical applications, you will end up with a car that isn't particularly good at anything. Get your vision and your budget together and build your car to do one thing really well, or build it to do everything pretty well.

When you know what you want to do and you understand the rules, you can usually come up with a comprehensive shopping list. That's where this book is designed to help you, by going over many common modifications people make and the major options on the market. You can read what's involved in a given modification before you decide to dive in yourself, take it to a pro, or leave that part on the shelf.

Step Four: Define Goals and Objectives

You need to be realistic about what you can afford and what you plan to do with your car. Modifying your car always costs more than you expect. Double your estimate and it'll

Great performance enhancements like this front-mounted intercooler on an R53 Cooper S can put you right into the top competition classes, so check before you turn a wrench.

still cost more than you expected. So make an accurate budget and realize that Rome wasn't built in a day, and neither will your car be done next weekend, or next month. That's why you see so many people driving around with half-finished cars.

My suggestion is that you start with a notebook. I'm a fully gadget-enabled modern guy, but I still use a paper notebook for each project car I have. The notebook stays in the car and I use it to log changes I make and results I notice. Some people prefer a spreadsheet or a blog—use whatever works for you. The point is to get into the habit of logging what you've done and the results you saw. The more objective data (lap times, dyno sheets, and so on) you can get, the better your log will be.

For most people, the car they're modifying is also the car they drive to work every day. There's usually not a lot of downtime available in the car's schedule. And some people aren't handy with a wrench, so take this to heart: If you've never done serious work on your car before, upgrading the brakes or swapping the turbo on your daily workmobile is a bad way to start.

Divide your shopping list into functional areas: Engine, Transmission, Suspension, Brakes, Interior, and so on. (This book is divided into chapters on that basis to help you.) In each functional area, list the things you want to do and the price of each item you need. Don't forget labor costs, gaskets, and fluids. If you're doing the work yourself, be sure to account for the cost of tools you need to buy.

With a good shopping list in your hands, and a total budget that will probably surprise you, it's time to prioritize.

Most new builders start with cosmetics. This is only natural but I think it's backward for a performance car. In general I like to improve stopping and handling before I put money into the engine, and I leave cosmetics for last. Who wants to scratch or dent an expensive paint job when a wrench slips?

With your itemized and prioritized list of modifications, you should be able to make a budget and a schedule for work that fits your finances and your calendar. Don't sweat it too much if you get behind on the schedule—everyone does. Right now the trick is to enjoy the journey as much as the destination.

Step Five: Have Fun and Don't Overextend Yourself

One key to a successful performance build is to make sure you reward yourself from time to time. There's nothing as satisfying in a project as being able to tell the difference when you've made a change. So schedule your modifications to make sure that you get a noticeable goodie from time to time. Maybe that means putting in the racing seats before the urethane bushings, but that's OK if it keeps your interest in the project.

There's a trap out there that you have to keep in mind, because it can grab you and cause no end of pain. The trap springs when you become financially overextended. The world is full of cars for sale where the owner has $25,000 in receipts and is looking for $10,000 or best offer by next weekend because he has to pay the mortgage. Don't be that unhappy person if you can help it. It's worse if your car is half-done, because if you can sell it at all, it's probably worth less than when you started.

The truth about building custom cars is that unless you find a nice, cheap, low-miles all-original 427 Cobra in a barn somewhere and take it to a big-time auto auction, you're not going to make a profit building and then selling your car. You're not even going to get your cash expenditures back out of it, so don't view this hobby as an investment. There's no reason to think that the person who buys your car will even think any of your modifications are worth keeping. For your own protection, you should view this process as building yourself a unique car that you customized for your own tastes and no one else's.

Finding a group of like-minded people in your area will help you keep your project going. The Internet is a nice tool for learning and discussion, but folks on the other side of the country can't help you change your brakes, or give you a ride to pick up your car from the mechanic. A local club is also a good way to get access to specialty tools. If one member has an engine hoist, then everyone has an engine hoist, and you can spend your budget on a tool that no one else has yet. Treat your club right, and you'll always have help when you need it.

The last thing to say about having fun and sticking with the project is that you should make sure that the car stays drivable, registered, and insured as much of the time as possible. Nothing will kill your enthusiasm for a project car as fast as spending money that just disappears under a tarp in the garage. Keep yourself behind the wheel to keep the rewards of your project coming back to you, and that will keep your enthusiasm strong.

CHAPTER 2

INCREASING ENGINE POWER

An internal-combustion engine is a marvelous piece of technology. It runs, for years in most cases, under some very challenging conditions. Using pump gas that would have destroyed the engines our parents had in the 1950s and 1960s, our street cars pollute less, get more miles per gallon, and make unbelievable horsepower and torque. For the most part, modern engines run longer, smoother, more reliably, and produce more power per cubic centimeter of displacement than any mass-produced engines ever sold to the public before.

"There's no substitute for cubic inches," A. J. Foyt said famously, and he was right to a point. But you can make a little 1.6-liter MINI engine into a powerhouse and still run it on pump gas. Modern technology such as BMW's Valvetronic infinitely variable valve timing in a naturally aspirated engine, or a turbocharged or supercharged engine, with real-time engine management based on data from multiple sensors gives the modern tuner a distinct advantage over the shade-tree hot rodder of days gone by. The tradeoff is that the shade-tree mechanic could sit and twiddle three or four screws on a carburetor until the car ran right. Today, we don't have that option. It takes the right equipment, software, and knowledge to make reliable power.

This chapter takes a look at the engine components along the combustion path. At its most basic level, an internal-combustion engine is an air pump. Air comes in the front, and goes out the back. We'll examine how air is sucked in through the intake and air filter and pulled onward through the turbocharger or supercharger, then pushed through

This well-dressed engine in Stephan McKeown's R53 includes an MSD coil pack, Dinan cold air intake, larger intercooler, and more that you can't see. And, of course, it's squeaky clean! (Photo courtesy Stephan McKeown)

the intercooler to the intake manifold and the combustion chambers. Then, we'll follow the exhaust as it makes its way through the manifold (or "header"), through the turbo again (if so equipped), down through the catalytic converters, and finally out the tailpipe.

How an Engine Does its Work

There are a bewildering array of products out there that claim better flow, more pounds per square inch (PSI) of boost, a cooler intake charge, and generally *more power*—which is what you're after. There are replacement ECUs and software reflashes, cold-air intake systems, upgraded turbochargers, and bigger exhaust pipes.

The main thing to remember is that all of the components in a car's engine function as a system. And because an engine is a system based on the flow of gases, the tightest point in the system generally governs the total output. The classic demonstration is to attempt to breathe through a drinking straw while running on a treadmill. What this means in real terms is that you may see an incremental improvement in power by relieving a restrictive component in the system, but real power gains require thoughtful modification to the entire system for the most efficient flow and greater energy output.

The Science of Combustion

A tablespoon of gasoline and a quart of air have a finite amount of energy potential. We can change that potential into different forms of energy such as heat, motion, and light by putting the fuel and air into an internal-combustion engine. We can theoretically create perfectly efficient engines and drivetrains, but we can never get more energy out of that combination of gas and air than the individual elements hold. So to make more power in our cars, we have to put more of those elements through the system, and make the system as efficient as possible.

Inefficiency can include such flaws as not burning all of the fuel we put into the combustion chamber —these are the "unburned hydrocarbons" that are measured in many emissions tests. This happens when the air/fuel mixture is incorrect. The theoretically perfect mixture is called "Stoichiometric" (pronounced *stow-ee-kee-o-MET-rik*) and is about 14.7 parts air to 1 part gasoline. However, perfect mixture changes all the time based on altitude, boost, ignition timing, and heat in the combustion chamber. This is important because if you have imperfect mixture, you're not getting all the energy you can out of the fuel and air.

Older cars relied on carburetors to feed fuel into the system. The carburetors were adjusted (generally by hand) until they achieved something close to the right mixture. Easy enough to work on, but not tremendously accurate. The penalty for misadjusting an engine's mixture

The consequences of detonation are severe. The pieces of piston missing from this hole in the middle ended up all over the engine.

on the rich side is fouled plugs, smelly exhaust, and low power. But the penalty for going too lean in the mixture is detonation, when the fuel/air mixture explodes in the combustion chamber. In any engine, this leads to piston failure, rod failure, burned valves, low power, and nothing at all that is good.

You can see that in a modern engine, the consequences of bad mixture are even worse. A modern high-compression engine coupled with lower-octane pump gas requires that the compression, spark, and mixture must be carefully controlled. We use computers and fuel injection to do this because the old tapered needles or sequential jets (little holes in brass tubes) simply aren't adaptable or accurate enough.

If your engine is boosted with supercharged or turbocharged air, you can blow it up before you even realize that there's a problem. Technology comes to the rescue with the modern MINI's array of sensors and probes that keep track of your engine's condition, millisecond by millisecond. The information from those sensors allows your engine computer to make decisions about how much fuel to give, when to strike the spark, and in the case of the R56 Cooper, when and how much to open the valves and let gases flow.

About Dynamometers

An experienced tuning technician can assist you in fine-tuning your engine programming by using a dynamometer (also known as a dyno) to provide real-time power readings as the technician adjusts the ECU programming.

There are bench dynamometers that measure the engine's power before it's installed in the car; there

INCREASING ENGINE POWER

Dynamometers are a tremendous tool for performance tuning, but don't put too much stock in big numbers on the dyno. It's the incremental difference between changes that you care about.

The new Peugeot/BMW engine in the 2007-and-later models has enormous performance potential. With a small twin-scroll turbocharger, the 1.6-liter R56 MINI gets pulling power that was formerly the province of V-8 engines.

are chassis dynamometers where you park the car on a set of big rollers and drive; and there are chassis dynamometers that bolt directly to the wheel hubs.

Just for fun, you can also download the Dynolicious software application that works with an Apple iPhone or iPod Touch. This software uses the device's internal accelerometer to calculate approximate horsepower and torque. It's cheap, reasonably accurate for the price, and fun to use!

All kinds of dynos operate by measuring the engine's ability to overcome resistance and do work, and it's important to remember that every dyno's readout is adjustable. Given the same car and the same conditions, any particular dyno may read relatively higher or lower than another. This doesn't matter. What matters is the relative improvement you get on a given dyno when tuning your car. People love to brag about their dyno sheets. Tuning shops obviously want their customers to walk away happy and they want a reputation for getting more power out of the same car than their competitors.

In the course of developing this book, we took the project R53 to a chassis dyno for a baseline reading while it was still completely factory stock. That particular dyno told us that our sturdy little 2005 Cooper S was delivering 188 hp at the wheels—quite an accomplishment for a car that the manufacturer claimed had just 168 hp at the flywheel!

When you see any dyno sheet, do not pay too much attention to the peak horsepower and torque, but to the entire area below the lines. The more total area underneath the lines, the better the power. After all, how often and for how long do you run your MINI at its 6,950-rpm redline?

The MINI Engine

There have been two basic engines in the North American MINI line. Both engines are 1.6-liter, 16-valve, inline 4-cylinder models designed for transverse mounting in a front-wheel-drive car.

The first engine was used on the 2002–2006 R50 and R53 models, and on the R52 Convertibles until 2008. It is an SOHC design, with a few modifications for a supercharged version. In its basic (R50 Cooper) form, the engine produces about 114 hp and 110 ft-lbs of torque, and gets about 30 mpg. In its supercharged form, different components are used to reduce the basic compression ratio, but compression is restored through the boost provided by the attached supercharger. This engine uses port fuel injection, in which fuel is sprayed at the intake port of the cylinder head. This engine makes 163 to 215 hp, depending on its factory tuning.

Starting with the 2007 model year, the R56 engine is the result of collaboration between Peugeot and BMW. This engine is a DOHC design that uses direct fuel injection. Direct injection means that the fuel injectors spray fuel directly into the combustion chamber during the intake stroke. This allows much finer control of fuel/air mixture and engine system timing than is possible with port injection.

In its naturally aspirated form, the R56 engine produces 118 hp and 114 ft-lbs of torque, and gets about 32 mpg in real-world combination driving. In turbocharged form, the engine produces between 172 and 208 hp, and between 177 and 192 ft-lbs of torque, depending on the engine's state of tune. Additionally, the turbocharged engine has an overboost feature that raises the engine's torque output to 192 to 207 ft-lbs for up to 15 seconds of hard acceleration.

For both generations of MINI engines, performance improvements generally fall into three categories: changing bolt-on components, altering the engine-control-computer programming, and performing fundamental machine work to the short block. For almost all street and competition performance enhancement, modifications are limited to bolt-on components and ECU programming. (Changes to bore, stroke, head porting, crankshaft design, and other deep engine work are beyond the scope of this book.)

PROJECT
Upgrading the Ignition with MSD Parts

Over time, ignition coil packs, plug wires, and spark plugs degrade in their performance. Usually this happens so slowly that the driver never notices it. But if you replace old stock parts with new performance parts, you'll notice a difference in starting and in smoothness at all RPM. This kit should not yield a noticeable horsepower improvement (unless your old kit was in really bad shape) but you will notice a positive difference, and you'll see why when you remove the old coil.

For this project, we installed a new MSD ignition coil pack and a set of MSD's best wires on the project R53. In addition, we changed out the stock spark plugs in favor of a set of NGK Iridium plugs.

The MSD coil pack costs about $90, and the MSD 8.5-mm Super Conductor plug wires cost another $90. A fresh set of NGK Iridium plugs runs about $60. The good news is that this is a job you can do in your own garage in just minutes, so you save on labor. You need a 10-mm wrench and a spark plug wrench capable of picking the plugs out of their deep wells.

Before you dive in, you need to realize that the bolts holding the stock coil to the top of your engine won't fit the holes in the MSD coil. You need new bolts with flat washers to install the MSD unit, and they don't come as part of the kit.

Bolts and Washers

MINI Madness and Alta Performance both deliver four appropriate bolts and washers with the coil when you buy the MSD unit.

The bolts you need are M6x60 mm. That is, they have 10-mm heads, about 2⅜ inches long. If you don't have a set of bolts for the new coil, go to the hardware store and buy them before you begin. You also need four M6 flat washers.

 The coil pack sits right on top of the engine on all MINIs through 2006, so you can't miss it. Start by removing the electrical harness from the back of the coil pack. There's a sliding clip you have to move to the left to get the harness free. Then pull each of the plug wires off the original coil and out of your engine. The 3-4 side of the coil faces the rear of the car, while plugs 1-2 connect at the front.

You can easily see that the #3 terminal (driver's-side rear) on the stock coil is corroded. If your car is like most MINIs, the other three terminals are likely to show some corrosion as well. This corrosion adds resistance to the ignition system and robs the plugs of their full spark potential.

You can see the corrosion on the #3 plug end of the stock coil. Just about all MINIs with more than 40,000 miles have developed this corrosion.

The new coil is mounted and the bolts are ready to be tightened. Use just 9 ft-lbs of torque, because the nuts in the valve cover are made of brass.

Using a 10-mm wrench or socket, remove the four bolts that hold the coil to the engine. There are four rubber pads that sit between the bolt heads and the coil, and four more that sit between the coil and the engine. Place these pads on the new bolts and under the new coil and prepare to install it.

The MSD coil is not marked 1 through 4 like the stock unit, so for reference, as you stand in front of the car looking at the engine, the #1 cylinder is on your left, then #2, #3, and #4 is on your right. The #1 spark plug wire will connect to the coil at the front-left of the coil, #2 at the front-right, #3 rear-right, and #4 at rear-left. However, leave them off for now.

Bolt down the new coil to 9 ft-lbs of torque. If you don't have a torque wrench that can measure that finely, just snug the bolts. Remember, these are just small parts and the receiving nuts are brass, so do not torque them too tightly.

3 If you're changing plugs at this time, make sure you get them installed correctly and torqued down according to the manufacturer's instructions.

4 Install the new plug wires according to their numbers. Make sure you get the right wires in the right places. Wire #2 is the shortest, followed by #1, #3, and #4 is the longest. The MSD wire kit includes a set of clips that are labeled 1 through 8. The clips come on a nifty little device that helps you slide them right onto the wires.

5 As you press the new wires onto the plugs, make sure

Remember that there is a little clip on top of the wiring harness that needs to be pushed to the left to remove the harness. Don't force it.

The finished product. It looks great, and helps your car run better, too. Preliminary experience suggests that this coil, wire, and plug combination reduces or eliminates the tendency of MINIs to stumble at cold startup on summertime gasoline.

each wire clicks into place and is completely sealed onto the valve cover. Finally, replace the wiring harness connection to the coil.

And that's all there is to it! When you fire up your engine, you should notice that it's smoother and more eager to start and run. The MSD coil is more powerful than the stock unit, and the MSD wires have less resistance than the stock wires, so you're going to get a more powerful spark. There's no scientific proof, but it's also distinctly possible that the snappy red cover on the MSD coil and the sexy red MSD ignition wires will make your MINI just a little bit faster.

Engine Air Intake Upgrades

The first and easiest step in improving engine performance is to look at your MINI's air intake. You can gain about 10 hp and 10 ft-lbs of torque here, and maybe a little more. If you do nothing more than purchase an aftermarket high-flow air filter, you will see some benefit. But for just a few hundred dollars, you can take the first step toward a high-performance engine.

What you want is to have the least restrictive system you can possibly find that will provide clean cold air to your engine. You really do need a filter, though, especially with a supercharger or turbocharger, since all kinds of stuff can get sucked into your system otherwise. Nothing good has ever been reported about feeding a small rock into a supercharger or turbo compressor fan.

Another improvement that goes with an improved air filter is what racers call a cold-air box. If you remove the stock air box, a bare aftermarket air filter pulls in air that has passed through the car's radiator or intercooler (or both) and is hanging around the hot engine bay. To bring in truly fresh air requires some ducting and separation of the intake point from the rest of the engine bay. Get this done right and it will set you apart in both performance and engine bay dress-up.

Cold-air intake kits are available from virtually every MINI aftermarket manufacturer. Kits for the R53 and R56 Cooper S are plentiful, and some offer replacement upgrade filters for JCW cars. Kits are also available for R50 and R56 Coopers. DDM Works, for example, has a nice kit for the R50 for just $189—and that's an affordable upgrade.

This is what happens when something other than air gets sucked into a turbo intake. Always use a good filter and make sure that every molecule of air in your engine has been filtered.

Mass Airflow and Manifold Absolute Pressure

R50 and R53 MINIs use a MAP sensor to determine how much air is being used by the engine. MAP stands for manifold absolute pressure. This device measures the air pressure in the intake manifold and, in the case of the R53, lets the ECU calculate the flow from the supercharger to determine how much air is being used.

R55, R56, and R57 MINIs use both a mass airflow (MAF) sensor and a MAP sensor in their intake flow. The MAF sensor is a delicate little device that tells the ECU how much air is coming in through the air filter. MAF sensors use a "hot wire" design that measures the amount of air passing through by the "wind chill" on the filament. A secondary intake-air-temperature sensor corrects the MAF output for the temperature of the incoming air. Because the MAF output depends on accurate cooling of the hot wire, these devices are very susceptible to dirt and oil. It is vital that you use a high-quality air filter (and don't over-wet the oiled varieties!) to keep your MAF sensor clean and functioning correctly.

It's important to know what system your car uses because intakes are built to accommodate a MAF sensor or not. If your car uses a MAF, make sure your aftermarket cold-air intake has a mounting point for one. Another factor to consider is the size and shape of the pipe where the MAF sensor lives. The MAF measures airflow by the cooling of the hot wire, and the ECU calculates how much air it has by assuming that you're using the stock intake. If you change to an intake tube that is even slightly smaller or larger, the ECU will not make the correct calculation.

PROJECT
Upgrading the Air Intake on an R53 Cooper S

For this project we installed and tested four different cold-air intakes from different manufacturers: Madness, Alta, M7, and Craven Speed. All of these kits use quality parts and the same fundamental design ideas. The top half of the stock air box is removed and each kit provides a replacement that allows in more cold air from the cowl area while protecting the intake air from the heat of the engine bay. Each of these kits retails for $199 to $249.

Yet even in their similarity, there are distinct differences between these kits:

- The Madness kit uses a K&N filter element, while the other three offer foam elements of varying sizes. The M7 kit uses the largest filter, by a significant factor.
- The M7, Craven Speed, and Alta kits eliminate the rear panel to draw high-pressure air from the cowl area. To achieve the same effect, the Madness kit provides a replacement rear panel with a ventilation hole similar to that used in the JCW kit for the R53.
- The Craven Speed kit features a clear plexiglass top that seals the intake area. The M7 kit uses a metal top and the Madness and Alta kits use rubber seals fitted up against the underside of the car's hood to achieve the same effect.
- The Craven Speed kit eliminates the bottom half of the air box and the front-mounted cold-air duct. The other three

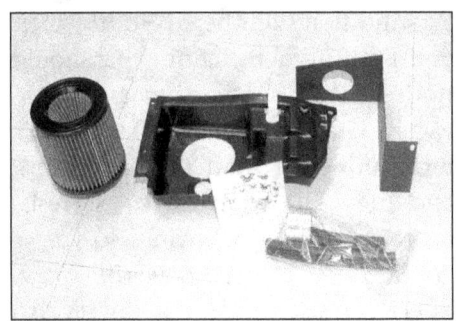

The Madness cold-air intake for the R53 uses a K&N-style filter and creates a hole in the back panel as with the JCW kit.

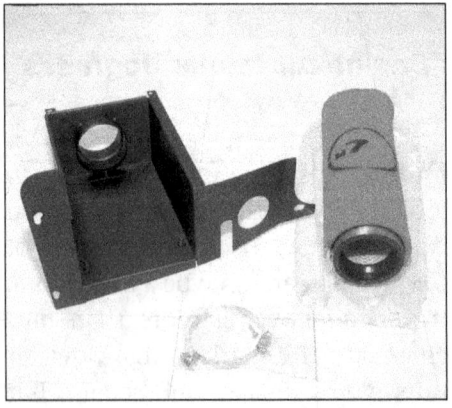

The M7 intake kit has the largest filter of the bunch, and removes the back panel to accommodate the extra length.

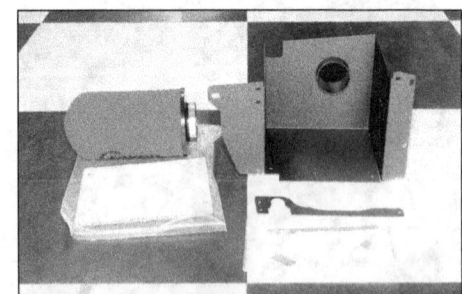

The Craven Speed cold-air intake uses a plexiglass panel above the filter to make the kit a nice dress-up item for your engine bay.

INCREASING ENGINE POWER

products continue to use the bottom half of the stock box and its integrated ECU box.

- The Alta kit provides a smooth silicone intake tube from the filter to the supercharger inlet, replacing the stock corrugated plastic tube. The M7, Madness, and Craven Speed kits all use the stock tube.

The Alta kit is unique with its blue silicone intake tube. This makes a nice dress-up item in the engine bay, but it's a challenge to install.

Because the total air through the engine is limited by the amount the supercharger can pump, each of the candidate intakes yielded about the same 10-hp boost. Each intake was installed in less than an hour. The Alta intake was the most difficult installation due to the intake tube replacement, but it was not significantly more difficult than the others.

Every intake comes with its own specific instructions, but to install a new cold-air intake on an R53, follow these basic steps:

1. Disconnect the negative pole of the battery. Then lift off the battery positive junction box. It hooks to the left side of the stock air box.
2. Remove the air inlet hose from the air box.
3. Remove the stock air box top half and the filter. You need a T-25 driver to remove the two Torx-style mounting screws. Also remove

The stock air box is what you see when you start this project. You'll gain 5 to 10 hp and several ft-lbs of torque when you swap it for an aftermarket cold-air intake.

This is the stock filter after 40,000 miles. Grunge is not an ingredient for high performance. Even with the aftermarket filters, you need to clean or replace the elements from time to time.

the top from the ECU case to the right of the air box and slide out the two clips that hold the ECU wiring harnesses in place on the computer. You can now remove the ECU and set it aside.

4. Remove the bottom half of the air box and the ECU box, if required for the kit you're using, and

Here's the R53 engine bay with the stock filter box removed. Note the rubber caps on the bolts that hold the back plate in place.

undo the two raised ball screws that hold the rear panel and support the air box in place. Then remove the two T-30 screws that hold the rear panel to the car. Remove the rear panel.

5. Install the new heat-shielding upper half of the air box as instructed for your kit.

The Craven Speed kit goes in easily, and the plexiglass top plate helps protect the ECU.

6. Install the new air filter. Note that virtually all such filters come pre-oiled from the factory, so you don't need to add oil. But take a moment to note the maintenance schedule for your filter so you can clean and oil it as needed.

The Madness kit fits well and installs easily. You can't see it, but the filter has an inverted cone in its end, maximizing its surface area.

7. Replace the ECU and carefully reattach its two wiring harnesses. There is a gap provided in the replacement rear panels or bridges provided in each kit to accommodate this wiring harness. With the Craven

CHAPTER 2

Speed and Alta kits, you mount the ECU inside the heat shielded box of the kit. For the others tested, the ECU returns to the stock box attached to the bottom half of the air box.

The M7 kit is all business, and it completely removes the back panel to fit the extra-long filter. There's just a hint of the red filter element visible.

8 For the Alta kit, install the silicone intake tube. There's an additional connection on this tube that leads to the crankcase vent.

The Alta kit comes with your choice of color on that nifty silicone intake pipe. This pipe is smooth on the interior surfaces, eliminating the ridges and folds of the stock unit.

9 Reconnect the battery and turn on the key for 10 seconds to re-initialize the ECU. Then start the car and carefully inspect the engine bay for good connections and correct operation.

PROJECT
Upgrading the Air Intake on an R56 Cooper S

The R56 air intake is fundamentally different from the R53 intake. Where the R53 uses the distinctive Cooper S hood scoop to duct air to the intercooler, the stock R56 has a front-mounted intercooler, but simply wastes the hood scoop. All R56 cold-air intakes remove the blocking plate to direct cold air to the intake, which is so obvious you have to wonder why MINI didn't do that in the first place.

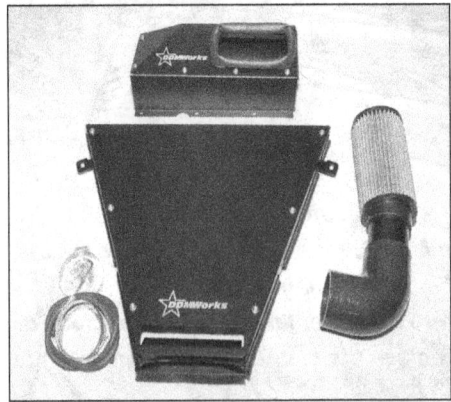

The DDM Works R56 cold-air intake makes use of the hood scoop and that big triangular funnel to duct air to the filter in the box.

The Alta kit eliminates the stock air box entirely, but again offers Alta's signature smooth silicone pipes in a variety of colors. With the R56 exhaust on the front of the engine and a duct from the hood scoop, they won't be sucking much hot air when the car's in motion.

This project installs the DDM Works Racing Intake System (RIS) kit. This kit retails for $448 and includes a powder-coated steel air funnel that ducts cold scoop air to the back of the engine compartment and into a new air-filter box with a K&N-style filter. The stock MAF location is moved slightly to accommodate a silicone elbow tube.

Other kits on the market, such as the Alta and Madness products, are of a similar design. The Madness kit uses an ultra-light carbon fiber air funnel and air-box top. The Alta kit omits the funnel and simply removes the hood scoop blocking plate and air-box top, replacing the box top with a heat shield and a full silicone tube inlet path to the turbo.

Every intake comes with its own specific instructions, but to install a new cold-air intake on an R56, follow these basic steps:

1 Looking at your stock R56 engine bay, the air-filter box is an oblong plastic container that runs parallel to the engine between the valve cover and the firewall. The inlet tube and MAF sensor are bolted to the air box and run forward to the turbocharger on the right side of the valve cover. First, remove the two Torx screws that hold the inlet tube and MAF to the air box. Remove the MAF housing and inlet tube from the air box and discard the rubber O-ring.

2 The top of the air box is held on with four screws along its front edge. Remove those four screws and you can lift and pull to remove the top of the box. The rear is held in place with tabs and slots. Don't force it. Just a gentle lift and pull is

INCREASING ENGINE POWER

enough. You can now remove the flat-panel air filter as well.

3 Unplug the wire loom that leads to the MAF sensor. Then loosen the hose clamp that connects the MAF housing to the turbo inlet tube and remove the MAF housing carefully.

4 Install the MAF housing onto the new intake-air box top. New bolts and nuts are provided, along with spacer washers to fill the bolt length between the box and the MAF housing. Make sure that when the air box is installed, the wire connection on the MAF housing points forward, and that the airflow arrow points away from the air box structure. This should be easy because you cannot bolt the MAF housing in place with the arrow pointing in the wrong direction.

Different R56 cold-air kits move the mass airflow (MAF) sensor to different locations, but it's most important that the airflow across the meter happens in the correct direction.

5 Install the filter directly onto the end of the MAF housing that extends into the air box. Snug-down the provided hose clamp around the junction.

6 Install the new air box by sliding its tabs into place and affixing the new top box to the stock bottom half with the provided replacement screws.

The DDM Works cold-air intake is a clean-looking installation, with the filter well isolated from hot-air sources.

7 The new air box has moved the MAF housing in relation to the turbo inlet tube, so attach the silicone elbow tube to the MAF housing and point the open end to the front of the car. Insert the short length of metal tube into the silicone elbow and the stock turbo inlet tube. Tighten all hose clamps.

8 Reconnect the wiring loom to the MAF housing. The plug fits only one way.

9 Remove the padded heat shield from the underside of your hood. Next, remove the blanking plug from your hood scoop. You have to remove the hood scoop insert retainer from the underside of the hood to do this.

The DDM Works scoop goes on in two pieces, and looks good when you're done with the project.

10 Install the underhood duct according to the manufacturer's instructions. Some of these ducts are one piece, but the DDM product is a two-piece frame and skin. All ducts for the R56 use the stock holes in the underside structure of the hood and plastic expansion retainers to secure the duct. The duct is V-shaped, with the broad end of the V oriented forward, toward the hood scoop. The narrow end of the V is open and designed to flow air into the top of the air box when the hood is closed.

 Cover Your Engine

Cover your engine with a blanket when working with the retainers and screws on the underhood duct (or any time you're working in the engine bay). A dropped washer or screw can get wedged between parts and cause a world of trouble.

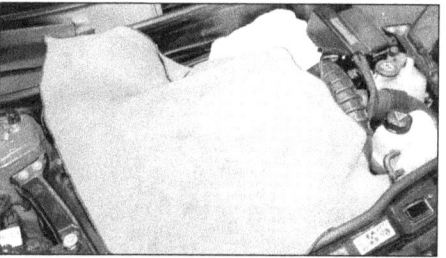

Any time you're working on the hood of the car, especially if you have the engine open, you should cover everything with a blanket. If you drop a washer or a nut into your engine, you'll go crazy trying to find it.

11 Finally, there is a vacuum tube that runs along the top of the engine and intake assembly that may interfere with the DDM underhood duct. The DDM kit provides a rubber vacuum tube to replace the stock hard line. You have to loosen a bolt and reorient the engine end of the tube to install the rubber vacuum tube.

12 Carefully close the hood, making sure that the underhood duct opening aligns with the opening in the top of the air box. Then start the engine and gently test-drive the car, listening for rattles or any other indication of a problem.

Take a moment to inspect the turbo inlet connection when you're done. It's easy to knock that inlet pipe loose, and then you're sucking in unfiltered air, missing your MAF sensor, and your car will throw a Check Engine light and put you in safety mode until you get it fixed.

Check Connections

Carefully inspect your work before you test-drive the car, particularly the connection from the inlet tube to the turbocharger at the front of the engine. With all the manipulation you performed, it's easy for this connection to come loose. Any disconnected tube can cause the Check Engine light to come on shortly after you start the car. If this happens, check the intake air path and make sure all tubes are properly connected. If you find and refit a disconnected tube, the light may remain on for an hour or so. If the light does not go off soon, seek professional help.

Exhaust Component Upgrades

The fuel charge in a MINI engine does its work by expanding as it burns, pushing a piston down in the cylinder. Once the fuel charge has accomplished this task, the main thing you want to do with the leftovers of combustion is get them out of your car as efficiently as possible, although turbocharged cars scavenge a bit more energy out of the gas on the way out. This very simple function is accomplished by the exhaust system, and that is the best place to easily bolt on some low-cost horsepower.

But before you work on your muffler, bear in mind that the exhaust system is also a critical emissions-control system. There are federal and state laws that govern what you can and cannot do to your car.

Common Sense

A note of common sense: Always replace all gaskets and worn fasteners when replacing exhaust components. Exhaust leaks are easy to avoid and a pain to fix.

Catalytic Converters

The catalytic converter has been the cornerstone of automotive emission controls for more than 35 years. Controlling emissions from street cars is an important environmental concern. Cars today are far cleaner than in decades past, thanks in large part to improvements in catalyst technology. While extreme high-performance applications generally include removing one or more catalysts from the exhaust system, it is a violation of U.S. federal law to do so on a car registered for use on public

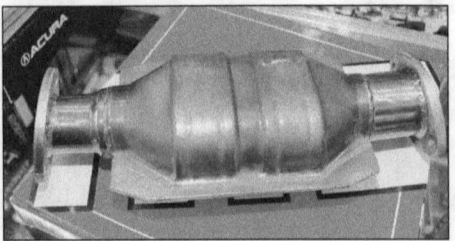

This catalyst is the principal air-quality device in use today. It is protected by federal law, and you need to understand the implications of removing or bypassing the catalysts in your car.

roads. Moreover, removing the catalysts makes it harder, if not impossible, for your car to pass emissions testing. Keeping your catalyst is no barrier to high performance. Your entire engine management system is designed to work with the catalyst and provide good performance.

The catalytic converter is a muffler-type device that uses a ceramic or stainless-steel alloy web that holds reactive catalyzing material (usually palladium or rhodium). When the exhaust gases pass through the catalytic converter and heat the catalyst, a chemical reaction occurs that helps change carbon monoxide to carbon dioxide, and helps to burn off any unburned hydrocarbons that remain in the exhaust stream before it exits the car.

Cat-Back Exhaust Systems

As the name implies, a cat-back system replaces the factory exhaust from the last catalytic converter to the exhaust tips at the rear of the car. This section of the exhaust system is where the mufflers are found. Desirable features in this part of the power system are velocity and free flow with as few bends as possible.

Because of differing chassis underbody configurations and rear bumper

INCREASING ENGINE POWER

designs, MINI exhaust systems are not shared among different platforms. Make sure the system you buy fits your car. Cat-back exhausts are readily available for all MINI models.

Stock MINI exhausts are 2.0 to 2.25 inches in outside diameter (OD). Most aftermarket cat-back units use stainless-steel pipe at 2.5 inches OD. Inside diameter for this kind of pipe is about 2.25 to 2.375 inches, depending on wall thickness. This is big enough to flow all the gas that the MINI is capable of generating, and to flow it substantially faster and easier than the stock unit. Some products move up to 2.75 or 3.0 inches OD for the R56 Cooper S, but 2.5 inches is standard for all other MINIs.

When choosing an aftermarket exhaust, apart from tubing size, look for smooth bends and joints in the pipe and unrestricted mufflers. Generally speaking, the freer the flow, the louder the exhaust, so there's a trade-off you need to understand before you buy. If you plan to drive your car daily, excess noise can become annoying and may be illegal. If you are building a dedicated track car, noise is usually less of an issue (within the bounds of your track's noise limits).

You can reasonably expect to gain 5 to 15 hp from a good cat-back exhaust. The actual gain will depend on several factors beyond the product you choose: What model MINI are you upgrading? Have you already upgraded your cold-air intake and exhaust header? Have you installed a reduction supercharger pulley or raised the boost on your turbo? All of these factors influence how much benefit you see from a cat-back upgrade. In general, you'll see the best results if the exhaust is the most restrictive part of your system before the upgrade, and most people perform the easy exhaust upgrade before they do the more difficult header upgrade.

PROJECT
Upgrading the Cat-Back Exhaust on an R53 Cooper S

This project installs the Magnaflow cat-back exhaust system on a 2005 R53 Cooper S. This product uses 2.5-inch OD T-304 stainless tubing, dual mufflers, and includes a resonating chamber in the main pipe. With our previously installed cold-air intake ("Upgrading the Air Intake on an R53 Cooper S") and a supercharger pulley, we can expect to see about 13 additional horsepower and up to 16 ft-lbs of torque from this project.

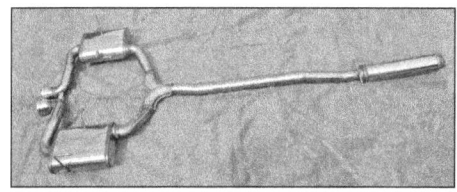

A clean design makes for good exhaust flow on this Magnaflow R53 cat-back system. Note that there are differences in the rear hangers between 2002–2004 and 2005–2006 R53 cars. Be sure to specify the correct model year to your exhaust vendor.

If you have access to a safe automotive lift, this project is easy and convenient. You can do the work using only jack stands, but it will take longer and be more difficult.

Follow the manufacturer's specific instructions, but in general perform these steps:

The stock rubber exhaust hangers on a MINI are very good, but you can buy poly hangers inexpensively for a nice touch to your installation.

Short-Shifter Kit

If you're considering installing a short-shifter kit (as described in Chapter 6), now is a good time to do it, because you have to disconnect the exhaust and remove the central heat shielding in order to get at the shift linkage. You might as well make both upgrades now.

1 Disconnect the battery and raise the car. Remove the rear underside shield from the muffler area. It's held on with four 10-mm nuts.

2 Unbolt the stock cat-back exhaust from the exhaust header at the catalytic converter. Then remove the exhaust tunnel brace, which is held on with six 10-mm nuts.

Rubber Hangers

Spray some WD-40 lubricant on the rubber exhaust hangers. Then use a large screwdriver or small pry bar to lever the rubber hangers off the muffler hanger posts. Be very careful taking off the center support. Work it off gently, as the rubber hangers are easy to break.

THE NEW MINI PERFORMANCE HANDBOOK

Support the front end of the exhaust on a spare jack stand or something else that is sturdy. Next, unbolt the inboard rubber exhaust hangers and the muffler hanger straps. The exhaust should drop out.

3 The exhaust-tunnel brace is mounted to the exhaust pipe using two stock rubber hangers. Remove the brace from the stock system and install it on the new resonator pipe. Then install the resonator pipe section to the header, but leave the bolts loose for now.

Bolt the resonator to the stock catalyst loosely at first. You'll tighten everything front-to-back when it's all in place.

4 Place the supplied exhaust clamps on the exhaust extension pipe and muffler components and connect the extension pipe and the muffler section of the new exhaust to the car. The stock rubber hangers can be reused on the outboard sides, or you can upgrade to poly hangers if you like. The stock rubber hangers on the inboard sides must be reused. If you have problems with exhaust rattles, poly hangers can often fix them.

The stock center support on the R53 is critical for holding up that long stretch of pipe to the rear end of the car. There are two special exhaust hangers on the topside of this piece.

5 Adjust the fitment of all parts and then, working front to back, tighten the bolts and clamps throughout the system. Strap-style clamps must be installed very tightly to seal. Make sure the exhaust is centered in its space at the bumper and that adequate clearance is provided all around. Run your hands along the top of the exhaust path and anywhere that the heat shielding is too close to let your fingers by, press it up and out of the way.

Different exhaust tips let people know you've got something special in your car even when it's not running. The Magnaflow exhaust went in easily and fits snugly. It should be worth 10 to 15 hp on the road.

6 Replace the rear underside shield and reconnect the battery. You are ready to test-fire the car.

PROJECT
Upgrading the Cat-Back Exhaust on an R56 Cooper S

Installing an exhaust in any R56-based car (including R55 and R57) is somewhat easier than the same project in the older cars. This project installs the Borla cat-back exhaust system on a 2008 R56 Cooper S. This product retails for about $900 and uses 2.25-inch OD T-304 stainless tubing, a single muffler, and includes a resonating chamber in the main pipe.

WARNING: *This unit, like many R56 exhausts, requires you to cut the existing pipe downstream of the second catalyst and slip-fit the Borla product over the stock pipe. Other kits, designed for track use only, eliminate this second catalyst. Obviously, it's hard to walk this modification back if you change your mind later.*

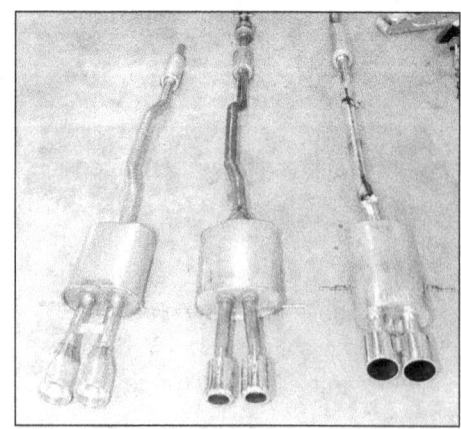

From left to right, here are three exhaust systems for the R56 Cooper S: the Borla unit, the stock system, and the larger-diameter MINI Madness cat-back pipe.

INCREASING ENGINE POWER

If you have access to a safe automotive lift, this project is easy and convenient. You can do the work using only jack stands, but it will take longer and be more difficult.

Follow the manufacturer's specific instructions, but in general you will perform these steps:

1. Disconnect the battery and raise the car. Loosen the circumferential clamp that holds the one-piece stock exhaust system to the downpipe from the turbocharger.

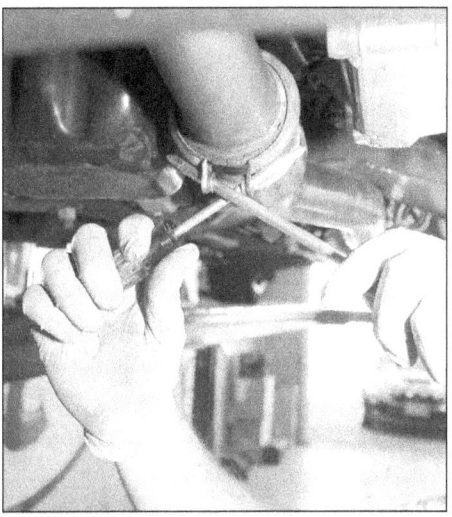

There's a trick to removing the circumferential clamp. Just cross two screwdrivers and pull your hands together to liberate the clamp and move it aside. Use the same technique to put it back in place.

2. Remove the stock center support from under the exhaust. This is a black rectangular stamping that is attached to the chassis with four bolts. Then spray the rubber hangers with WD-40 and pry the stock exhaust system away from the rubber hangers. The stock rubber hangers can be reused, or you can upgrade to poly hangers if you like. Be careful and support the exhaust, because when you remove the last hanger, it will fall.

The R56 exhaust is very simple compared to the R53. You can see the stock rubber hangers easily on either side of the muffler.

3. With the stock exhaust out of the car, use a reciprocating saw, cutoff wheel, hacksaw, or exhaust-tubing cutter to cut through the pipe just in front of the resonator. This leaves most of the pipe attached to the catalyst.

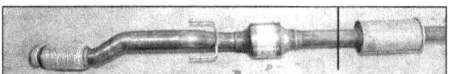

To install the Borla R56 exhaust, you have to cut the stock unit between the catalyst and the resonating chamber. This means you really can't go back to stock without welding or placing a slip fitting back over the stock pipe.

4. Assemble the pieces of the new exhaust, but leave the fittings loose for now. Get a friend to help lift the new exhaust into place and install it on the rubber hangers. Or you can install the new exhaust in pieces and then fit it together.

5. Replace the stock center support and, working front-to-back, tighten the fittings on the new exhaust. Pay attention to orientation, because misalignment anywhere in the system will make the new tailpipes sit off-center in the bumper space.

Exhaust Headers

The exhaust header (also known as the exhaust manifold) attaches directly to the body of the MINI engine at the exhaust ports on the cylinder heads. On the R50, R52, and R53 engines, the exhaust ports face the rear of the car. On all R55, R56, and R57 cars, the exhaust ports face the front of the car.

On a normally aspirated or supercharged Cooper, the exhaust header leads directly to the catalytic converter and then through the exhaust pipe to the muffler and out the back of the car. On a turbocharged car, the exhaust manifold ducts gases to the turbocharger before they find their way to the catalyst and then out of the car.

The main thing you want in a header (and throughout the exhaust system) is efficient flow of gases on their way out of the car. This means a large pipe with a few smooth bends and no restrictions. It's good for this pipe to be wrapped or coated on the outside to keep heat in the exhaust gas until it exits the car. It's also good for this pipe to be made of stainless steel, or coated on the inside, to reduce friction and more efficiently move the gas through the system to the exit. Finally, long primary tubes of equal length verging into a conical collector help to tune the exhaust by reducing back-pressure, which is the amount of work your engine has to spend to push exhaust through the system.

Any exhaust header made to fit the R53 Cooper S also fits the R50

CHAPTER 2

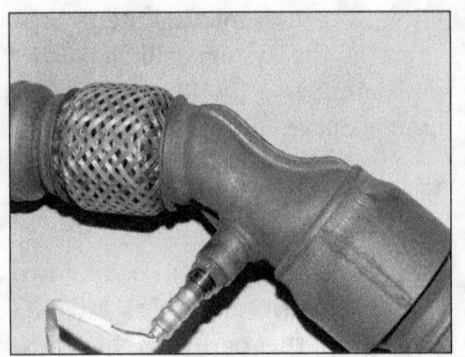

The stock header has a narrow point right at the oxygen (O_2) sensor. An aftermarket unit eliminates that choke point, and offers you the choice to use a catalyst or not.

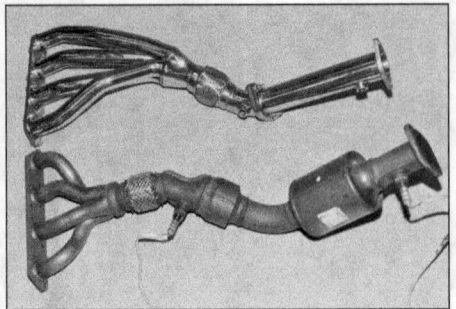

The Madness header with catalyst delete tube compared to the stock unit. Not only does the Madness header eliminate choke points, but the primary tubes are longer and straighter, and the 4-into-1 collector is smoother for improved flow. You can order the same header with a catalyst for your street car.

and R52 Cooper. These are generally sold as "off road and racing only" parts, due to the laws governing replacing catalysts on street cars. The short exhaust manifold for the R56 Cooper S is designed to flow exhaust through the turbocharger, through a "downpipe" with a catalyst, through a second catalyst in a connecting mid-pipe, through the muffler, and out of the car.

In general, replacement exhaust manifolds are not made for the turbocharged R56 models. However, you can purchase and install an upgraded downpipe for better flow. These downpipes may or may not include a high-flow catalyst. There are also replacement mid-pipes (also called connecting pipes) that may or may not include the second catalyst. Supersprint makes an entire line of upgrade exhaust parts for the R56 MINI, including a high-performance header for the R56 Cooper. Note that all of these parts must be considered "race track only," due to federal emissions laws.

You can expect up to a 10-hp boost by replacing the stock header with a free-flowing aftermarket unit with no catalyst, assuming you already have an intake and a free-flowing cat-back exhaust installed. If you keep the catalyst, your gains will be lower, but you'll pollute far less and still pass the emissions test.

PROJECT

Installing the Madness Exhaust Header on an R52 Cooper S JCW

This project also works on any R50, R52, or R53. Removing the stock exhaust header on a first-generation MINI engine is somewhat tricky, but can be done conveniently if you have access to an automobile lift. If you have to work with jack stands, it will be a bit harder, but still achievable.

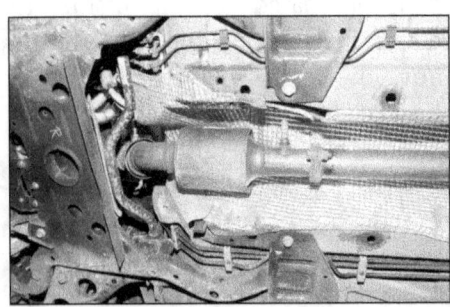

The stock header is easy to find under the car. It's right behind the front subframe.

The R50/52/53 engine exhaust system is two pieces: header and exhaust. The exhaust portion of the system is simply the pipe and mufflers. The header portion includes the manifold, two oxygen (O_2) sensors, and the catalyst. This Madness replacement header provides installation locations for both O_2 sensors, and has a removable section where the catalyst is installed on the stock unit. The particular header we installed does not include a catalyst, and is therefore not legal to use on a street car, but you can purchase the same header with a catalyst.

This procedure was performed on a 2006 R52 Cooper S JCW edition. Follow these steps:

1 Raise the car to a comfortable working height on the lift, and allow the exhaust system to cool before you begin.

2 Disconnect the header from the exhaust first. These bolts have been heated and cooled many times and are often difficult to loosen. Spray them with some penetrating oil while you wait for the parts to cool.

Look for this O_2 sensor plug on the driver's side, just in front of the catalyst.

INCREASING ENGINE POWER

3 There's a plug for the downstream O₂ sensor just forward of the catalyst on the driver's side, right next to the brake lines. Unhook that plug and remove the header with the O₂ sensor still attached. It's easier to remove the O₂ sensors once the header is out of the car.

You will need to undo some of the heat shielding to get the O₂ sensor wiring clear. It's easier to remove the sensor when the header is out of the car.

4 Remove the heat shielding at the driver's side of the lower curvature of the header. The O₂ sensor wiring runs behind this shield, and the stock header cannot come out of the car with this shielding in place.

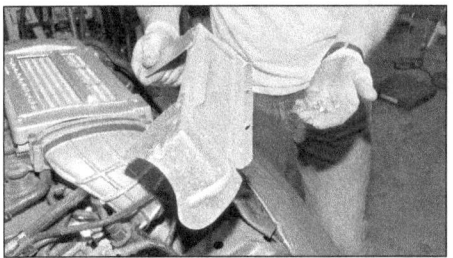

Just two bolts hold the upper heat shield to the engine.

5 Lower the lift and raise the car's hood. There is another heat shield covering the top of the header that must be removed. The heat shield is held in place with two 13-mm bolts into the back of the engine. If you have a strut tower brace, you need to remove it to gain access to the heat shield.

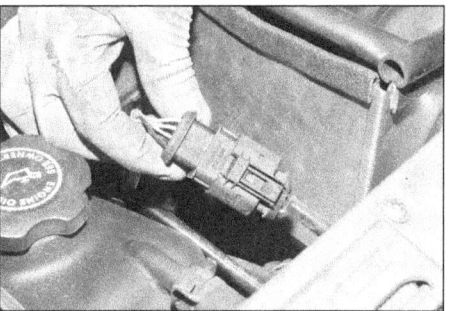

The plug for the upper O₂ sensor lives behind the engine between the oil filler cap and the air box. You need to unplug this sensor before you remove the header.

6 Find the plug for the upstream O₂ sensor. This plug is found down in the depths between the valve cover and the intake air box. Unplug the O₂ sensor and make sure that the wire is disconnected all the way to the O₂ sensor.

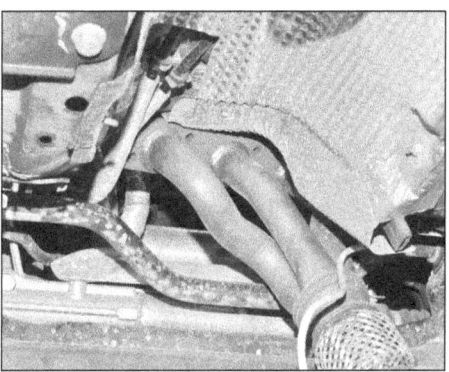

When everything is disconnected, you can work the header out of the car just by carefully moving it to clear obstacles. The new header goes on the same way; just carefully insert it and move it upward to meet the engine.

7 Working from above, remove the eight 10-mm bolts that hold the header in place. Then raise the car again and wiggle the header out and down. You might have to move the gear-shifting cables out of the way and work around the heat shielding, but it will come out.

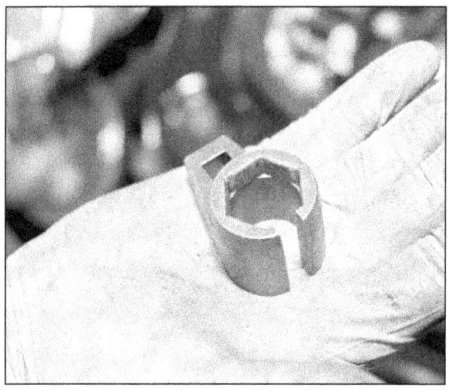

Always use a proper O₂ sensor wrench to remove or install a sensor. O₂ sensors are delicate and relatively expensive devices, and the tool doesn't cost much.

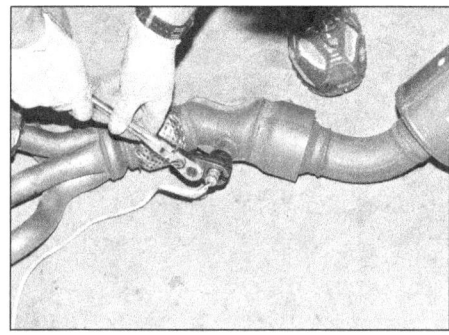

The O₂ sensor wrench applies even pressure all around the sensor body. Sensors are often stuck after years of heat cycling.

8 With the header out, you can remove the O₂ sensors. These are frequently frozen in place and difficult to remove. You can use a standard 22-mm wrench to remove an O₂ sensor, but if at all possible they should be removed with a special O₂ sensor wrench or socket attachment. These sensors are somewhat delicate and expensive, and the O₂ sensor wrench grips all sides of the sensor body for firm and even pressure. Put some high-temperature anti-seize coating on the O₂ sensor threads before you reinstall them in the new header. This will make the removal job easier next time.

THE NEW MINI PERFORMANCE HANDBOOK

CHAPTER 2

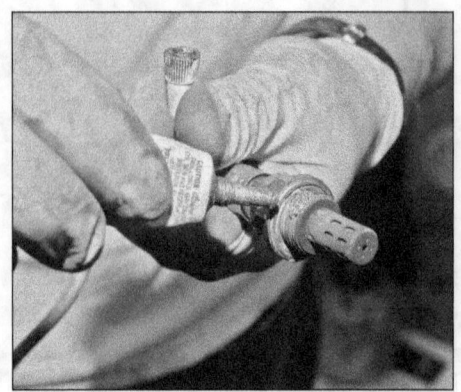

To make this job easier next time, apply a dab of high-temperature anti-seize compound to the threads on the O₂ sensor. Be careful not to get any on the sensor itself!

You can see here how the sensor tip extends into the exhaust stream. Make sure that the upper sensor goes back to the upper location and the lower one to its accustomed site as well.

9 Put the O₂ sensors in the new header. If your new header deletes the catalyst, the engine management system displays a Check Engine light unless you modify the downstream O₂ sensor by soldering-in a diode designed to fool the computer into believing that that O₂ sensor is reading normally. The wiring kit and instructions to perform this splice come with the racing header kit. Splice the diode into the sensor wiring and you can then replace the O₂ sensor normally. Or, simply install a new high-flow catalyst.

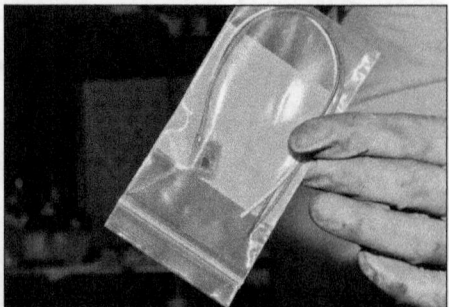

Because this header deletes the catalyst, the diode splices into the wiring harness to prevent the system from throwing a Check Engine light. This diode emulates the signal from a happy O₂ sensor.

Note that the exhaust gasket for this header fits in only one orientation. The bolt holes will not line up if you install it backward.

10 Before you install the new header, take a moment to orient the gasket that fits between the header and the engine. The holes on this gasket line up correctly in only one orientation. Once you have the gasket ready, install the new header to the engine. It's handy to have an assistant at this point to help from above, because someone needs to start a couple of the attachment bolts to hold the header and gasket in place. The header bolts take a torque of just 18 ft-lbs, so don't over-tighten them.

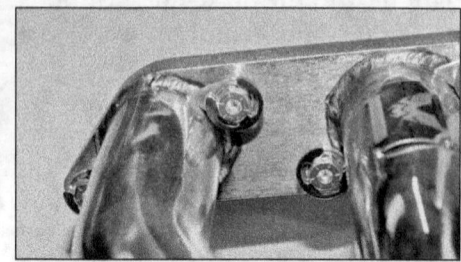

These special header bolts come with the Madness kit. The teardrop-shaped clips ride on the header tubes to prevent the bolts from ever coming loose, and they are held in place with circlips. It's a nice detail for your engine.

11 Reconnect the O₂ sensors to their wiring harnesses and route the wires out of harm's way. Then replace the heat shields and their fasteners.

From below, the racing header shows a clear, smooth path for the exhaust gases.

12 Connect the new header to the exhaust system. The stock copper gasket is designed to be reused, but if you can get a new one, it's always better to use a fresh gasket.

Supercharger Upgrades

The supercharger used on the R53 Cooper S is an Eaton M45 belt-driven "Roots" design. This means that the supercharger uses two helical gears turning in a case to pump air toward the engine. The R53 supercharger is mounted to the front of the engine, and driven using a replaceable pulley on the left side as you face the engine.

Water Pump

The R53 engine's water pump is mounted to the opposite end of the supercharger and runs on the same motion from the supercharger pulley. Overdriving the water pump has not yielded any cooling issues under normal operation. Regardless of the installation of reduction pulleys, the lubricant for the water pump drive has been known to slowly leak in some cases. This leads to destruction of the water-pump drive gears in the supercharger housing. If this happens, the supercharger makes horrible noises, and when the gears break, the water pump ceases to operate. This is an expensive fix, and there's no known easy way around it.

The R53 supercharger system design is unusual in that the throttle body is placed before the supercharger in the intake air stream. This is contrary to the usual engineering rule that you never throttle the intake of a pump. The way the MINI system gets around this rule is through the use of a bypass valve downstream of the intercooler. When you lift off the throttle, the supercharger's boost is not needed, and so the bypass valve opens and allows the output pressure of the supercharger to recirculate back to the input side of the pump.

Because the supercharger is always spinning at a multiple of engine RPM, boost is always available if you supply the supercharger with air from the throttle. When the throttle closes, you don't need boost any more so the boost is dumped back into the intake stream continuously until it is needed again. What this does is allow the R53 to respond immediately to throttle changes and apply boost only when needed.

If you install a boost gauge (as described in Chapter 6), you will see that much of the time you're driving, there is vacuum in the intake manifold. Intake air is still being burned in the engine but boost is not needed at that moment, so it is dumped. However, when you step on the throttle and deliver air to the supercharger, the bypass closes and boost peaks immediately. This is in contrast to a turbocharged engine, where there's always some lag from throttle to boost.

From 2002 to 2004, the Cooper S used a first-generation supercharger. The advent of the JCW kit in 2004 included an upgraded supercharger with coated vanes on the impellers. Starting with model year 2005, all supercharged models received this upgraded supercharger until the end of R52 Cooper S production in 2008. If you have an early Cooper S, you can obtain about 5 hp simply by upgrading to the later unit.

Because the supercharger drive pulley is replaceable, you have some control over the relative speed at which the supercharger turns and, thus, how much boost the supercharger provides. The stock pulley

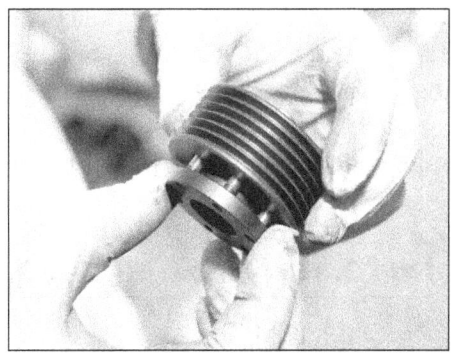

The replacement 15-percent-reduction pulley clamps down on the supercharger shaft where the stock one is a press-fit from the factory. This makes it easy to remove if you need to take your car back to the stock configuration.

Pulley

If you change your pulley to provide more boost, you're changing the rules on your engine control computer. The computer can compensate, but for best results you should plan to reflash your ECU to balance the change to the supercharger and account for the increased boost in your fuel map.

turns the supercharger at just over twice the engine speed, or 14,317 rpm at a redline of 6,950 rpm. The stock setup produces about 8 to 10 psi of boost.

By reducing or increasing the diameter of the supercharger pulley, you can change the drive ratio of the supercharger and control the boost. The effect is similar to changing gears on a bicycle—if you have a large crank pulley driving the belt, reducing the size of the supercharger pulley makes the supercharger turn faster at any given engine speed. Thus you have a choice between the factory's JCW pulley at 11.3-percent reduction and an array of aftermarket pulleys at 15- to 19-percent reduction, producing 15 to 17 psi of peak boost.

At 15-percent reduction, your supercharger will be spinning at about 16,464 rpm at the engine's 6,950-rpm redline. At 19-percent reduction, your supercharger will be spinning at 17,037 rpm at redline, only about 600 rpm more! But before you go out and get a 19-percent pulley, note that there have been engine failures attributed to the 19-percent pulleys, but the 15-percent pulleys have an excellent safety record.

PROJECT
Installing the Madness Supercharger Pulley

For this project, we installed the Madness 15-percent-reduction pulley on the project 2005 R53 Cooper S. This pulley retails for $149, plus $50 to rent the pulley removal tool. If you have friends who are interested in a group buy, you can save by renting the removal tool just once and performing several installations.

WARNING: *You must use a special pulley removal tool to complete this job because the stock pulley is a press-fit onto the supercharger shaft. Virtually all reduction pulley retailers will sell, rent, or loan you a pulley changing tool with the purchase of a pulley. If you attempt to cut, pound, yank, or otherwise force the stock pulley off its shaft, you are likely to damage the supercharger beyond repair.*

You may also wish to obtain a belt tension relief tool to make this job easier. If you purchased a pulley of greater than 15-percent reduction, you also have to purchase a shorter replacement serpentine belt. In any case, you should also purchase replacement spark plugs that are cooler than the stock plugs, to compensate for the increased boost. These plugs are often suggested by the retailer when you buy the reduction.

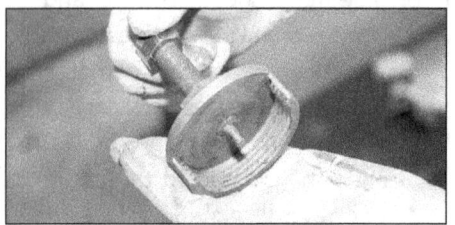

You absolutely need to use a pulley removal tool to do this job. The tool costs about $100, or it can be rented from most retailers. If you have several friends with R53 MINIs, consider jointly investing in a pulley tool.

1 Disconnect the battery and then remove the engine mount bolt on the left side as you face the engine. Then disconnect the electrical ground strap between the left engine mount and the engine. Remove the oil dipstick and set it aside. If your R53 is a 2002–2004 model, you must also remove the engine vibration damper, and the air box, ECU, and skid plate to remove the right-side engine-mount bolt. This bolt must be removed so you can move the engine to the right and then up, in order for the early crank pulley to clear the frame rail.

2 Loosen but do not remove the 16-mm bolt on the belt tensioner, which is located on the left side of the engine, underneath the output of the supercharger. You may also find it convenient to remove the hood opening sensor, which is in the working area.

Disconnect the battery and remove the ground cable. This allows the ECU to reset and learn the new boost rate more quickly.

Loosen this lock bolt to let the tensioner move so that you can remove the serpentine belt from the stock supercharger pulley.

Working from below, jack up the engine to reveal the pulley in its working location. You have to be able to get the tool onto the pulley and remove it.

3 Jack up the engine using a floor jack under the left side of the cast-aluminum oil pan. This is the most dangerous part of this job, so go slowly and be careful not to break anything or pull anything loose. When you jack up the engine,

INCREASING ENGINE POWER

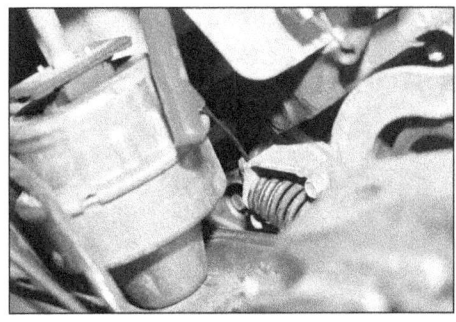

When you take the slack out of the serpentine belt, a hole in the rod that runs up the center of the tension spring is revealed. Stick a hex wrench or screwdriver through that hole to hold the tensioner while you work.

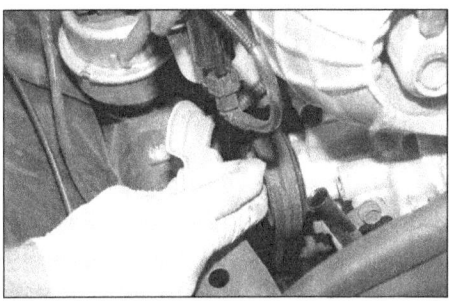

With everything undone, remove the tensioner lock bolt and move the whole tensioner assembly aside to provide working space.

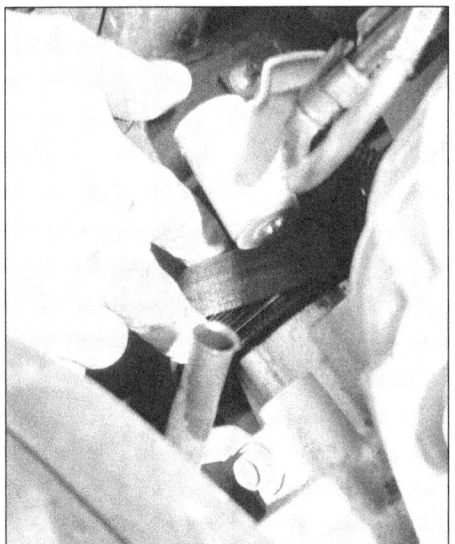

Carefully remove the serpentine belt from the supercharger pulley, but leave it attached to the rest of the pulleys on the engine.

don't force it too high. You only need to be able to get the tool onto the stock supercharger pulley.

4 There is a shaft that runs up the center of the serpentine belt tensioner spring. Compress the tensioner spring. There is a hole in the shaft where it extends through the tensioner casting. Insert a small screwdriver or T-handle Allen wrench into the hole in the shaft to hold the tensioner together while you remove the pulley. Then remove the 16-mm bolt that holds the belt tensioner in

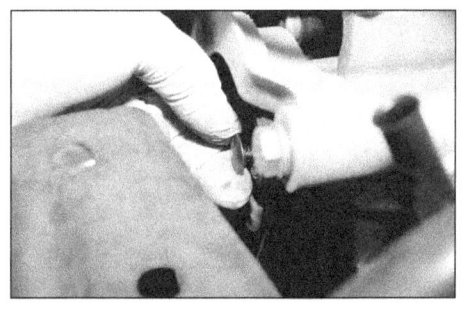

There's a center cap in the stock pulley. Remove that cap to reveal the supercharger shaft. The center bolt of the removal tool fits in it to press on the supercharger shaft.

Slip the pulley-removal tool onto the pulley so it holds the pulley evenly as you apply pressure to pull it off the shaft.

place. The belt tensioner then moves aside enough for you to gently take the belt off the supercharger pulley.

5 There is a plastic cap that fits into the body of the supercharger pulley. Remove this plug to expose the hole in the center of the pulley. Place the pulley removal tool on top of the pulley with the centering shaft in the central hole of the pulley. Use a large adjustable wrench to hold the body of the pulley removal tool while you use a 24-mm wrench or socket to turn the pulling

Use a good 24-mm socket and an adjustable wrench to turn the bolt in the pulley removal tool and pull the pulley off the shaft.

The pulley comes off in the tool. It is critical that you not damage the supercharger shaft in any way, or the supercharger will destroy itself.

THE NEW MINI PERFORMANCE HANDBOOK

The supercharger shaft is barely tapered and, once inside the supercharger, it is directly connected to the compression vanes.

The aftermarket pulley slides right onto the shaft. Press it gently until it's all the way on and seated. Tighten it with those Allen-head screws—but not too tight.

The pulley goes on and tightens up in just moments. Now you're ready to reassemble.

bolt. The tool places even pressure on the pulley to pull it off its shaft.

6. With the pulley removed, you can see the supercharger shaft. The replacement pulleys on the market are not a press-fit, but rather have a tightening collar that uses 4 to 6 small Allen-head bolts to secure the new pulley on the shaft. Place a dab of red Loctite on each bolt and reassemble the pulley. Slide the pulley onto the shaft until it stops. Using a star pattern (as when tightening lug nuts), gently snug-down the bolts to secure the pulley to the shaft. Torque spec on the Madness pulley is 60 inch-pounds.

WARNING: *Inch-pounds are a much lighter torque than foot-pounds— 60 inch-pounds converts to 5 foot-pounds. If you don't have a torque wrench capable of reading inch-pounds, that's just hand-tight with a small Allen wrench. Don't overtorque these bolts or you'll strip them!*

7. Move the belt tensioner back into place and restore the 16-mm bolt snugly, but do not torque it down. Remove the retainer you inserted step 3 and make sure the belt tension is good. Then tighten the 16-mm tensioner bolt.

8. Lower the engine back onto its mount (or mounts, if you're working on a 2002–2004 model) and reassemble the parts you removed in Step 1.

Intercooler Upgrades

When you compress air, it gets hot. Hot air is not as dense for combustion as cold air, so it helps performance to cool the air after it has been compressed by the turbocharger and before it enters the engine. Cooling the compressed air is the function of the intercooler— it's just a radiator for air. MINI mounts its stock intercoolers for the R53 supercharged car on top of the engine and provides a hood scoop to collect cool outside air and direct it through the intercooler. For the R56, the intercooler is mounted in front of the radiator, right in the main airflow. This is a better location for the intercooler, because the increased air collection area and better rearward venting improve cooling efficiency.

Several intercooler upgrades are available for both R53 and R56

The stock intercooler on the R53 is a good unit, but you can find others that are a bit bigger and cool more effectively. The plastic air duct is essential to good operation.

models. For the most part, these are simply larger units installed in the stock locations for each model. The 2006 JCW GP edition came with a larger intercooler from the factory. Installation of these larger intercoolers

This Alta intercooler is larger than stock, and uses rubber trim to make sure all the air flows where it will do the most good.

is straightforward and can be performed with reference to a standard MINI repair manual.

Air diverters are also available to ensure that more air passes through your intercooler, and these are generally effective and inexpensive.

The bottom line on larger intercoolers is that you will not see a large horsepower improvement simply by using a larger intercooler or an air diverter. However, that's not to say that they don't have value, especially if you live in a very hot climate or have increased your boost (and thus the heat of your charge air) dramatically. Every little bit helps.

There are also alternate-design intercoolers for the R53 that flow air straight through the intercooler intake, rather than directing the air downward toward the engine heat source. These are more expensive, but also more effective than simply adding a row or two to the stock design.

At the exotic end, there are water-based intercoolers for the R53. These generally incorporate the stock intercooler encased in a water jacket. There is an additional front-mounted radiator, a reservoir tank, and a recirculating pump. The water-intercooling system is closed and does not share fluid with the car's regular cooling system. Using this kind of system, you can keep the charge temperature low, which means more horsepower from a dense air charge. The Madness water-to-air intercooler system costs $1,549, and others cost as much as $2,700, so these are generally used only by the most highly modified cars.

Pressure Tube Muffler Delete

The R56 turbocharged engine comes with a muffler in the flow path to the intercooler. Replacing this restrictive part with an aftermarket tube increases flow from the turbo to the engine. Several leading aftermarket manufacturers make bolt-on replacements for this restrictive muffler.

Turbocharger Upgrades

All R56-based cars use a twin-scroll turbo for better performance across the entire working range of the engine, and specifically to eliminate power lag from low RPM. A twin-scroll turbo design uses dual turbine inputs into dual scrolls (also called "volutes") around the turbine wheel. The engine takes exhaust from two cylinders and runs that gas through one scroll of a particular size, and runs the other two cylinders of exhaust through a different-size scroll. Both volutes contain the same volume, but they each have a different radius. There is an outer volute scroll and an inner volute scroll. The fact that they have different radiuses affects the angle at which the air strikes the turbine wheel. One volute is tuned to help spin-up the turbo at low RPM, and the other to accentuate high-RPM performance. By using two scrolls of different sizes in the housing, MINI expanded the operating range of the turbo and the performance band of the engine overall.

Many enthusiasts will be happy to know that they have already improved their turbo's performance by moving to a less-restrictive exhaust system. Using a larger-diameter downpipe, higher-flowing catalyst, and larger-bore exhaust pipe reduces the amount of pressure at the turbo outlet to the downpipe. Reducing the pressure at the turbo's outlet produces a greater pressure differential from the intake side of the turbine wheel to the output. This pressure difference helps accelerate the turbo's spool-up significantly.

Robert Young is a scientist and engineer with Forced Performance, a well-known manufacturer of turbochargers. He explains the airflow

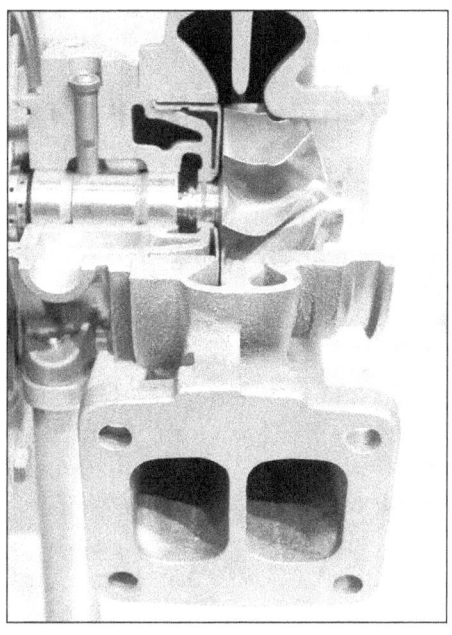

In this cutaway, you can see how the twin-scroll design used in the R56 requires two parallel but differently formed volutes to bring exhaust gas to the turbine wheel. The different shapes optimize the turbo for both low-RPM spin-up and high-RPM boost pressure.

This cutaway shows the whole inside of a turbo. On the left, you can see the compressor wheel. In the center is the shaft and its oil passages. On the right, you can see the turbine wheel.

issue like this: "You can't lose sight of the fact that all the air that you're going to use to make your horsepower has to come in through the air filter, and go out through the tailpipe. The whole path has to be de-restricted. If you were watering your lawn, you wouldn't go right in the middle of your hose and splice in a soda-pop straw. If you looked at your hose while you were watering your lawn and you realized not much water was coming out, and you looked at the length of hose and realized it was kinked in the middle, you'd unkink it and fix your problem. That's basically what you've got to do with turbocharged engines. You've got to figure out where the kink in the hose is—where's the restriction?—and correct it."

You can find out more on this topic by reading the FAQs under Info Center at www.forcedperformance.com.

PROJECT
Installing the John Cooper Works Challenge Turbo

The upgraded turbocharger used in the European R56 John Cooper Works Challenge racing MINIs can be used to upgrade the induction system on any 2007-or-later (R55, R56, or R57) Cooper S, and it's a direct replacement. Combined with an ECU software reflash, you can get up to 15 psi of boost with this installation.

Other kits are available that use high-quality turbochargers, such as the Garrett GT28RS, but these must be considered custom installations. When you upgrade to a turbo capable of supplying so much more boost, you are necessarily going to have to modify the fuel injectors and ECU mapping, probably to the extent of installing a custom standalone unit.

To perform the direct replacement turbo upgrade, follow these steps:

1 Raise the car to a comfortable working height on your lift or tall jack stands, and allow the exhaust system to cool before you begin. Then disconnect the battery. You'll be working near the alternator, and the positive terminal is unshielded. If you touch it with the heat shields as you remove them, sparks will fly.

2 Remove both O_2 sensors from the turbo downpipe. The upper sensor is accessed from the top of the engine, right out in front. The lower sensor is at the bottom of the turbo downpipe, accessed from underneath the car. O_2 sensors are frequently frozen in place and difficult to remove. You can use a standard 22-mm wrench to remove an O_2 sensor, but if at all possible they should be removed with a special O_2 sensor wrench or socket attachment. These sensors are somewhat delicate and expensive, and the O_2 sensor wrench grips all sides of the sensor body for firm and even pressure. Put some high-temperature anti-seize coating on the O_2 sensor threads before you reinstall them. This will make the removal job easier next time.

3 Remove the upper heat shield from the turbo. The shield is held in place with three 10-mm bolts across the top of the shield. You can now see the turbo assembly from above. The turbo sits right out in front of the engine, with the exhaust

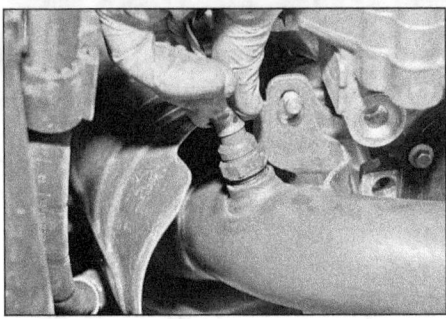
The lower O_2 sensor is on the downpipe, right where it comes out the bottom of the engine bay.

The upper O_2 sensor on an R56 is right out in front, on top of the downpipe.

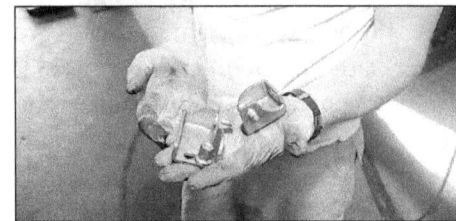
These brackets hold the downpipe in place. They have to be removed in order to get the downpipe out.

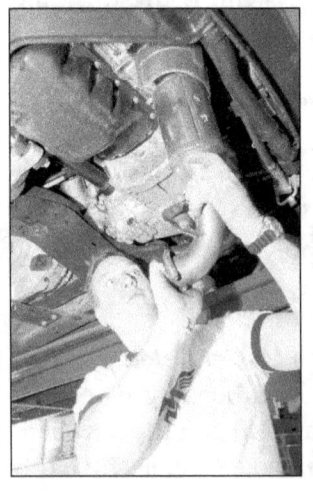
When everything is disconnected, the downpipe comes out easily from below.

INCREASING ENGINE POWER

manifold mount and the downpipe on the left with the turbine. The compressor half of the turbo is on the right. Air comes to the turbo from the intake filter through the upper flex tube and the pressurized air leaves the turbo for the intercooler from the lower tube. In the middle of the turbo are the oil lines.

4 Remove the turbo downpipe. The upper connection is held in place with three nuts on studs that extend from the turbine housing. From under the car, loosen the circumferential clamp that holds the exhaust system to the downpipe and remove the brackets that hold the bottom end of the pipe to the engine. After you remove the downpipe, remove the lower heat shield. This is the shield that is likely to contact the alternator positive terminal as you work.

The R56 exhaust manifold is small—just long enough to bring the gases to the turbo with maximum energy. It's held onto the engine with a series of 10-mm nuts on fixed studs.

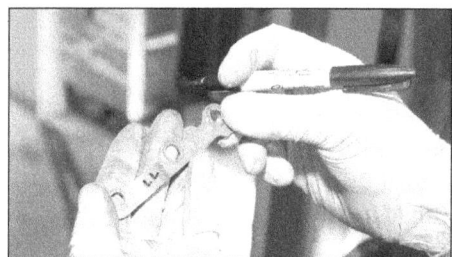

Mark the braces that help distribute the torque that holds the exhaust manifold to the engine. They are each unique and fit in only one location and one orientation.

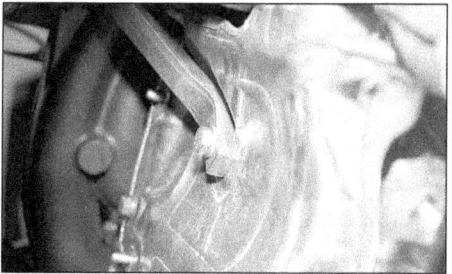

Looking up from below the car, there is a brace that is just a piece of bent metal. This brace supports the turbo assembly, and must be removed.

Again, looking up from below, use a long extension and undo the brace at the bottom of the turbo.

5 With the downpipe out, you can now see to remove the ten 11-mm nuts that hold the manifold and turbo to the engine. There are four bracing bars that help distribute the force of the manifold nuts across the top and bottom of the manifold mating face. Each of these bracing bars is a little different, so mark them according to their position on the car: lower left, upper left, upper right, lower right. There is also a turbo brace to remove to provide clearance to some of the lower manifold nuts. You access this brace from underneath the car. Also, you must remove the turbo oil drain plug from underneath the car, and this is best done with a long extension on a socket wrench.

6 Remove the air hoses from the right side of the turbo. The pressure air fitting is barbed, and the pressure hose that runs to the intercooler is also formed inside, so you might have to work a little to get this hose off.

Carefully remove the banjo bolts that supply oil to the turbo. Be sure to conserve the washers. You need one on each side of the banjo fitting.

7 Remove the oil inlet and outlet banjo bolts from the top of the turbo. Be sure to save the copper washers, as they can be reused. On the right-hand side of the turbo, locate the shiny metal canister and remove the vacuum tube from its connection. This tube controls the turbo's waste gate. Also on the right side, remove the electric connection to the black bypass valve. If your new turbo does not include its own bypass valve, you will have to transfer the stock unit. This is a simple matter of three small screws.

With the manifold off the car, you can see right into the exhaust ports. Make sure that all traces of the old gasket are cleaned off the mating face.

THE NEW MINI PERFORMANCE HANDBOOK

CHAPTER 2

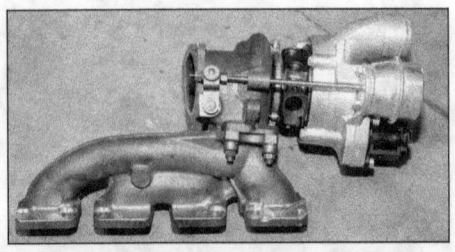

You can see how the exhaust manifold delivers gases to the turbo, and how the turbo is divided into the turbine side and the compressor side.

8 With everything disconnected, simply lift the turbo and manifold out of the car. The turbo unbolts from the manifold with four nuts.

Looking at the replacement turbo, you can see the inlet tube on top, the pressure output tube at about 9 o'clock, the waste gate actuator on the bottom, and the black bypass valve at about 3 o'clock.

> **TECH TIP — Pipe**
>
> This is a good time to replace the intercooler pipe. The stock unit has an internal muffler, and a straight-through pipe delivers better flow.

9 Clean and inspect all mating surfaces. This is a pressurized system, so clean mating surfaces are necessary to achieve a good seal. Use new gaskets when reassembling the new turbo.

The pressure outlet hose can be difficult to install. You don't want it to blow off, so use a screwdriver to help it over the barbed end of the turbo outlet.

10 Install the new turbo onto the manifold and bolt the turbo and manifold to the cylinder head. Reconnect the oil lines, bypass valve wiring, vacuum tube to the waste gate, and air hoses. Replace the oil drain and the turbo brace from underneath the car. Replace the lower heat shield and then the downpipe. Do not yet replace the upper heat shield, however.

The advantage of using an upgrade turbo made with the same housing is that everything just fits right together with no fuss.

11 When you are reinstalling the O_2 sensors, put five to six counterclockwise turns into the cables so they don't end up twisted after you have tightened the sensor in its bung. Don't forget to place a small dab of anti-seize on the threads (never on the sensor itself!) to help them come out easier next time.

12 Reconnect the battery and turn the car on for several seconds to allow the ECU to reset itself. Then start the engine and inspect the turbo for oil, exhaust, and pressure leaks. Take out the upper O_2 sensor one more time, replace the upper heat shield and the O_2 sensor. Then carefully test-drive the car, watching for the Check Engine light.

Turbo Downpipe

In a turbocharged R56, the turbo sits front-and-center relative to the engine, mounted to the exhaust manifold. The downpipe comes out the left side of the turbo body and routes exhaust flow down to the exhaust system. The stock downpipe includes a catalyst.

Replacement downpipes are available, and make an easy substitution at the same time you upgrade the turbo. The procedure to change a downpipe is the same as the procedure to change a turbo (step 1 through step 4), and then simply reverse the steps with the new downpipe.

Bear in mind that the stock downpipe contains a catalyst and it's illegal to remove that catalyst on a car intended for street use. Some downpipes feature a high-flow catalyst, and those will probably pass emissions testing.

Turbo Bypass and Blow-Off Valves

On an R56 MINI, the stock turbo system incorporates a bypass valve, which is housed in a black plastic unit attached to the turbo body. This

INCREASING ENGINE POWER

This black box is a bypass valve that redirects pressurized air back into the intake stream when you let your foot off the throttle. Because the throttle on your MINI is electronic, so is this valve.

Many aftermarket blow-off valves vent air to atmosphere. This doesn't hurt anything, but leads to a momentary rich fuel condition because that air has already been metered into your engine's intake stream and fuel allocated for it.

The waste gate is a valve that opens to allow exhaust gas to bypass the turbine when maximum boost is reached. You can fool the waste gate with a manual boost controller and get some extra boost, but it's not without risk to your engine.

valve performs the same function as a blow-off valve (BOV) on other turbocharged engines. This bypass valve is the source of the "whoosh" sound you hear when upshifting under hard acceleration, and it performs a very specific service to the engine.

When a turbocharged engine is under boost, there is a tube full of pressurized air from the turbo compressor outlet to the throttle body, and with the MINI's front-mount intercooler this tube of compressed air is about 4 to 5 feet long and moving very fast. It takes a fraction of a second for a given puff of air to make it from one end of that tube to the other.

When your MINI is running at its 6,950-rpm redline and you lift your foot off the throttle and the throttle plate closes, there's nowhere for that air to go. It slams into the throttle plate and the pressure wave bounces all the way back to the turbo. The turbo compressor fan and the shaft go from 110,000 rpm to 10,000 rpm in an instant. When you shift into the next gear and step on the gas, suddenly the turbo has to accelerate from 10,000 rpm all the way back up to 110,000 rpm again. That causes turbo lag.

The bypass valve allows that air to escape and not cause the turbocharger to lose 100,000 rpm of shaft speed instantaneously. The bypass valve can open and the pressure is released and redirected back into the intake stream. The turbo can continue spinning so that in a second, when you're back on the gas, spin-up time to maximum boost is reduced.

For most situations, the stock bypass valve is sufficient. But if you've got a custom turbo application and you've reworked your engine for a lot of boost, you may want to consider an aftermarket BOV. Some BOVs recirculate the vented air back into the system like the stock unit, which helps the engine management because all that air has been accounted for when it went by the MAF sensor. The engine is budgeting fuel for that air, and you can momentarily run rich if the air is lost on a shift. On a street car, you'll probably prefer to maintain strict air/fuel ratios and a smooth idle. Most aftermarket BOVs are the "vent to atmosphere" design. These simply release pressure to the outside. There's nothing wrong with this, but you'll want to make sure your engine

tuner accounts for the BOV when tuning.

Turbo Waste Gate

Another part of the turbo system that you hear about is the turbo's waste gate. This device is part of the stock boost control. When the turbo is producing as much boost as the engine is designed to take, a valve opens in the exhaust turbine side to allow some exhaust flow to bypass the turbine wheel.

In extreme-high-performance engines, it is sometimes necessary to upgrade the waste gate, usually to make the gate spring firmer to maintain high boost levels. But these engines are well beyond the usual level of street tuning and at that point the car has a completely custom-designed turbo system.

Related Turbo and Supercharger Upgrades

Several classes of upgrades are generally used with turbocharged cars, though very few MINIs are ever built to use these exotic upgrade parts.

CHAPTER 2

Manual Boost Controllers

Manual boost controllers are normally used to coax a little more boost out of a turbocharger. But be aware that in a MINI, boost is controlled through the ECU, and a reflash or ECU upgrade should really be your first choice for modest increases in boost pressure because that also remaps your fuel program and ignition at the same time, maintaining balance.

Manual boost controllers operate oppositely of a waste gate. Manual boost controllers bleed off some of the boost signal to the actuator until a particular boost pressure is reached. A manual boost controller is usually installed in a vacuum/pressure tube that goes to the waste gate actuator. However, because the R56 MINI is controlling boost at the ECU, the computer compensates for the waste gate not opening by applying more actuating force, triggering the bypass valve, or even shutting the throttle plate. Remember, your MINI uses an electronic throttle. The ECU can override your foot position and shut things down if it senses danger.

So, as a general rule, if you're not putting in an aftermarket big turbo kit and a standalone ECU, a manual boost controller is not an easy way to get marginally higher boost from a MINI.

Intercooler Sprayers

Many turbocharged cars use a device that sprays water onto the intercooler to improve its function. Spraying the intercooler works just like spraying any hot object—the evaporation of the water helps cool it, and that temperature drop is passed on to your air charge. MINI has no such device from the factory, but numerous aftermarket versions are available from quality suppliers for all intercooled MINI models. Some exotic aftermarket coolers even spray liquid carbon dioxide onto the intercooler in place of water.

Water/Alcohol Injection

Water injection is a technique that comes to street use from the more exotic and expensive echelons of the racing world. Cars with large, powerful turbochargers are prone to detonation due to high air temperatures caused by extreme boost levels. A water/alcohol injection system squirts a very small amount of water into the intake stream to reduce combustion-chamber intake charge temperatures enough to avoid detonation and to help burn the air/fuel mixture more efficiently.

Several leading MINI aftermarket houses sell water/alcohol injection systems. However, this kind of installation is necessary only if you have upgraded to a larger turbo capable of boost in excess of 16 to 18 psi.

Fuel System Upgrades

The stock MINI fueling system is based on the engine management map of the stock MINI. There is enough

---

PROJECT

Diverting the Windshield Washer to Cool the R53 Intercooler

You can make your own intercooler sprayer by following these steps:

1 Cut a windshield washer line and place a plastic tee fitting in the tube, or redirect the rear window washer line. From the tee or rear washer line, run a tube to the intercooler.

2 Mount the line pointed at the intercooler and attach a spray nozzle. Any small directional windshield washer nozzle from the auto parts store should do the trick. Be sure to aim it at the left (hot) side of the intercooler, where it will do the most good.

There is no reason this modification cannot be used on the R56 front-mount intercooler, but it will be a longer and more difficult installation.

---

adjustability in the system to accommodate a supercharger pulley reduction or a modest increase in turbo boost. Your engine tuner should tell you when improving fuel flow is necessary, and many aftermarket products also include information about necessary fuel flow requirements.

Radiator and Oil Cooler Upgrades

The stock MINI cooling system should be sufficient to keep your engine running in the correct temperature range unless you are making well-over-stock horsepower. When you come to the point that you're taking the car to the race track and you need to upgrade the cooling system, bear these considerations in mind:

- Have you maximized airflow to your existing radiator and oil cooler?
- Is your thermostat functioning as designed?
- Are you underdriving your water pump? This is a consequence of changing the supercharger pulley on the R53. The water pump spins 15 to 19 percent faster, moving the water

INCREASING ENGINE POWER

through the system more quickly, reducing the time for cooling in the radiator.
- Does your car have an automatic transmission, and if so, does the radiator you're considering include a compatible transmission cooler?

With your radiator and oil cooler needs well-understood, you can order upgraded direct-fit replacements from several aftermarket MINI retailers.

Naturally Aspirated Engine Upgrade

For the most part, this chapter has focused on the R53- and R56-based, forced-induction engines. The primary reason that the Cooper does not get much engine performance development compared to the Cooper S models is simply the low cost to purchase a forced-induction model and thereby get a fully supported high-performance car. However, there's plenty you can do to give your naturally aspirated R50, R52, R55, R56, or R57 MINI Cooper a little kick in the pants for some more power.

The two places where you'll pick up the most power are at the intake and exhaust. A basic cold-air-intake kit and a cat-back will get you about as far as you can go without getting into the engine internals. The R50 engine also responds well to an MSD ignition kit. The Supersprint exhaust we installed sells for $450 at PRO MINI.com. You can buy a Magnum Force cold-air intake along with it for $169. Add $240 for the MSD kit and you've claimed most of the available horsepower for well under $1,000. You can also install a replacement header, but it costs another $1,000 for only marginal gains.

PROJECT
Installing the SuperSprint Cat-Back Exhaust on an R50 Cooper

This project covers the single best thing you can do for an R50 Cooper's performance: de-restrict the exhaust. Combined with a cold-air intake, you've done the lion's share of the easy horsepower improvement you can get with this car.

1 Disconnect the battery and raise the car. Unbolt the connection that holds the one-piece stock exhaust system to the header.

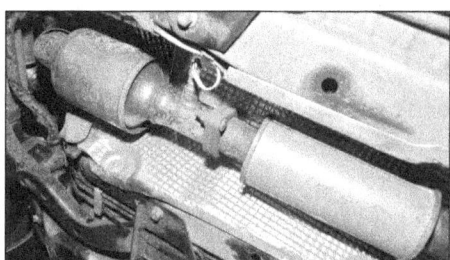

The interface between the exhaust and the header is the same as on other MINIs. Just undo the two nuts from the studs and be careful not to damage the copper gasket.

2 Remove the stock center support from under the exhaust. This is a black rectangular stamping that is attached to the chassis with six bolts. Then spray the rubber hangers with WD-40 and pry the stock exhaust system away from the rubber hangers. The stock rubber hangers can be reused.

There are two of these 10-mm bolts that hold the muffler strap around the stock muffler. Undo them and the muffler comes right out.

3 Find the muffler can at the rear of the car and undo the muffler strap. Be careful, as the exhaust falls out on the ground when you undo this strap.

4 Use some WD-40 to lubricate the stock muffler hangers and remove the top of the strap from the hangers. The Supersprint kit comes with two new strap tops. One is labeled 2001 MINI and the other is labeled 2002 MINI. All North American MINIs use the 2002 design. Lubricate the studs and press them into the hangers so that the strap hangs at an angle with respect to the car's centerline. Test-fit the muffler half of the system if you're not sure how to install the hanger strap.

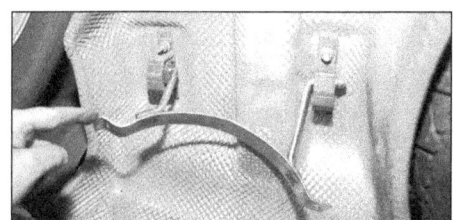

SuperSprint gives you two muffler hangers. You want the one that is labeled for 2002+ Coopers. Note that the muffler comes through at an angle, and so the hanger is also mounted at an angle.

5 Assemble the two pieces of the new exhaust and install the center support on the provided studs, but leave the fittings loose for now. Get a friend to help you lift the new exhaust into place and install the bottom half of the muffler strap hanger. Or you can install the new exhaust in pieces and then fit it together.

6 Working front-to-back, tighten the fittings on your new

THE NEW MINI PERFORMANCE HANDBOOK

exhaust. Pay attention to orientation, because misalignment anywhere in the system will make your new tailpipe sit off-center in the bumper space. Note that the nuts provided with the system are bronze and therefore soft. Don't over-tighten them or you'll strip them out.

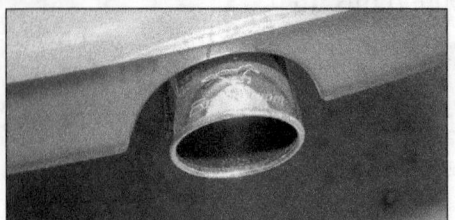

The SuperSprint is a well-made product and an easy install. This unit is good for a substantial power gain in your Cooper.

7 Drop the car and reconnect the battery. When you start the car, you'll hear an aggressive new undertone to your exhaust, and you'll be surprised how much power you just gained!

Turbocharging a Cooper

For some Cooper owners, adding a turbocharger may seem like an attractive way to boost horsepower and torque. The short answer to this temptation is: Don't do it! It will cost you more than the price difference between a Cooper and a Cooper S to make the conversion, and when you're done you will have a ticking time bomb under your hood.

The most critical factor is the compression ratio. Simply put, this is the relative size of the combustion chamber at top dead center (TDC) compared to the size at bottom dead center (BDC). There's a complex formula to calculate the exact ratio, but generally if your chamber is 50 cc at TDC and 500 cc at BDC, your basic

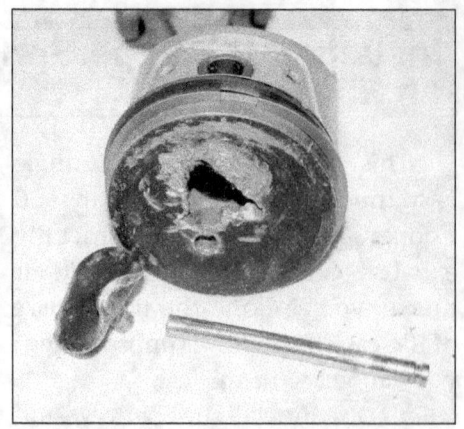

The danger when you start pumping up the power in your engine is that you may exceed the designed strength of any number of components. Broken engines are part of the high-performance game, so be careful or be ready.

compression ratio is 10:1. An R50 MINI Cooper has a factory compression ratio of 10.6:1 and an R56 Cooper has a compression ratio of 11:1. For comparison, an R53 Cooper S has an 8.3:1 compression ratio, and an R56 Cooper S is compressed at 10.5:1.

In general, turbocharged and supercharged engines start out with a lower compression ratio because boost raises the cylinder pressure. So, the naturally aspirated Cooper engines have higher-compression-engines and different engine management software than their Cooper S siblings. If you put boost into an engine designed for high compression and normal atmospheric pressure, you risk detonation and big holes in your pistons.

Controlling the Engine: ECU Upgrades

In older cars, fuel delivery and ignition tuning were controlled by the operation of mechanical parts. You adjusted this system by fiddling the

The ECU is a solid-state computer that lives next to the air filter in an R53.

carb, twisting the distributor, and setting the point gap with feeler gauges.

Today, all those functions are performed by the ECU, also called the engine management system, the "chip," or simply the computer. The ECU controls the timing and force of the spark, and also controls the amount and timing of fuel delivery through the fuel-injection system. In R56-based Cooper S models, the ECU controls the amount of boost pressure from the turbocharger. The ECU includes a top-speed and maximum-RPM governor.

The ECU is your car's brain, and it operates using input from various sensors throughout the intake, combustion, and exhaust systems. It adjusts mixture- and timing-based indications of air density coming into the engine combustion performance, exhaust gas composition, and temperature. In cars with Acceleration Stability Control (ASC), Dynamic Stability Control (DSC), Dynamic Traction Control (DTC), and Electronic Differential Lock Control (EDLC) traction control, the ECU may take input from the brakes or differential to detect a loss of traction, and respond by making changes to reduce torque to get the car back under control.

INCREASING ENGINE POWER

Building a High-Performance Cooper

Jeff and Scott Bibbee are the father-and-son team who founded Texas Speedwerks. The intrepid duo have built an R50 Cooper for autocross and trackday competition. Their effort shows the depth of work required to coax ultra-high performance from a naturally aspirated Cooper.

"I had spent some time on basic horsepower modifications—intake, cat-back exhaust, and MTH engine management software. But then I found a "take-off" Cooper S head from a local owner who had the JCW kit installed a few years back, so I decided it was time for more," Scott says.

Jeff and Scott's business partner, "Dr. Mike," spent more than 80 hours porting and polishing the Cooper S head, meticulously machining the ports and runners to maximize air velocity, and he did it all by hand. The process of porting and polishing a head is laborious, but it removes material that hinders airflow into and out of the combustion chamber.

"We reused the stock Cooper S valves, as we didn't think any bigger valves were necessary for the NA Cooper motor. My dad and I lapped the valves in by hand after we cleaned everything up with a Scotchbrite setup on Mike's drill press," Scott continues.

Scott then chose a Shrick Cooper cam, which offers significantly more lift and duration than the stock R50 cam. When he reassembled the car, Scott also installed a Milltek header and catalyst to increase exhaust flow.

"Immediately, the car was a completely different animal. Off the line, the car was noticeably quicker—but, between 4,000 rpm and our new redline of 7,000, the car was an animal. A couple years later, Jan Brueggemann from Revolution MINI came to Dallas and tuned the car. We picked up 6 to 7 more peak horsepower, but the magic came from an additional 6 to 7 ft-lbs of torque throughout the power band. This made street driving even better," Scott says.

Right now, Scott's R50 may well be the most powerful naturally aspirated Cooper anywhere. "Right now, the wheel horsepower is 145, and close to 140 ft-lbs of torque," he says. Scott has a couple improvements planned that he believes will make even more power. A custom intake manifold with runners and a plenum matched to the system and yet another aftermarket header are in the works.

"We figure the new intake manifold will correct a slight dip between 3,000 and 4,000 rpm that we were seeing on the dyno, as well as offering more power on the top end. A new header will complement the final product, maximizing port velocity on the other side," Scott says.

Prior to Jan's tuning, this car participated in the *MC2 Magazine* Dynamic Track Collective shootout at Spring Mountain Raceway in Pahrump, Nevada. Even with 40 hp less than other cars, this Cooper was still sixth fastest of 12 cars entered. "Had we been on R-compound tires like all the other competitors, I think we would have been up in third place," Scott says.

Scott Bibbee of Texas Speedwerks has built an R50 Cooper that makes about 145 wheel hp without forced induction of any kind. This is the old-fashioned way of making horsepower, by careful optimization and craftsmanship. (Photo courtesy Scott Bibbee)

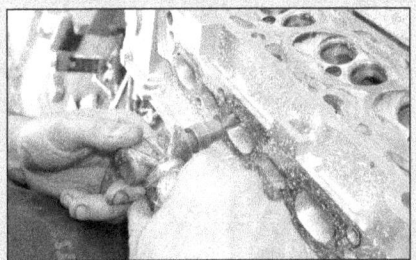

Mike works carefully to expand and smooth out the exhaust ports on this R50 Cooper head. With a naturally aspirated engine, everything you can do to increase flow helps you make power.

You can see how the intake ports have been opened and smoothed to bring as much air as possible into the combustion chamber with every stroke.

CHAPTER 2

Expert Interview: MINI Madness on ECU Upgrades

George Mehallick founded MINI Madness and started modifying MINIs as soon as the first ones were sold in the United States. In the course of his development efforts on R53 and R56 Cooper S ECUs, he's seen it all and knows what works and what doesn't.

Q: Most people modifying MINIs are just looking for more street performance. When should they think about changing their ECU programming?

For the R53, they should reflash the ECU after they install a reduction pulley on the supercharger. We don't recommend anyone driving an R53 with a pulley for more than six months without an ECU programming change. The reason is that when you add another 4½ pounds of boost to the system, the car doesn't think that's a good thing; it thinks it's a bad thing and it doesn't know why it's happening. Instead of seeing a small change in boost pressure based on atmospheric conditions or altitude, it's seeing big changes. So it does its best to try to adjust. But the processing power of the computer is not robust enough to make changes that fast. The default mode of the ECU is to dump fuel into the system to compensate. It also retards timing to try to adjust. This is all happening because its baseline has been altered. So we give it new programming to reset that baseline. Now that the computer knows a new baseline that matches what it's seeing, it can make better decisions.

Q: What about the turbocharged R56?

For the R56, changing the ECU programming is what you do instead of changing the pulley, because the ECU controls the boost from the turbocharger.

Q: What are the benefits of a reflash?

It'll improves fuel mileage and performance. We can also push the performance limits a bit based on what's been done to the car and what kind of fuel the car will be drinking. If we know the car's going to be running on 100-octane unleaded racing fuel, we can use different settings than if it's running on 91-octane pump gas.

Q: Many street performance enthusiasts may want to walk these changes back eventually. Can they do that?

Yes. They can simply go to the dealer and have them reflash it back to the stock programming.

Q: What's the practical difference between a reflash and a piggyback ECU unit?

A reflash is the cleanest solution from a hardware perspective. It's seamless because you don't have to cut into your wiring. The other thing that's nice about a reflash is that you have access to the full spectrum of the computer. Whereas with a piggyback unit, you have a very limited scope of things, because the piggyback intercepts signals from sensors in the car and then manipulates those signals before sending them on to the ECU. So you can't change the RPM limit or the top-speed governor.

Q: Do you usually change the RPM limit and top speed with a reflash?

Yes, we remove the top-speed limit and raise the rev limit by about 500 rpm. We do this because the engine makes power right up into that range, and it's amazing what a 500-rpm difference makes in shift points, especially on a race track.

Q: What about a standalone ECU?

Those are limited to race cars only. The thing about the MINI is that there are actually several computers. You've got a body computer module that controls the water temperature, fuel level, speedometer, lights, and air conditioning. That's directly connected to the engine-control module, and if you replace the ECU you have turned off all that other stuff. You have to put in separate gauges with their own senders, and figure out how to control all those functions.

> **Q: So, it seems like a reflash is the right answer for most people. How much should someone expect to pay for it?**
>
> Typically from $700 to $800, depending on who's doing the work. It's not custom to the point of sitting on the dyno with a particular engine with particular modifications, but we have several canned programs for different common setups. So we ask a customer a series of questions like "What mods do you have on your engine?" and "What kind of fuel are you using?" and then select a program to meet those needs. One thing about our program is that ours is a one-time fee. If you buy a reflash from us and then change your engine needs, we'll update that reflash for free. Another thing to note is that people are leery of reflashes and they worry that the dealer will be able to detect the reflash, but it's really not detectable.

All MINIs use OBD II–compliant ECU computers. These computers use flash memory—similar to the re-writable memory chip in a digital camera or thumb drive. Information is retained in the memory even if you completely disconnect its power source.

When automakers build a car, they play it safe with the ECU programming. They need to meet emissions standards, fuel-economy standards, and perhaps most importantly, longevity standards for their products. So they program the ECU to accept whatever kind of fuel the cars may be forced to drink, a wide range of altitudes at which the cars may have to operate, and a big safety margin to keep the engines from blowing up.

Obviously, then, the ECU is an excellent place to find some additional performance. But it's also about the most difficult thing for the average car owner to really understand. ECU programming is complex, and the vast majority of us are not qualified to tinker with it. But there are products on the market with proven programs that will optimize your car's performance with the specific hardware modifications you have made.

For the MINI, there are three levels of ECU upgrade: a packaged or custom reflash of the stock ECU, a "piggyback" unit that works in addition to your stock ECU, and a complete standalone replacement-ECU computer. It is not fair to say that any of these options is inherently better than the others; each of these options has its place, depending on your needs. Reflashing your stock ECU is cheaper and far easier than buying a piggyback unit, and a piggyback is generally cheaper than a full computer replacement.

You can get great street- and light-competition performance improvements from a simple packaged reflash that you can install yourself. A custom reflash generally requires an experienced tuner, but the result is uniquely tailored to your car and your performance needs. Some piggyback units require massive intervention and hacking into the car's wiring harness. At that point, you're better off going with a full standalone ECU, which requires custom wiring and is really suited only to dedicated racing cars. For the vast majority of drivers, a light-duty reflash does the trick.

Several aftermarket retailers are working on plug-and-play reflashes that plug into your OBD II socket, but at press time only the Shark Injector for 2002–2006 Cooper S models is on the market. Read the installation instructions for that product carefully before you buy it.

Stock ECU

If you upgrade to a standalone system, be sure to hang on to your stock ECU in case you ever need to restore the stock setup.

There's one more thing you need to know about changing the ECU: It's an emissions-control device and covered under the same federal law that governs catalytic converters.

CHAPTER 3

IMPROVING HANDLING

Your MINI is one of the best-handling cars ever offered to the motoring public. The modern MINI is heir to a 50-year tradition of competing far outside its power class, based primarily on a good, balanced suspension placed under a chassis optimized for great driving performance. Other cars have addressed suspension and handling after the body or engine was determined; with a MINI, the great handling is built in right from the first line drawn on a clean sheet of paper.

By placing the wheels at the four corners of the vehicle, the original MINI designers ensured a stable platform, with improved interior space as well. By choosing a transverse-mounted front-wheel-drive design, the designers ensured that the little car would place most of its weight low, above the front wheels, for better traction and quick steering. And by keeping the whole

Cornering

A low-powered car can build up and maintain speed if it handles well, but a poor-handling car has to slow down for every corner.

Speed Reading

If you are interested in learning more about suspension design and development, there are several good books on the market that go into far greater detail about the science that governs suspension work. Carroll Smith's *Tune to Win* and Fred Puhn's *How To Make Your Car Handle* are great resources.

Autocrossers are perhaps the best suspension tuners in the world. Because their sport depends on razor-sharp car placement and precise handling, they know how to get the most out of their suspension. (Photo courtesy Craig Wilcox)

assembly lightweight and on a short wheelbase, they made sure that the MINI would be lively and eager on a curvy road. The designers of the new MINI retained all those benefits and added a modern suspension and steering system.

But that doesn't mean you can't improve things. Every production car is a product of many compromises. A smooth ride versus stiffer shocks and springs, or the tendency to understeer rather than oversteer, for safety. The factors designed into the stock suspension are not unchangeable, and you can tighten-up your MINI to race car specs, or just cinch-up a few loose places and enjoy a car that competes with others at twice the horsepower and twice the price.

WARNING: *Automotive suspensions use tremendously powerful springs that are held under compression when normally installed. Do not attempt to release any automotive spring without the proper tools and instructions or you could seriously injure yourself or even be killed. It costs just a few dollars to have a professional shop install springs, and it's money well-spent if you don't have the right tools to do it safely.*

Suspension Terms and Concepts

While we're examining the suspension system, this is a good time to explain a few terms that are often used but are sometimes not well-understood. Three terms heard frequently in any discussion of suspension are camber, caster, and toe. Along with ride height, these measurements are the basic building blocks of suspension alignment. More advanced concepts include roll center, bump steer, Ackerman steer,

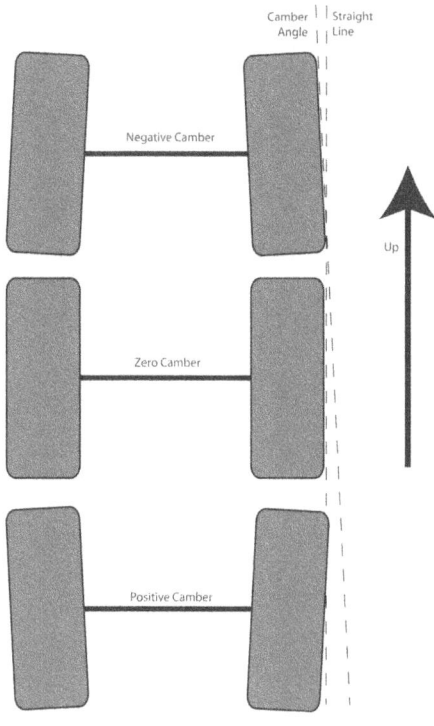

This diagram shows what camber looks like against a true vertical line. Park your car on a flat surface and use a carpenter's square or plumb bob and you can observe your car's camber.

sprung/unsprung weight, slip angle, and torque steer.

Camber

Camber is the angle made by the plane of the wheel and a truly vertical line drawn next to the wheel when viewed from the front or rear. Simply put, if the wheel angles in at the top, this is called "negative" camber. If the wheel angles out at the top, it's "positive" camber. And if the wheel is straight up and down, it's "zero" camber.

For maximum grip, you want zero camber on the outside wheels while you're cornering. That's key, because you have to account for suspension compression, body roll, and tire deflection while the car is sitting still. Most suspensions move toward

Springs

Replacing your stock springs with lowering springs gives you a bit more negative camber all on its own. This may be enough to suit your needs.

positive camber as the car leans while cornering. In nearly every case, any gain realized as the suspension compresses and the front wheels turn are less than that lost due to body roll, so you start with a bit of negative camber. Also, tires deflect a bit under cornering (taller 60- and 70-series tires much more so than low-profile tires) and you have to take that into account, too. With aftermarket parts, all four wheels on a MINI can be adjusted for camber.

Caster

Caster is the angle between the actual steering axis (a line from the upper ball joint to the lower ball joint and through to the floor) and a true vertical line drawn up the diameter of the wheel. Generally the top ball joint is set slightly farther back than the lower ball joint. A rolling wheel naturally tries to follow its steering axis, which is why if you release the steering wheel in a turn, the car begins to straighten itself out. For ordinary driving purposes, caster has a wonderful effect: enhancing stability and helping your car go in a straight line. Caster is a function mostly limited to the front wheels, but caster also affects rear wheels to the extent that they are subject to bump steer.

Too much caster can make a car harder to steer and sluggish to turn down into corners, but on a MINI, you can't adjust more caster into the

CHAPTER 3

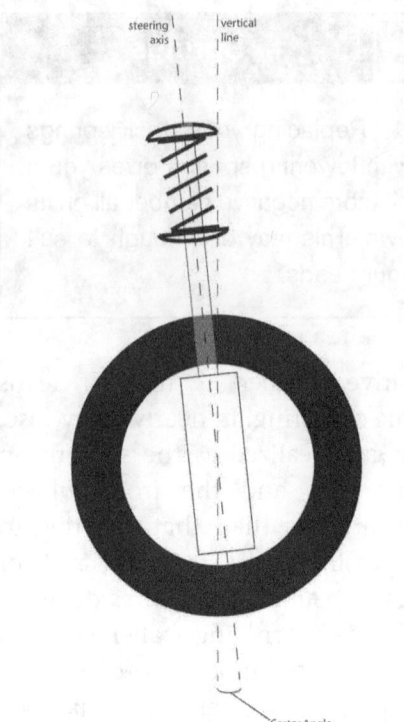

Caster is harder to see on a car, but it's there. This diagram shows how caster is created by suspension geometry.

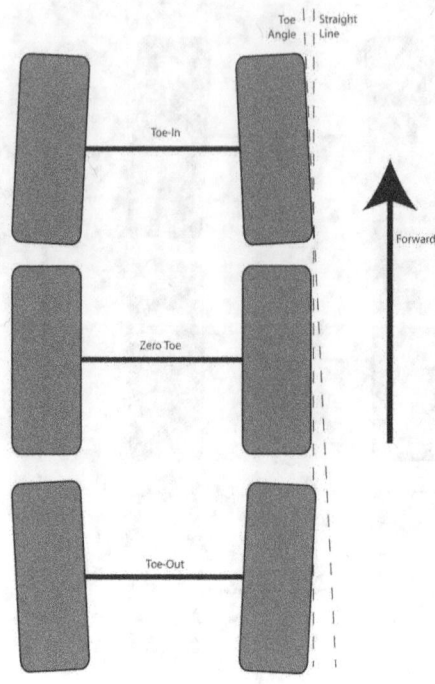

This diagram shows toe settings as seen from above the tire. It's hard to see toe with the naked eye, because the body lines of most cars are not truly parallel.

car beyond the stock setting without major suspension upgrades. Note that the caster setting also affects camber as you turn the wheels, so take that into account when you choose components that allow you to adjust caster or camber. The more caster you create, the more negative camber you get on the outside wheel when you turn the wheels. In the recommended camber settings (negative 1 to 1.5) the effect of stock caster has already been integrated, but if you start playing with caster, you need to understand that you're also dialing in more camber when turning.

Toe

Toe is the angle between two lines drawn parallel to the planes of a pair of tires. This is the easiest of the three to explain. If the fronts of a pair of tires are closer together than the backs, that's toe-in. If the backs are closer together, that's toe-out. Look at your feet if you're not sure. Put your heels apart and toes in, that's toe-in. Heels together and toes apart, that's toe-out.

In general, most street-driven cars want a little bit of toe-in—just about 1/16 inch or so. This is so that when the car is driving in a straight line, both wheels are trying to drive toward the car's centerline. This enhances stability at the cost of a little bit of friction. It also means that you have to turn the steering wheel a little farther to get both tires pointing into a turn. Conversely, if you set your car up with toe-out, both tires are trying to drive away from the car's centerline in straight-line driving, which increases a feeling of "wandering" on the road, especially on a rough surface. But if you want to turn, a bit of toe-out on the front wheels means that just a slight movement of the steering wheel causes both tires to head into the turn, increasing turn-in response. For the best straight-line speed, you want zero toe—all wheels exactly parallel.

Note that the steering arm angle changes the toe setting when you change the ride height of your car because you are moving your wheels up or down relative to the fixed point of steering attachment on the chassis. Ideally you want the steering rods level (parallel with the ground) to minimize bump steer. In addition, adjusting camber or caster causes a change in toe, making toe the last piece of the alignment puzzle to be adjusted.

Roll Center

A car's roll center is a matter of great concern to automotive designers and race car engineers, but they have the advantage of being able to design or adjust their cars to whatever specification they like. The rest of us are limited to minor adjustments to the design that the engineers give us.

The simplest explanation is that a car's roll centers (one in the front and one in the rear) are the points around which the car's body wants to rotate under cornering forces. At rest, these points are located roughly along the centerline of the car between the front- and rear-wheel centers, and a little bit above ground level. The roll axis is an imaginary line through the car's front and rear roll centers. The tricky part is that the roll axis moves around a bit based on every movement in the car's suspension as you drive.

IMPROVING HANDLING

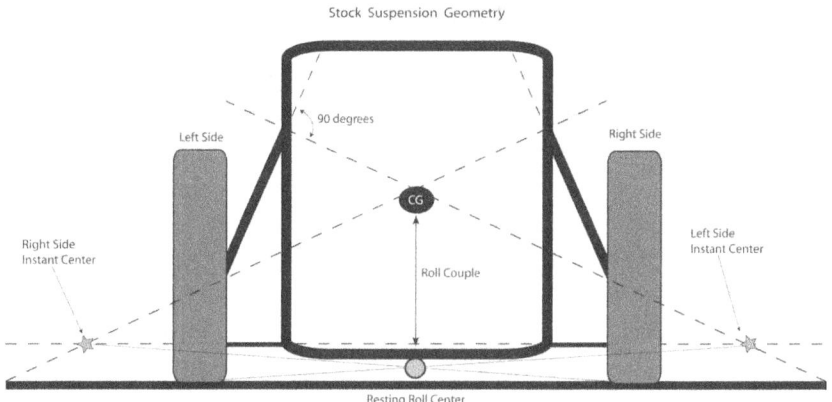

This somewhat complex diagram shows how automotive engineers figure a car's roll center. The details are not critically important, except to note that the MINI's designers put its roll center above ground level and you want to keep it there.

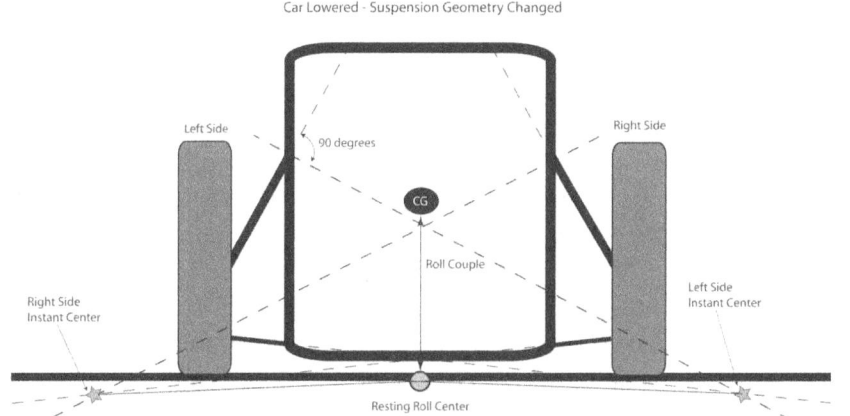

Just by installing lowering springs, you have altered the car's roll center. Maybe not this much, but some. You need to restore it to its original location.

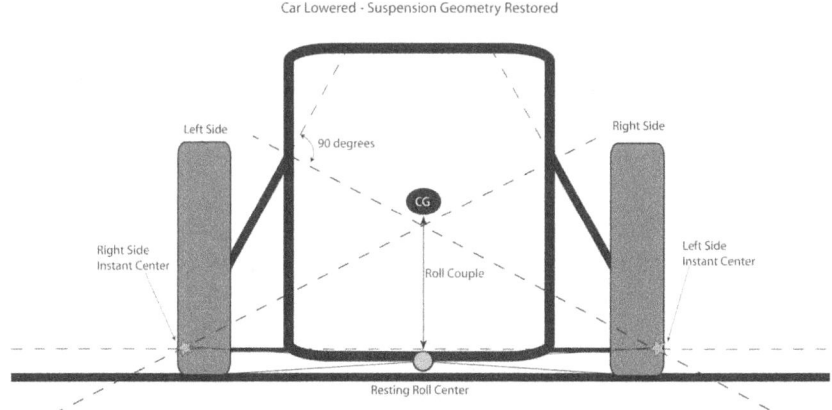

By restoring the stock suspension geometry, you have raised the roll center again while you've kept the lower center of gravity. As a bonus, you have reduced your roll couple.

In addition to roll centers, your car also has a center of gravity, and the distance between the height of the center of gravity and the roll axis is called the roll couple. The roll couple acts as a moment arm—a virtual lever—trying to tip your car over when cornering. A long roll couple makes tall SUVs feel "tippy," and a short roll couple is part of what makes your MINI feel stable.

If this all sounds like a lot of confusing engineering talk, that's because it is. What you need to know is the general effect of the suspension changes you are contemplating.

When you put lowering springs on your MINI, you lower the center of gravity, but you also lower the roll axis. You can restore the stock suspension geometry by lowering the outboard end of the lower control arm by about the same amount as your lowering springs dropped the chassis, thus raising your roll center back to the stock specification, but keeping the lowered center of gravity. Congratulations! You just reduced your roll couple.

To recap: By lowering your car an inch or so, and then raising the roll center by about the same amount (it doesn't have to be precisely the same), you can keep the stock roll center and predictable suspension geometry, and also shorten the roll couple moment arm and reduce the

> **Tire Diameter**
>
> When you're thinking about changing your wheel and tire size from stock, bear in mind that this also changes your suspension geometry and roll center. Smaller-outside-diameter tires lower your roll center.

leverage applied to your car. This change also reduces the amount that the roll center moves side to side in cornering. All of this yields a more stable platform as you drive.

You can take it too far, however. If you put the roll center high enough to be at the same height as the center of gravity, you would have zero roll in cornering, but you can't cheat physics out of overall weight transfer when you corner. Having the roll center too high also alters the wheels' camber curve, and your car will want to rise up on its suspension in cornering. Keeping the roll center about where the factory put it is a good compromise.

Bump Steer

Bump Steer is simply the change in your tire's steering orientation that happens as the suspension travels between full extension (droop) and full compression (jounce). Because each steering rod is fixed at the inboard end, but the suspension allows the wheel assembly to move up and down, the outboard end of the steering rod describes an arc. If that's hard to visualize, hold your arm straight out in front of you. Your elbow is the inboard end of a tie rod, and your hand is the outboard end. If you bend your arm at the elbow, your hand describes an arc. If your hand was holding onto the steering arm on a wheel, that wheel's steering direction would be changed as your elbow bends.

Thus, bump steer means that if the tire is exactly parallel to its mate when the car is at rest, it will be pulled out of parallel when the suspension is compressed in jounce, or extended in droop. You experience bump steer as the sensation of having the steering wheel "yanked out of your hand" when you hit a pothole or bump. You may also notice that when you run over such an obstacle, your car changes direction. That's bump steer in action.

Ackerman Steer

Ackerman steer is another concept that comes into play as steering input moves the front wheels. Simply put, if the front wheels are parallel when steering is centered, the geometry of the control arms on the wheel assemblies and in the steering rods may cause the wheels to move out of parallel as you deliver more steering input. Typically, the inside front wheel points into a turn more than the outside front wheel. The goal is to cause both wheels to orbit around a single central point. Because the inner wheel is in a tighter orbit around that point, its angle of steering needs to be more extreme.

For high-performance driving, engineers alter the steering geometry to create "reverse Ackerman," which is getting the outside wheel to describe a tighter angle than the inside wheel. They do this because they know the outer wheel will be taking most of the pressure and controlling the total amount of slipping, and the goal is to correct for slippage with the increased steering angle.

The amount of bump steer and Ackerman steer in your car is a function of the geometry of your suspension and steering system. You can't do much about it in a street-driving context, except to keep these factors more or less where the MINI engineers put them, while you go about making some smart changes to improve handling. If you make changes without considering these factors, you can experience unintended negative consequences in your handling.

Sprung and Unsprung Weight

When talking about suspensions, you hear the term "unsprung weight" from time to time. What this means is simply that portion of a car's total weight that is not supported by a spring. Usually, this means the wheel/tire combination; the hub, brake, and a portion of the lower suspension arms; and bottom of the strut/shock assembly on each wheel.

In general, the higher the un-sprung weight, the greater the impact on the suspension as you traverse bumps and other "upsets" to your vehicle. The reason is simple—the suspension has to control more bouncing mass as you drive.

Your tires take up some of the shock when you go over a bump, but if you've got very-low-profile tires (such as the run-flat designs on heavy wheels, as installed by the factory on the Cooper S), they won't absorb very much. If you have high unsprung weight, that much more shock is transferred to your suspension and your car.

So for better handling and steering, you want to keep the unsprung weight as low as possible through the use of lighter wheels and other suspension components. But, as always, there are tradeoffs to think about. For example, you might decide that larger brakes are a good investment despite the increase in unsprung weight that they carry.

Slip Angle

Slip angle is the difference between where your tires are pointed and where you're going. In hard cornering you can usually feel the tires slipping, but slippage happens any time you turn the car. As the tires roll and the contact patch continually changes from one section of the

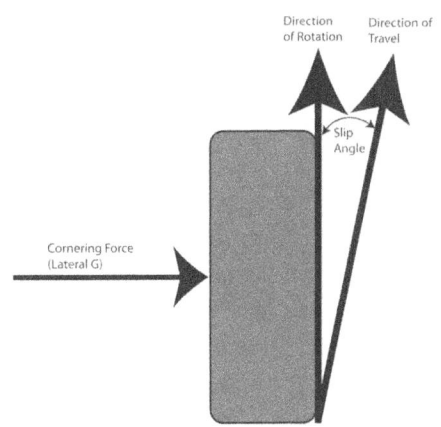

Every time you corner, each tire on your car has a slip angle. The beauty of modern tires is that they can tolerate much more extreme slip angles than tires of a few decades ago. That's part of what makes your MINI so much fun to drive.

tread face to the next, there's some natural give that has to happen just because the tire is made of rubber and is designed to be flexible.

What's interesting about slip angle is that it is constantly changing as you move into and out of a corner, and at any given moment it's not the same for the front tires compared to the rear, or from side to side. Each tire has its own slip angle, constantly changing.

Slip angle is not a setting you can change. Rather, it's a means of describing what is happening with a tire. When a car is understeering, we say that the slip angle ratio (front to rear) is greater than 1:1. That is, the fronts are slipping more. If the converse ratio applies and the rears are slipping more, that's oversteer. The greater the slip angle, the more the tire is scrubbing as you corner.

Slip angles are a good thing, because if your tires didn't slip at all they would hold traction perfectly right up to the point that lateral G forces overcome that traction, which would happen at a surprisingly low speed. Modern tires are very well designed to hang on to some traction even at very high slip angles.

The point of explaining this is that when you make changes to the suspension, the changes come through in the tires' slip angles. Changes to the car's roll axis, roll stiffness (springs and sway bars), and alignment all affect working slip angles.

Torque Steer

Torque steer is an effect you feel under hard acceleration where your car wants to veer left or right (and sometimes alternating) on its own. In older front-wheel-drive cars with unequal-length driveshafts, this problem was severe even in low-powered cars. The MINI has equal-length driveshafts and a well-designed steering system, so the problem is reduced. But if you have a Cooper S of any year, you've also got a lot of torque. Yet a bit of torque steer is better than the alternative, which is spinning your wheels.

If you turn off the DSC and really lay into the throttle on a Cooper S, you can induce wheelspin; especially if the traction on that particular patch of street is reduced in any way. As traction changes from moment to moment between your front wheels, you experience the feeling as the car wanting to steer itself. If your car has a limited slip differential, the feeling can be even more dramatic, and can also be experienced as understeer when you're accelerating through a corner.

Finally, if your R53 is equipped with DSC or ASC, those systems will apply a little brake to the spinning tire to redirect torque to the tire that still has grip, and this can feel like torque steer. The DTC and EDLC on the R56 is more advanced and reduces the sensation of torque steer.

MINI Suspension Design

The MINI suspension is fundamentally the same across the entire product line. Small differences exist in parts from different models, but the design strategy remains the same.

Front Suspension

A MINI front suspension is relatively simple, as suspensions go. On each side of the car, there is an L-shaped lower control arm attached to the chassis in two places. The part is often called an A-arm (or wishbone)—on some cars they are actually shaped like a capital A. The A-arm is made from thick, stamped and welded sheet steel, and it supports the hub and bearing carrier assembly on a ball joint.

The bearing carrier includes one flange on which to attach the steering arm, and another flange on which to attach the brake caliper. The brake disc is centered on the hub and is held down by a Torx screw, the brake caliper, and the wheel. The front axle comes through the bearing carrier assembly to spin the hub, and it is held in the hub by a large nut. At its top, the bearing carrier attaches to a MacPherson strut assembly, which includes a support structure, a spring, a shock absorber, and a top mount that bolts into the chassis of the car. There is an anti-sway bar that connects to the two front struts with drop links and is attached to the chassis in two places.

On any R50, R52, or R53 with the stock front suspension, camber and caster are set for you. The bottom of the strut fits snugly into the top of the bearing carrier and one bolt is used to hold it in place. The strut top is fixed, and does not allow for camber or caster changes, yet the entire assembly is put together with soft rubber bushings that allow quite a bit of flex. But that's why there's an aftermarket, to provide firm bushings and adjustable components.

On the R56, you have about -0.5 degree of front camber adjustment you can set. There is a screw or plastic pin at the top of the strut tower, and the holes through which the strut is mounted are slightly elongated. Simply remove the screw or pin and loosen the strut top nuts. Press the strut toward the center of the car and retighten the strut top nuts.

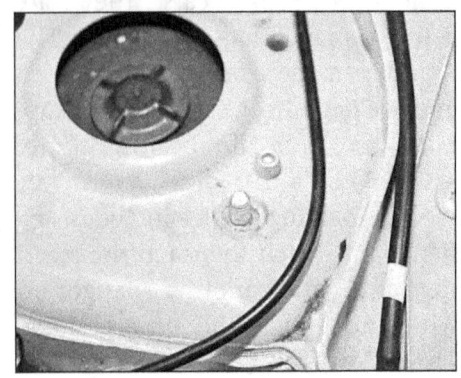

You can see the slotted hole in which the strut top bolt rides. If you remove that peg, you can get about 1/2 degree of negative camber right away into your R56-based MINI.

Rear Suspension Design

On each side of the rear of the car, there is a hub and bearing carrier assembly contained in a large, stamped and welded trailing arm on R50/53 models, and an aluminum trailing arm on R56-based models. Each side also has two lateral control arms that attach to the chassis inboard of the hub assembly, and these attach to the rear end of the hub assembly at its top and bottom. These control arms limit the lateral movement of the rear wheels, while the trailing arm limits fore and aft motion.

The rear bearing carrier includes a flange on which to attach the brake caliper, and a mount for the rear strut. The brake disc is held in place by a Torx screw, the caliper, and the wheel. The MacPherson strut assembly is bolted to the inboard side of the trailing arm, and includes a support structure, a spring, a shock absorber, and a top mount that bolts into the chassis of the car. The rear anti-sway bar is attached to the chassis in two places toward the center of the car, and uses drop links to attach to the trailing arms on either side of the car.

With the stock rear suspension, you can adjust toe at the leading end of the trailing arm by loosening the bolts that hold the main bushing carrier in place. All other relevant settings are fixed through 2004. Starting in 2005, you can adjust rear camber a little (-0.5 degree) at the outer end of the lower lateral control arm. But again, remember that the assembly is put together with those soft rubber bushings. You can tighten your suspension quite a lot with just a little effort and expense by using aftermarket adjustable lateral control arms and poly bushings in the rear trailing arm.

Be wary of dialing in too much camber in the rear. You want only about -1.0 degree on each side or you will start to increase understeer in corners.

Shock and Spring Upgrades

In any discussion of modern cars, you hear the word "strut" used synonymously with the word "shock." This is accurate enough—if they need new shocks, most folks buy a new strut assembly. But the strut is properly the assembly that functions as the upper control arm of the front suspension, and the shock absorber is simply the insert that damps suspension motion.

Shock absorbers (also called dampers) are a critical part of the suspension. More than anything else, they keep the wheels in contact with the ground by absorbing the spring recoil when you drive over a bump. Without shocks, the springs can literally launch the car into the air when they are suddenly compressed by a bump and then release their energy. The shock absorbers "catch" the car and make the springs release their energy over time. Moreover, shocks make the car's ride more comfortable and confident. You should always keep your shocks in good condition.

When people talk about shock absorbers, they sometimes use the terms "jounce" or "bump" and "rebound" to describe compression and extension resistance, respectively. A shock absorber resists both jounce and rebound, but it may not resist both motions equally. If you have adjustable shocks, you can set the resistance level to harder or softer settings, but sometimes only in the rebound direction. If you have purchased double-adjustable shocks, you can set jounce and rebound resistance separately.

A common mistake people make with adjustable shocks is to set them up as stiffly as possible. Stiff shocks seem like high performance because you can feel every bump—you may think you can tell the difference between driving over a dime and a nickel, but that's not necessarily helping keep your tires on the ground. Most adjustable shocks are quite stiff to begin with, so start with them on their softest setting and work your

Expert Interview: Texas Speedwerks on MINI Suspension

Jeff and Scott Bibbee are experts on MINI suspension. As the owners of Texas Speedwerks and avid autocross and time-attack competitors, they know the value of getting a MINI's suspension just right.

Q: As professionals in the field, what do you think are the strengths and weaknesses of the stock suspension?

Scott: The obvious strengths are the go-kart handling right out of the box, which is not to say that it can't be improved, but the car handles really well as delivered. MINI did their homework on setting the car up, but the downside with any mass-produced car is that it has to be what the factory considers safe. In most situations, that means understeer. They would prefer that if you take a corner too fast, the front end will push and you'll hit a curb rather than the rear end coming around and doing something nasty.

Jeff: To say that another way, they put too much shock and not enough spring on the car.

Scott: The U.S. manufacturers do the opposite. They prefer to overspring a car and underdampen it. That's why we have a reputation for building cars in the U.S. that wallow all over the road. That's because the spring is doing most of the suspension control, versus having a matched system. It gives you a softer ride, but not necessarily good handling. Both situations give you less control over the car.

Q: If the problem is too much shock and not enough spring, do you recommend less shock and more spring?

Jeff: Our philosophy is to leave the shock alone and beef up the spring. On the MINI, that seems to work better than anything else.

Scott: The optimal solution is to match your shocks and your springs. You want to make sure they're working in concert with each other to provide the best control over the attitude of the car. That's what the high-end suspension manufacturers are doing. They will match valving in their struts to meet the spring rates that work best for a particular car.

Q: How did you develop your custom springs?

Scott: We took all three variants of the stock shocks: the basic MINI, the Cooper S, and the JCW, and we came to a compromise on the spring rate based on the dyno plots of those three shocks. But they're not that different. The Cooper S struts and the JCW struts provide a little more dampening force, but the springs are exactly the same.

Even though our springs are significantly stiffer than the OEM springs, they're matched to the valving of the shock and the whole system works together to provide the ride characteristics that you expect—a great ride, but at the same time you have controlled handling, good cornering, and less body roll.

Q: How much will your springs lower the car?

Jeff: On the R56, a little more in the front than the rear, and on the R53 we lowered it a little more in the rear than the front. But on average our springs will drop the car about 3/4 of an inch. You'll get an additional half-degree of negative camber on all four wheels.

Q: Are your springs progressive?

Scott: Absolutely not. We don't believe in progressive springs. The reason is that progressive spring rates get higher the more you compress the suspension. So when you're in a hard corner, it's going to compress the springs more on the outside than on the inside, which means the effective spring rate on the outside has increased significantly more than the inside. Unfortunately, that leads to unpredictable behavior in mid-corner if you start to adjust the attitude of the car with the throttle.

Q: If I take off my stock struts and buy a set of Bilsteins or Koni adjustables, do I need a different set of springs?

Scott: As we said, our springs are a compromise, because we wanted them to work with the OEM shocks as well as any aftermarket offerings. Those Konis are single-adjustables. That means you're only

Expert Interview: Texas Speedwerks on MINI Suspension *CONTINUED*

able to adjust the damping and the rebound in a set ratio. If you turn them up to full stiff, they will eclipse the springs, but there aren't a lot of springs out there that can deal with that. Bilsteins have a fixed 3-to-1 ratio between damping and rebound, and they work perfectly well. We have people running on OEM struts and on Bilsteins and Konis. The result is always the same: The handling is better because the spring rate is higher.

Q: What do you think about sway bars? Do you advocate a change?

Jeff: Yes, we do. Out of the box, the R53 has way too light of a sway bar in the rear. The front sway bar on the R53 and R56 is perfect. We do not recommend a change in those. Now, you can overdo it, but we found that the sweet spot is a 19-mm bar on the rear. People who go to a 22-mm rear bar often find that their car is really twitchy and unpredictable in curves because it wants to step out and oversteer, particularly because it's so light in the rear end. The thing about a whole lot of rear sway bar is that you'll get out of sorts in a really fast and sometimes violent sort of way, and that's never a good thing.

Q: How about adjustable end links?

Jeff: We did not think that adjustable end links were very important, until we did an experiment. We set up a cone on a skid pad and we tried to corner around the cone with the stock end link settings. We took pictures of Scott turning around the cone. The inside rear lifted about 5 inches and the front end plowed. Then we took it back to the pits and set the sway bars to neutral and ran the same experiment at the same speed and the car cornered flat. That made believers out of us.

The end links we sell have ball joints on both ends and they're fully adjustable. The way you use them is you put the driver in the car on a flat, level surface, and then you pick one side or the other and loosen up the adjustable end link rod. Then you start to turn the rod. And when you turn it one way, it's stiff. You want the rod to be loose, so you can turn it with two fingers. That's when there's no preload on the sway bar.

Adjustable end links are another fine-tuning mechanism to get your car handling much better. Remember, if you've got coil-overs you can't corner-weight your car unless your sway bars are neutral.

Q: What do you think about poly bushings?

Scott: Most consumers like a nice, pliable, quiet ride, so automakers make their cars with soft rubber bushings. So if you replace your suspension bushings with a firm set of urethane bushings, you'll get a more precise feel of what the wheels are doing, but the downside is more NVH [noise, vibration, and harshness] and more of a "darty" feeling to the car. You'll get a very significant difference by upgrading your bushings to urethane, and even more if you go with a heim joint or a pillow ball.

Q: Do you think the MINI needs strut tower bars?

Scott: Absolutely not. We have seen no time difference on the track with or without those. The MINI's unibody is very rigid, and over time they'll probably provide a little bit of longevity to the body. For a full-blown race car, you're probably going to tie your cage to those points anyway, but for a street car they're mostly just bling.

Q: What are the issues for someone who wants to go all the way with suspension development?

Jeff: Well, that's a huge question. We tell people not to do a whole lot to their car at once. We tell them to do a few things and then learn to drive the car again—baby steps. So we tell people to do the springs and sway bar and then quit. Then if you're not satisfied, you can go in and do the rest.

Q: When should someone think about coil-overs?

Scott: There are a few different types of coil-overs on the market. There are basic coil-overs that allow someone to set their ride height using the springs and shocks that the company has engineered all the way up to a quad-adjustable coil-over where you can independently adjust the low- and high-speed damping and the low- and high-speed rebound. And there's everything in between. People on the high-end cutting edge of things have pure race cars that never drive on the street. On the other end there are the people who just want their cars to look cool. For the manufacturers, they have to look at what the majority of their customers want. And most people want improved handling, but they also want some ride comfort.

We deal with KW exclusively. KW offers three off-the-shelf systems. They have variant 1, which is ride height only. They have variant 2, which is single-adjustable for damping as well as ride height. And they have variant 3, which has independent rebound and damping adjustment as well as ride height.

The thing about people who ask about the variant 3 kit, unless you're a hard-core track guy or you have a whole lot of experience tuning suspensions, you don't want the variant 3. You can chase settings until you're blue in the face, but the majority of people out there really don't need more than single-adjustables. The variant 3 kit is overkill for most people.

Q: How much can you really lower a MINI with coil-overs?

Jeff: What we found out about coil-overs is that there's a point of no return when it comes to lowering your car. When you get to about an inch and a half of lowering, the aerodynamics underneath the car get so bad that you can't control it.

Scott: It's not just that; there's also suspension travel. On a MINI, you've got limited suspension travel. If you lower the car too much, you take all the stroke out of the suspension and you end up with a car that will bind on the bump stops, or the spring will bind and then bad things happen. It's all about balancing everything out.

Q: What about camber plates?

Jeff: We tell people that if they're going to go to the expense of putting coil-overs on the car, they should at least put camber plates and adjustable rear control arms on the car so they can get the camber set up right all the way around.

Scott: Next to a rear sway bar, the most dramatic change you can make is adding negative camber to the front. The factory sets up the car to be neutral in the front and to have more camber in the rear to promote understeer. Camber in the front is critical to be able to go fast and maintain tire life. You need to maintain as much contact patch as you can. Camber plates really make a huge difference in the car. You not only get crisper turn-in and more cornering prowess, your track tires will last longer.

Q: Any final thoughts?

Scott: The thing about the MINI is that it's not the most powerful car in the world, but you can make it handle better than 99 percent of cars on the road. My Cooper is a perfect example. On sticky street tires, we've seen 1.2 Gs in a corner at the race track. Suspension tuning is the key to going fast in a low-horsepower car. It's all about maintaining your momentum in the corners, and that's all about how well your suspension is set up. There's nothing more important than that.

way up through the range. Chances are you'll find that a medium-soft setting gives you the best all-around results, especially if you've gone to stiffer and lower springs.

Shock Absorbers

In the case of the MINI, the shock and strut body are one piece, so we will call the assembly a "strut." There are a variety of struts made to fit your MINI. The MINI design is such that with some basic tools, you

Shock Absorbers

Jeff Reid is the vice president of Ohlins USA's automotive shock absorber division, and he recommends a balanced approach. "People mistake really stiff shocks for high performance—but that's not performance. Yes, your car's got some steering response because it's flat, but you need some compliance to get ahold of the pavement. If it's done right, you get both," he says.

do not need to have new struts installed by a professional. However, if you change springs at the same time you change struts, or if you change alignment settings, you should have your car professionally aligned afterward.

Some of the leading strut assemblies on the market include Bilstein, KW, H&R, Koni, and KYB. Different people prefer different brands, and some people have really strong preferences; each of these brands has a dedicated following.

Springs

At the easy and low-cost end of the suspension upgrade spectrum, you can buy spring kits that install into the stock strut body and are known to have pretty good spring rates for most MINI applications. It's a good idea to replace the shock/strut assemblies at the same time as the springs, but it's not necessary if your stock units are in good shape. The job is easy enough to do that you can come back later and replace the shocks.

Coil-Over Suspensions

At the top of the suspension hierarchy, you can buy coil-over suspension kits. These kits replace the stock strut body with a threaded-body unit of a specific diameter and/or design that accepts springs of a specific coil diameter. Large adjustment nuts move up and down the outside of the threaded bodies to allow you to assemble and disassemble the unit without a spring compressor. You can set ride height individually on coil-overs, which allows you to set corner weights and spring preload. Because you can remove and install springs on your own, a set of coil-overs opens the possibility of multiple sets of springs of varying rates for different driving events.

Virtually every aftermarket retailer offers a kit designed for your MINI, including a set of springs chosen for your car's weight. The best coil-over kits include adjustment nuts that let you set the total height of the assembly as well as the compression on the spring. This allows you to set ride height and retain the full travel of the suspension while separately adjusting the effective spring rate.

PROJECT

Upgrading Struts with Springs, Bushings and Reinforcements

One of the most common handling projects that you can undertake yourself is to replace the stock shocks and springs with upgraded shocks and stiffer springs that also lower the car. Lowering the car looks great and helps handling because it lowers the car's center of gravity. Refer to the discussion on roll centers (page 56) for more information, and refer to the project below to install spacers to restore your stock roll center.

This project installs a set of Texas Speedwerks lowering springs on our project R53 Cooper S, but the instructions work for all MINIs. The springs are designed to lower the car about 3/4 inch, but we saw just about 1/2 inch of real lowering because we installed a set of Madness anti-mushrooming reinforcements at the same time. We also installed a set of Madness poly bushings on the rear struts, and we upgraded the rear trailing arm bushing (see page 71) at the same time. We did not replace the stock struts because they were working well and we wanted to test the performance with the Texas Speedwerks springs. For the record, the Speedwerks springs work great with the stock Cooper S shocks. They drastically reduce front-end lift and dive and they ride firm and smooth, but not harsh.

1 Raise the car to a comfortable working height on the lift or a set of sturdy jack stands and remove

the front and rear wheels. We'll start with the rear struts.

2 At the rear, there's a rubber cap covering the bottom strut attachment. Remove the cap and you can undo the 21-mm bolt that holds the strut bottom to the trailing arm. Undo the anti-lock sensor cables and the parking brake cables on both rear struts and the brake-wear sensor cable on the right strut of the car. Then undo the two 13-mm bolts that hold the strut top to the chassis. The strut comes right off.

3 Take the strut to your workbench and install a pair of quality spring compressors designed for use with MacPherson struts. These work from the outside of the spring. You cannot use internal

This rubber cap keeps dust, rust, and rocks away from your rear strut's lower mount. It's best to leave it in place.

IMPROVING HANDLING

compressors due to the shock rod running up the middle of the assembly. Compress the spring to take the pressure off the strut. The top of the rear shock has a 5-mm Allen (hex) head fitting to hold the central rod while you loosen the 16-mm nut that holds the strut together.

Wrench

If you don't have a 16-mm wrench—and most metric tool kits do not include one—a 5/8-inch SAE wrench or socket fits well enough.

Always use proper spring compressors designed for use with MacPherson struts on your MINI suspension. These springs are under a lot of tension and you can be injured if you try to undo them without protection.

4. With the strut apart, clean and examine the parts. There are rubber pads that cover the top and bottom of the spring. These pads are shaped so that the end of the coil fits snugly, supporting the whole bottom and top of the spring. There's a small metal bushing inside the stock rubber bushings at the top of the strut. Place that metal insert in the new poly bushing. Then you're ready to reassemble the strut.

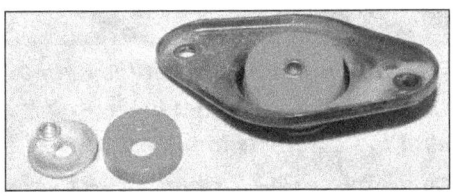

You can see how the bushings install in the top cap of the strut. The smaller red bushing fits on the other side of the cap with the washer and nut to hold it in place.

5. Use the spring compressors to compress the spring before you begin, or you'll never get the nut started. As you reassemble the strut, notice that the strut top is canted. You can twist the strut for final fitment, but make sure to line up the bottom mount and the canted top so that the high end of the cant is aligned with the tabs that hold the ABS sensor cable and the parking brake cable on the inboard side of the car. Make sure the spring ends stay snugly in their rubber perches and use the 5-mm hex wrench to be sure the top is on tight.

You can see where the end of the spring fits into the rubber pad on the strut. This keeps the spring from turning and moving around the strut body.

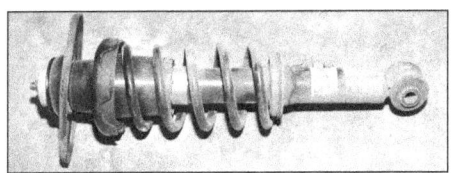

This is a MINI rear strut. Note that the cap is canted to provide proper suspension geometry.

Then reinstall the rear struts and attach the various cables to the strut bodies. You may find it necessary to temporarily disconnect the rear sway bar end links to line up the strut attachment points.

6. On the front end, there's an 18-mm bolt that squeezes the bottom of the strut into the bearing carrier assembly. You must remove this bolt because it holds a captive tab on the strut body. Also, go ahead and remove the sway bar end link from the strut body. Removing the end link requires a 16-mm wrench, and a 17-mm wrench or a 5-mm hex wrench to keep the tiny ball joint from turning. Also remove the brake line and ABS cable; on the left side, remove the brake-wear sensor cable. You can now wiggle the bottom end of the strut free from the bearing carrier. Undo the three 13-mm nuts that hold the strut top to the strut tower and you can remove the strut.

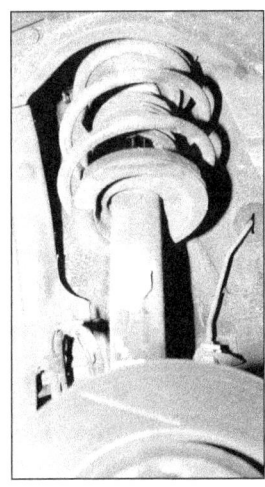

The front struts on a MINI are actually easier to remove and replace than the rears. Just a few nuts and bolts and you've got it out of the car.

CHAPTER 3

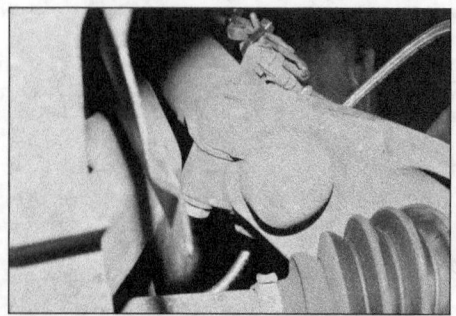

Here, you can see the single bolt that holds the front strut to the bearing carrier and hub. Just undo that bolt and wiggle the strut free of the hub assembly.

Take the cap off the top of the strut to see the one nut that holds the whole strut top assembly together.

This strut tower has been "mushroomed" out of shape by repeated bumps. You can see how the brace does not sit flat on the tower.

You also need to unhook the brake flex lines to replace the front struts. Just pull gently but firmly and the grommet will come loose.

The front struts go back together even more easily than the rears, especially when you've created some slack by installing shorter springs. This would have been a good time to replace the shock bodies, too.

The other side of the same car is still flat. This end of the brace is sitting flush with the tower surface.

Simply place the reinforcements on top of the struts while they're out of the car. They install in only one orientation. Note that you might need to put in longer strut top studs if you also want to use a strut tower bar.

7 Take the strut to your workbench and install quality strut spring compressors. Remove the central dust cap from the strut top. As with the rears, the top of the front strut has a 5-mm Allen (hex) head fitting to hold the central rod, but the 19-mm nut that holds the strut together is down in a hole. Unless you've got special sockets that allow you to insert a hex wrench while you work, you'll need to loosen that 19-mm nut with air tools and a deep socket. Do not put a pair of Vise-Grips or other clamps on the shock rod or you will destroy it. The good news is that the front struts can go back together without compressing the new springs because they are shorter than the stock units. Make sure the springs are lined up snugly on their rubber perches.

8 There are no poly bushings to reinforce the top of the front strut. It's made to turn with the steering and has an internal bearing. This is the part you can replace with a camber-adjustable strut top if you want more adjustment. However, if your strut towers are becoming deformed due to the constant abuse of road bumps, you can install reinforcements. Some reinforcements mount on top of the strut tower, but others are made of plates that go between the strut top and the strut tower. The plates fit on the strut top only one way, but you have to test-fit them in the towers to understand the correct orientation. Note that you may find that the studs on the strut top have been bent as the top has mushroomed and you may need to bend them back to fit.

IMPROVING HANDLING

9 Reinstall the front struts with the reinforcement plates attached. First secure the three top nuts to hang the strut in place and then align the captive tab and slide the bottom of the strut into the bearing carrier and attach the mounting bolt. There is no alignment adjustment to worry about here. Attach the various cables to the strut bodies.

10 If you are concerned about your roll center, install spacers such as the MINI Mania Precision Steering Amplifier kit under the front lower ball joints as described on page 72.

11 Take your car to a professional alignment shop for a full four-wheel alignment. You have lowered the car, so you will gain some negative camber. Be sure to tell the alignment technician if you would like to keep that camber. Your toe settings will also be changed.

The reinforcements show a bit of color when they're installed. They also give you back 1/4 inch or so of ride height if you're installing lowering springs.

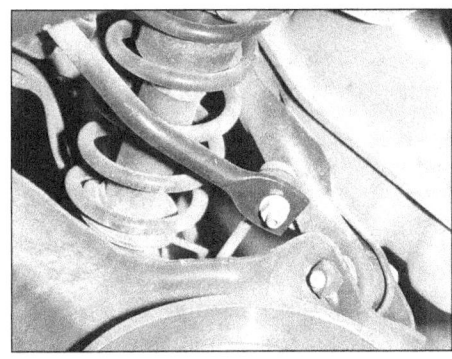

The stock rear sway bar is set up a little soft to allow understeer. That's good in a street car, but it's not high performance.

The stock front sway bar is perfectly adequate until you have a completely adjustable coil-over suspension. Save some money and leave it in place.

Sway Bar Upgrades

One of the most noticeable changes you can make in your suspension is a replacement rear sway bar. Changing the front or rear sway bar requires dropping the corresponding suspension subframe. You can replace a rear sway bar yourself, but if you decide to change the front sway bar, you should take that job to a professional.

Sway bars are designed to reduce body roll during cornering, but that's not all they do. Remember, sway bars limit the total amount of body roll, and that limits the lateral movement of the roll center. But you can't cheat physics, and that weight transfer due to centrifugal force has to go somewhere, so the tradeoff is that as you increase sway control, you also increase lateral load transfer to the outside wheel in a corner. In extreme cases, this shows up as a car's tendency to pick up an inside rear wheel in a corner.

 Front Control Arm

If you have the front end of the car apart for a sway bar, go ahead and replace the front control arm bushings as well. This work is best performed by a professional.

A stock R50 Cooper has a 22.5-mm front sway bar, while the Sport Package R50s and all R53 Cooper S models have a 24-mm front bar. In the rear, a stock R50 has a 16-mm bar, and the sport suspension R50 and all R53 cars have a 17-mm rear bar.

The R56 series is more complicated. R56 Coopers have a 21.5-mm front bar, or a 23.5-mm front bar with the Sport Package. In the rear, an R56 Cooper has a 16-mm bar, or an 18-mm bar with the Sport Package. The R56 Cooper S has a 22.5-mm front bar, or a 23.5-mm with the Sport Package, and a 17-mm rear bar, or an 18-mm with the Sport Package.

There is no change in sway bars with the JCW package or the GP package in any year for U.S. models.

Depending on the size and setup of your sway bars, you can adjust your car's tendency to oversteer or understeer. Simply put, to increase understeer, increase the front bar or soften the rear bar. To increase oversteer, increase the rear bar and soften the front bar. Just remember that oversteer and understeer tendencies are affected by many factors in addition to sway bar choice, including tire choice, alignment, roll center, and tire pressure.

The best setup for your MINI is to use the stock front sway bar and increase the rear sway control, and

THE NEW MINI PERFORMANCE HANDBOOK

use adjustable end links on both bars. There's a good reason for this—your MINI's rear wheels aren't doing very much, so it's a good place to reduce body roll. Your MINI's front wheels, on the other hand, are busy pulling the car and steering, and the more traction you can get on both of those wheels, the better off you'll be. Add to this the native tendency of front-wheel-drive cars to understeer, and the fact that the factory designers want production cars to understeer, and you've got a powerful case to dial in a little more oversteer by upgrading the rear bar. If you're picking up the inside rear wheel in cornering, adjustable end links will help fix the problem.

Sway Control

A good feature in an aftermarket rear sway bar is a series of mounting holes for the end link. By moving the link away from the end of the bar, you can get increase sway control by reducing the leverage your wheels place on the bar. You can switch between street and track setup just by moving the end links!

PROJECT
Installing the Alta 19-mm Rear Sway Bar

For street cars and most competition purposes, an aftermarket 19-mm sway bar is what you want for sway control. Alta Performance makes a bar with three end-link mounting holes for easy adjustment, poly bushings for rigidity, and optional adjustable end links. This procedure was performed on the project 2005 R53 Cooper S, but it is applicable to any MINI. Follow these steps:

1 Raise the car to a comfortable working height on the lift or a set of sturdy jack stands and remove the rear wheels.

2 Remove the stock end links at the sway bar ends. These are held on with a 16-mm nut. You can use a 17-mm wrench to hold the backside of the stud or use a 5-mm hex wrench in the end of the stud. Remove the links entirely if you switch to adjustable links.

3 Remove the left rear strut. It's got a 21-mm bolt at the bottom (or 18-mm after 2005) and two 13-mm bolts at the top. Be careful when detaching the ABS sensor, brake-pad wear sensor, and brake line from the strut body.

4 There are four 16-mm bolts that hold the rear suspension subframe to the chassis. You can see the sway bar mounting clamps, and the subframe bolts are above the sway bar. Remove these bolts, and a fifth bolt at the center of the subframe on R52 convertible models. Move the subframe down enough to get at the sway bar clamps and bushings. You might have to gently use a pry bar to move the subframe and hold it.

5 Remove the sway bar clamps. Each clamp is held on with two 13-mm bolts. You can now carefully pull the sway bar out on the driver's side of the car. There are brake lines, a big central wiring harness, and other obstacles to avoid, so be careful and don't force anything.

6 Orient the new sway bar so that the end-link attachments point slightly downward when the bar is level. There is a ridge where the attachments are welded to the bar, and that ridge should be on top. Insert the new sway bar from the driver's side, carefully avoiding obstacles.

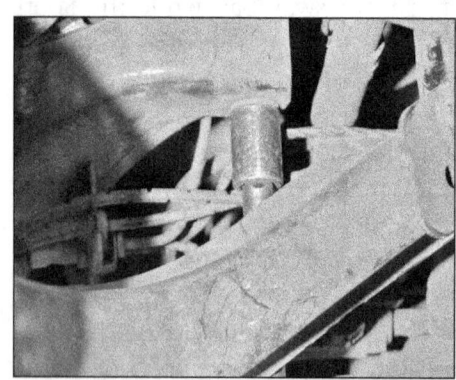

Here you can see the socket on an extension removing one of the outer bolts of the rear subframe. The other two bolts are inboard of this location on either side of the car.

The hot ticket is a 19-mm rear sway bar with adjustment holes and adjustable end links. This setup lets you go from a street to a track setup, and back again in a matter of moments. Be sure you install it right side up.

7 Give the new poly bushings a generous treatment of the provided grease and fit the new bushings and clamps over the sway bar. Line everything up with the stock mounting holes and use the stock bolts to attach the new bar to the car.

 Reassemble the rear subframe and tighten it down. It may be challenging to get the bolt holes lined up, but there are additional holes, and a little leverage will move the subframe into position. Next, reinstall the struts and sway bar end links. Finally, reinstall the tires and test-drive the new configuration.

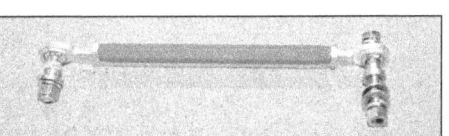

A set of adjustable end links like this will set you back a few dollars, but if you're autocrossing or driving hard, getting your sway bars set up for neutral preload with you in the car is one of the best things you can do for handling.

End Links

When you attach your stock end links or new adjustable end links to the new sway bar, use the attachment hole at the end of the bar first. That's the softest setting. At that setting your new 19-mm bar is 15 percent stiffer than the stock rear sway bar. You need to get used to that before you start playing around with even stiffer settings of 40 percent, and 77 percent stiffer on the inner end link holes. This bar increases oversteer, and you don't want to find yourself going backward through a corner the next time it rains.

Adjustable Sway Bar End Links

The theory goes that when your car is standing at rest, there's no torsion on the sway bars. That's not always true, but suppose for the moment that it is true on your car. When you climb into the driver's seat, your car is no longer standing at rest. You have compressed the left-side suspension somewhat with your weight. Now your sway bars are already pushing back on your suspension! You can relieve the preload —or set a preload of your choosing— on your sway bars if you get adjustable drop links, sold by many aftermarket retailers.

Adjustable sway bar links are simple to install and use. Sway bars are wide, U-shaped torsional springs. They ride above the front and rear lower control arms, and the ends of the U are connected to the rear control arms and upward to the front strut bodies with drop links. The stock drop links are fixed-length with ball-joint bushings. You can remove these easily and replace them with adjustable-length links. Then simply sit in your car and have a friend adjust them until the bar and link are about perpendicular to each other and there's no stress on the sway bars. Be sure to check that the sway bars and links do not bind or interfere with other components. Easy!

You can also use your adjustable links to create preload to help your car turn left or right, but improving one happens at the expense of the other, so be sure you understand the tradeoff.

Suspension Brace and Bushing Upgrades

All MINIs use a unibody design, which is to say, the chassis and body are made of stamped pieces of sheet steel, welded together. In hard cornering, the chassis is subjected to a great deal of pressure, and it will flex. Chassis flex works against the suspension by slightly changing its geometry at the worst possible time.

There are many different designs for strut tower braces. Some provide support against mushrooming, and some do not. All of them help make your steering more crisp and precise, however.

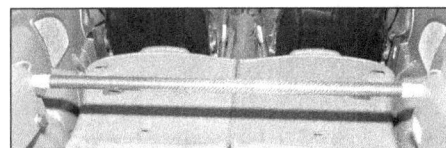

Rear strut braces install behind the rear seat. Some prevent you from putting the rear seats up, so choose carefully if you're not planning to delete the rear seats.

Ideally, you want the chassis to be as stiff as possible. The main points of flex are at the strut towers and suspension subframes, where the forces from the suspension are concentrated. Strut tower bars bridge the strut towers across the top of the engine bay, making an arch that helps stiffen the chassis.

Chassis stiffeners are also available to bridge the rear strut towers, the lower A-arms, and other points on the underside of the chassis. All of these bars help stiffen the chassis and improve steering and suspension response. All of them can be installed at home in minutes using ordinary hand tools. For ultimate chassis stiffening, however, you can't beat a good roll cage.

CHAPTER 3

PROJECT
Installing a Front Strut Tower Brace

A front strut tower brace is primarily a dress-up item for most street cars, but over time, it will help your MINI's chassis stay strong. The example bar in this project is the polished-aluminum PROMINI stress bar from www.promini.com. This procedure was performed on an R50, but it works for all MINIs. After the installation, this car's steering was noticeably quicker and more precise. Follow these steps:

1 On an R50 Cooper, you must install a PROMINI low-profile battery cover. This is a stock cover that has been cut and modified to provide clearance for the strut tower bar. Simply release the tabs, remove your old cover, and pop the new one into place.

2 With the car standing on its wheels normally, undo the six 13-mm nuts that hold the strut tops in position. Place the ends of the strut bar onto the strut top studs and loosely thread the nuts back on, but do not tighten them down yet.

3 Each strut tower end has a through-bolt to hold the central part of the bar to the end plates. Notice that the bar is offset and can be installed in only one orientation. Place the "fat" side of the bar toward the front of the car, with the body of the bar riding in the indentation of the new battery cover. Install the passenger-side through-bolt first.

> **TECH TIP**
> ### Strut Towers
> If your strut towers have mushroomed out of shape, you might find fitment to be challenging. In extreme cases, you might need a body shop to re-flatten your strut tower tops.

4 The driver's side of the central part of the bar includes an offset adjuster. Orient the adjuster hole to the lower right for easy installation. Line up the adjuster hole with the hole in the tower end and install the through-bolt.

5 Tighten the strut top mounting nuts, then the passenger-side through-bolt. Finally, use a crescent wrench, or 1-inch open-end wrench to set any desired preload on the bar and then tighten the driver's-side through-bolt. The hood should shut normally.

In the R50 engine bay, the strut tower brace path passes right through the top of the battery box.

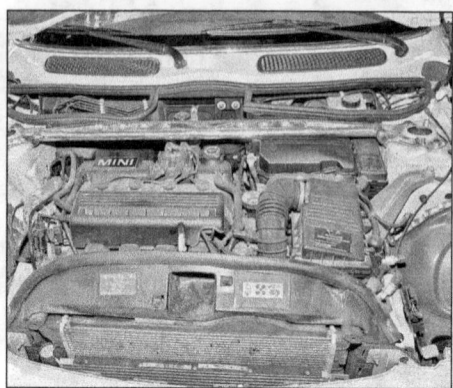
The PROMINI strut tower bar is a strong design, and keeps a low profile to use available space.

The PROMINI R50 kit includes a special battery cover that provides room for the strut bar to pass over the battery.

Suspension Bushings

All of the control arms and sway bars on a MINI use rubber bushings to attach to the chassis and hub assemblies. Among the first things any performance enthusiast does to improve handling is replace these rubber bushings with a firmer material such as polyurethane; sometimes metal bushings can be used.

A metal bushing may go by several different names—pillow ball is popular among tuners, while racers call the same item a heim joint or spherical bearing. Some military-spec or aviation applications call the same item a mono-ball bearing.

Regardless of the name, you're dealing with a spherical steel bearing in an enclosing bearing race. There is a hole through the sphere to allow you to fasten it at one end, and usually a male or female threaded end for the second attachment point. Pillow-ball

IMPROVING HANDLING

These bushings insert into the stock bushing to firm up the rear trailing arm. In combination with a rear sway bar upgrade and rear strut bushings, you'll really be able to feel your car's rear end tracking more precisely.

For the ultimate in precision and motion control, you can't beat heim joints, also known as pillow balls.

strut tops usually come assembled with the entire top structure. You generally buy these bushings premade, keep them lubricated, and throw them away when they're worn.

The reason these bushings are so highly prized is that the rotation of the ball in the socket allows a good range of motion for a control arm, while allowing virtually no unwanted slack in that motion. Where a rubber bushing compresses and deforms, a heim joint holds firm. The effect of heim joints on steering and suspension response is nothing short of amazing.

PROJECT
Upgrading Rear Trailing Arm Bushings

A major source of vagueness in the rear suspension is the large rubber bushing around which the forward end of the rear trailing arm pivots. The bushing itself is inset in a carrier and the trailing arm is held in place by one large bolt. The forces placed on the bushing are significant, and it benefits from a snug reinforcement. If you are replacing rear springs or upgrading the bushings on the rear struts, now is an excellent time to undertake this project. This procedure works for all MINIs.

1 Raise the car to a comfortable working height on the lift or a set of sturdy jack stands and remove the rear wheels.

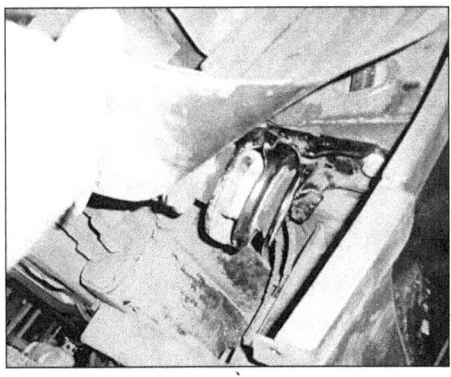

2 You can see where the trailing arm goes forward into the body of the car. Remove some of the plug clips that hold the plastic trim in place and move the trim aside. You can see the bushing carrier bolted to the underside of the body in a little pocket. (For the purposes of photographing this procedure the bushing carrier is out of the car, but you do not need to remove it.) This carrier sets rear toe, so do not loosen it unless you mark its position first.

3 On the outboard side of the bushing carrier opposite the trailing arm, there's an 18-mm bolt with a large plate washer. Remove that bolt, and the trailing arm comes loose.

4 Insert the two poly bushing supports into both sides of the stock bushing. You do not need to remove the stock bushing. Simply snug the inserts in place. The plate-style washer on one side and the body of the trailing arm on the other side

You can see the bushing inserts in the trailing arm pivot by pulling aside the plastic cover of the wheel well liner.

holds the bushing inserts in place. Move the trailing arm back into place. Replace the bolt and plate washer and thread it into place snugly, but do not torque it down yet.

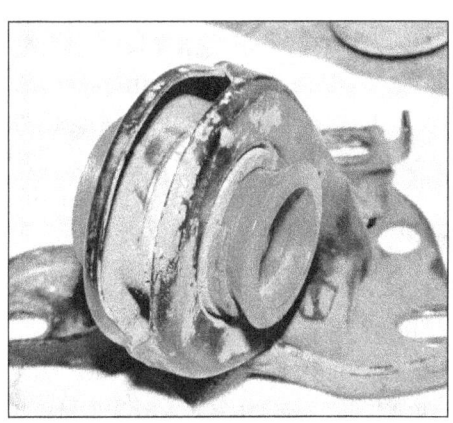

You don't need to remove the bushing carrier, but we did to take this picture of how the bushing inserts fit into the carrier.

5 Replace the rear wheels and lower the car to the ground. Bounce the car lightly as you roll it forward and back a few feet. When the rear suspension is at rest, torque the 18-mm bolt to 74 ft-lbs. Replace the plastic trim and its clips.

Other Suspension Parts Upgrades

There are several other areas where you can upgrade your suspension components. Some aftermarket products offer a new fixed-camber or -caster setting, while others allow complete adjustability. For street use, a mild fixed adjustment usually is sufficient; for autocross or track competition, you are likely to want to be able to make your own changes. Bear in mind that if you pick a variety of products from different manufacturers, they have not been tested together and may interfere with each other.

Strut Tops and Camber Plates

The strut top is also called a "hat" or "top mount." This is the cap that holds the top of the shock and holds the spring under compression. The strut top holds the strut in one position to keep the stock camber setting. The strut top fits into the strut tower and is held in place by two or three fairly small studs—just enough force to keep it located.

The stock tops allow a comparatively great deal of play in order to make the stock ride comfortable. Several manufacturers make hardened polyurethane or true metal bushing pillow ball tops that reduce the amount of play. These products offer

With a camber plate, you can dial as much camber into your front wheels as you would like. You can also better support the upper end of the strut with a pillow ball fitting. Some camber plates also allow you to adjust in a bit more caster.

a fixed camber adjustment—usually about negative 1 to 1.5 degrees—good for street performance.

The other part of a strut top that you can change for a performance upgrade is to add a camber-plate replacement strut top. Camber plates are slotted, so you can move the top of the strut in or out and tighten it in place to set the camber (and sometimes caster). Most full coil-over setups also include camber adjustment in their custom strut tops. There's a small tradeoff here: You'll notice increased noise, vibration, and harshness (commonly called NVH) in the car with a fixed top like this.

Positive Steering Response

There is a class of aftermarket products that increase caster by lowering the rear mount of the front lower control arms. These are called positive-steering-response kits. These parts help soften the resistance of the suspension to lifting under acceleration, which paradoxically prevents the car's body from lifting.

Newtonian physics tells us that the reaction to acceleration and deceleration has to go somewhere, and if it doesn't go to the suspension, it goes to the chassis. The suspension is made to absorb bumps, and the chassis is supposed to be rigid. So the main advantage of one of these kits is that the springs get to absorb the lift rather than the chassis, and this helps keep the tires in good contact with the ground. With the tires in better contact with the ground, you've got more cornering capability, and less tendency for the front wheels to lose traction under acceleration because of weight transfer through the chassis.

Finally, virtually all positive-steering-response kits come with upgraded bushings for the forward lower control arms, so you score a point there as well. The stock control arm bushings are large and made of soft rubber. The bushings deflect quite a bit under braking and accelerating and this deflection is expressed as a surprisingly large toe-in/toe-out change.

PROJECT

Installing the Mini Mania Precision Steering Amplifier

MINI Mania has created a convenient product to restore your suspension geometry if you have installed lowering springs. The Precision Steering Amplifier (PSA) is a set of aluminum spacers that drop the outer ends of your lower control arms about 3/4 inch. This project can be performed on all R50, R52, and R53 MINI Coopers with 17-inch wheels.

WARNING: *To use this product, you need to grind down the lowest point of the outer ball-joint nut to clear the stock 17-inch wheels, and grind a bit more off the nut to clear 16-inch wheels.*

1 Raise the car to a comfortable working height on the lift and remove the front wheels.

2 Locate the outer ball joint at the outer end of the lower control arm and undo the two 13-mm bolts that hold it to the bottom of the bearing carrier.

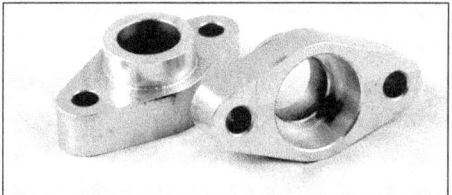

These spacers from Mini Mania allow you to restore steering geometry after lowering your car.

3 Pull the lower control arm free of the bearing carrier. You might need to tap gently with a rubber hammer.

4 Insert the PSA spacer and align it with the bolt holes.

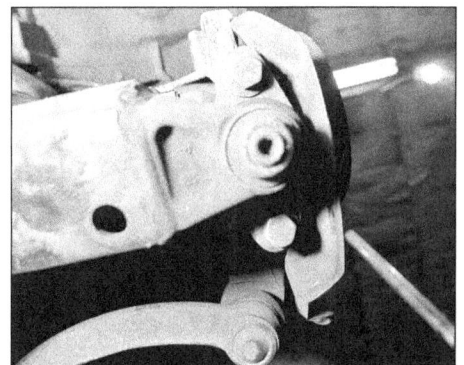

Remove the two bolts on either side of the ball joint. They come out easily, and then you can separate the ball joint from the hub.

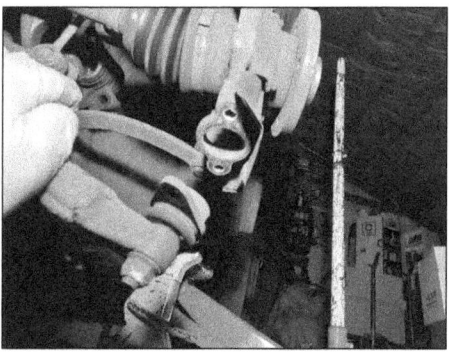

Wiggle the ball joint out of the bearing carrier and you're ready to install the precision steering amplifier spacer.

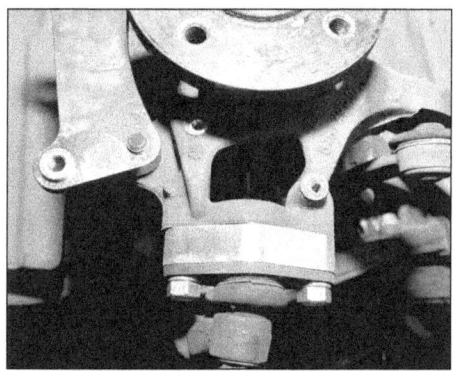

The spacer comes with longer bolts for reinstallation. The whole process takes just moments.

Replace the ball-joint end into the bottom of the PSA. Tap it gently with the rubber hammer to seat it well.

5 Place some Loctite on the threads of the long replacement bolts provided with the kit. Thread in the bolts and torque to 50 ft-lbs.

Even with 17-inch wheels, we had to grind quite a bit off the bottom of the ball joint to clear the wheels. If you have 16-inch wheels, you'll need to grind even more.

6 Use a body grinder, dremel, or mill file to remove some material from the bottom of the ball-joint nut (the lowest point on the end of the control arm). Test-fit your wheel and remove more material as necessary until there is no rubbing.

Wheel Spacers

Track is the measurement between the centerlines of the tires—the width of your car's stance. Your MINI has a nice wide track built into its basic design, but you can add a bit by changing the wheel offset or by using wheel spacers. Spacers are simply big thick plates that fit between the brake rotor and the wheel.

Increasing your car's track helps with stability in cornering by reducing lateral load transfer. Simply put, it's easier to tip over a narrow, tall box than it is to tip a short, wide box. The tradeoff is that it takes more effort to steer the car if you put spacers on the front, and you are increasing the length of the lever pressing on the lug studs, wheel bearings, and suspension when you're cornering. You might also experience tire rub against the fenders in hard cornering.

You should choose wheel spacers under three conditions: if you have installed brakes that interfere with your wheel spokes or you have changed your wheel back spacing and you need to move the wheels outward,

You can see the front wheel sits quite a ways out from the wheel well with a 15-mm spacer behind it.

if you're autocrossing and need the stability for cornering, or if you just want a wide and pugnacious stance for aesthetic reasons at a car show.

The downside to spacing out the rear end is that you reduce oversteer, which you've been trying to promote with other suspension changes. On the other hand, spacers increase stability. But if you put spacers in the front, you'll feel it in the steering. Because you've increased the leverage working on the suspension, you'll feel bumps more acutely, a front tire that is out of balance will shake your steering wheel more, and you'll increase bump steer. That increase in leverage also puts extra stress on the wheel bearings. You're pretty safe with the 5-mm spacers; 12-mm spacers will put some load on your bearings; and 15-mm is about the maximum you should ever use.

WARNING: *Wheel spacers are usually used in concert with wheel stud kits, but the PROMINI kit comes with extra-long lug bolts instead.*

Whatever you choose, you must use a longer bolt or stud than the stock MINI part to replace the length lost to the spacer. If you don't lengthen the lug bolts, you will not get full insertion into the hub and the outside front wheel will break off in a corner.

PROJECT
Installing PROMINI 15-mm Wheel Spacers

You can buy generic spacers at any performance auto parts shop, but you really should use spacers made specifically for the MINI. They have the right centerbore to fit on the hub boss, and provide their own boss to center the wheels. They also have a chamfered hole and a longer bolt to replace the T-50 Torx bolt that holds the brake rotor to the hub. Follow these steps to install the spacers:

1. Raise the car to a comfortable working height on the lift or jack stands, and remove the wheels.

2. Remove the T-50 Torx bolts that hold the brake rotors to the hubs. Line up the spacers on the hubs. You might need to tap them gently with a rubber hammer to get them all the way onto the hub boss. Install the replacement bolts that come with the kit. In the case of the PROMINI kit, these bolts use a 6-mm Allen-head fitting instead of the Torx—a big improvement!

3. Replace your wheels and use the longer wheel studs provided with the kit. Torque the wheel lugs to 90 ft-lbs.

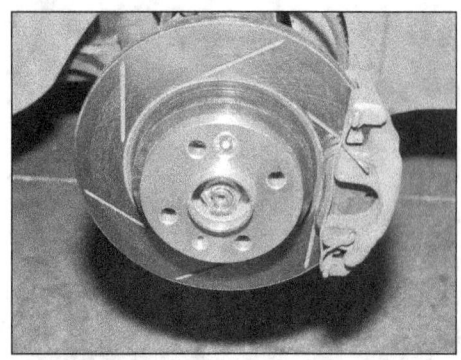

This is a high-quality spacer from PROMINI. Note that it is hub-centric, and provides a centering boss for your MINI wheels and a replacement locating bolt.

Wheel and Tire Upgrades

Your wheels are one of the most visible features on your car, and most people select them carefully for style. Everyone knows that good tires are critical to good performance, but your wheels are also an important performance component. The good news is that it's easy to make a wheel choice that is both stylish and a performance enhancement.

Wheels and tires are the final component in the power delivery chain—the parts that physically connect your car to the ground. Thus, they have a great impact on acceleration, handling, and braking. The consequences of tire selection are well known, but remember also that the weight and offset of the wheels affect

This autocross Cooper S is riding on SSR Type C wheels. These weigh just 11 pounds apiece, and they're a common choice for the sport. (Photo courtesy Dan Bryant)

the way the springs and shocks work, and the weight and diameter of the wheels affect braking ability.

If you plan to compete using special tires, you should buy an extra set of wheels and keep your competition rubber on them. Autocrossers, rallycrossers, racers, and winter sports enthusiasts should all have a dedicated set of doughnuts kept in good condition for playtime.

For now, let's look at some considerations to keep in mind when selecting wheels and tires.

The Physics of Wheels

Moment of inertia has nothing to do with the amount of time it takes you to get off the couch—but it has a lot to do with accelerating a car. Moment of inertia is a measurement of how much torque it takes to accelerate an object in angular rotation around an axis—to spin a wheel, for example.

Without breaking out the physics textbook, a small wheel takes less energy to spin-up than a large wheel of the same mass because the mass is concentrated close to the axis of rotation. This is why pure racing clutches are made so small—to help the engine spin-up faster. It's also why 20-inch-and-larger wheels (almost never seen on MINIs) are bad for both acceleration and braking performance. It takes more effort to get that wheel rolling, and it also takes more effort to stop it once it's moving.

To use an extreme example, monster trucks need huge, torquey engines in large part to get those giant tires moving, but the vast majority of MINIs are rolling on wheels of 17 inches or smaller. The differences in moment of inertia are tiny—between 15 and 17 inches. So don't worry about going to 17 or even 18 inches to clear your big-brake kit—it's no big deal.

Next, the wheels and tires are the biggest contributors to your car's unsprung weight. Remember that unsprung weight stresses the suspension and shocks. You don't have to buy the absolute lightest wheels and tires on the market, but be aware of weight when you're making your selections. You'll be surprised how heavy some wheels are, especially the stock wheels!

Finally, the wheel/tire combo affects acceleration not just by maintaining grip, but also because the total diameter of the tire affects the final drive ratio—a taller tire is just like a taller gear. There's a tradeoff between acceleration performance and top speed inherent in the diameter of the wheel and tire combination you choose, and the total diameter of the tires also affects the roll center a little bit.

Selecting Wheels

Selecting wheels should be fun—and the following information should help you get started. Most MINI-specific retailers know the fitment issues on wheels that they sell. A general-purpose wheel and tire shop may not. Another good source for this information is the Internet. MINI forums have archived information or current experience with the fitment of a wide variety of wheels.

Wheel Strength

The variety of wheel styles available on the market has never been greater than today, but be aware that not all wheels are equally strong. If you plan to do some hard cornering, be aware that you can put a great deal of stress on your wheels. You want your wheels to be strong enough not to flex or break under cornering, and you want them to be light as well. To achieve that end, look for wheels with many spokes, preferably designed in a web pattern. These are popular with racers for their light weight and strong design.

These stock MINI wheels are good and strong for racing, with multiple spokes and attachment points.

There are a few questions to ask yourself when selecting wheels:
- Will the inner diameter of this wheel clear my brakes, struts, tie-rod ends, and any aftermarket parts I plan to put on in the future?
- Will the outer diameter of this wheel, plus the tire I plan to run, clear my fender wells? Even if I lower the car?
- Is the width of this wheel suitable for the tires I plan to buy?
- Is the width of this wheel suitable for my car's suspension and wheel wells?
- Does this wheel have an offset within the workable range for my car?
- Is this wheel strong enough for my purposes?

Wheel Diameter and Width

Selecting a wheel diameter is probably the first thing you need to decide. Coopers come with 15- and 16-inch options, Cooper S models come with 16- and 17-inch wheel options, and JCW cars have an 18-inch option.

Wheel diameter is the distance across the center of the wheel from bead sealing surface to bead sealing surface, not from the edges of the rim. Measuring from the edges of the rim can add 1 inch or more to your measurement.

Your minimum wheel size is usually dictated by your brake plans, and occasionally by the tires you want to run. Most brake kits state the minimum specs for wheel diameter, but bear in mind that this is no guarantee that a particular wheel of the specified diameter will fit over a particular brake. Offset and wheel structure come into play as well. There's no test better than fitting the actual wheel/tire over the brake in your fender and checking for interference throughout your steering travel range.

The next factor to consider is wheel width. This is defined as the distance across the width of the wheel from bead sealing surface to bead sealing surface—again, not from the edges of the rim. Measuring from the edges of the rim can add 1/2 inch or more to this measurement.

You can generally find any given style of wheel in a range of diameters and widths, but generally speaking as the diameter increases, the available range of widths also increases. You won't find 18x5 wheels outside of a specialty shop.

The MINI standard 15-inch wheels are 5.5 inches wide. The 16-inch wheels are 6.5 inches wide. The stock 17-inch wheels are 7 inches wide, and the 18-inch wheels on the R53 JCW GP are also 7 inches wide. Aftermarket 16- to 18-inch wheels marketed to MINI owners for street use generally range from 7 to 8.5 inches wide, with the majority at 7.5 inches.

Wheel width is also a critical consideration in conjunction with the

This is by far the most popular wheel for the R53 Cooper S. Once again, it's based on the Minilite style, but it's a 17-inch sport wheel.

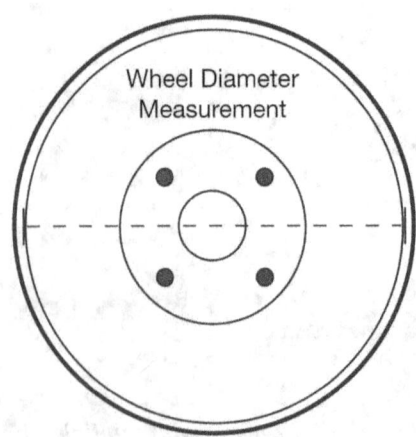

Measure your wheel diameter not from the edge of the wheel, but rather from the tire bead seating surface.

This wheel was based on the original Minilite wheels that were popular on the original Minis. Of course, those came in 10-, 12-, and 13-inch sizes, while the smallest wheel you find on a new MINI is a 15-inch design.

Aftermarket wheels come in a variety of sizes and styles, and if you've got nice brakes, you'll want to show them off with an open-face wheel.

IMPROVING HANDLING

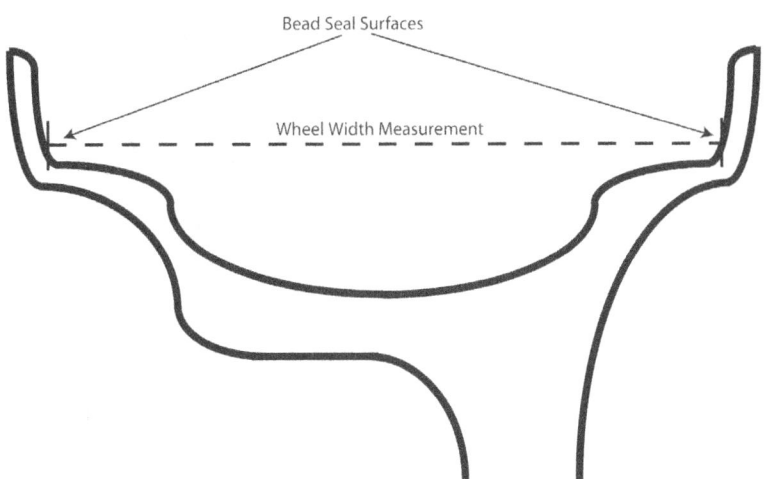

Again, the wheel width is not measured from the lip of the wheel, but from where the tire actually seats and seals.

tires you select. A tire uses air pressure to keep its lips sealed against the wheel (called the bead seal), and if your tires are too narrow and your wheels too wide, the lips will be stretched to meet the beads. This can lead to tires coming off the bead at high speed or during cornering, which can be disastrous. Conversely, if your tires are too wide and your rims are too narrow, the tire will be forced to balloon out from the rim and you'll get poor handling and a bad bead seal. In general, plan for your wheel width to roughly match the tread width of your tires.

Your tire retailer should be able to tell you if you have a width problem. But again, there's no test for wheel width as good as putting a tire on your car and moving the steering and suspension through its full range of motion while checking for rubbing.

Wheel Offset

Wheel offset is the last critical dimension to look at when selecting wheels. This dimension is also known as "ET." It is the distance between the back of the torque circle (the surface where you bolt the wheel to the hub) and the measured center of the wheel width. A wheel with positive offset is where the torque circle is outboard of the centerline of the wheel width. Negative offset is where the torque circle is inboard of the centerline. Zero offset is where the torque circle is on the centerline.

Correct offset is important to ensure that the wheels clear the brakes and to avoid fender rubbing. All stock MINI wheels are designed with positive offset of +45 to +52 mm. The 15-inch stock wheels use a +45-mm offset, while almost all stock 16- and 17-inch wheels use +48-mm offset. The stock 18-inch wheels fitted to JCW cars are offset +52 mm.

Aftermarket wheels have a slightly broader range of offsets, from as low as +35 to +55 mm. In general, the greater the diameter of the wheel, the more the offset tends higher the higher the offset. That's only 20 mm (about 3/4 inch) of difference between the high and low limits.

In general, if you keep wheel offset pretty close to stock for the diameter of your wheel, it shouldn't cause wheel clearance problems. If you get too far out of tolerance range, you are likely to have rubbing problems. As always, test-fit the actual wheel if you're not sure.

A related term is *backspacing*, which is simply the distance from the wheel's mounting face to the inboard edge of the wheel. If you select wheels much wider than stock, you need to check the backspacing in addition to the offset to make sure that the wheel doesn't rub on the struts or on the inner fender wells when you turn. Obviously, offset affects backspacing.

Wheel Weight

As you know, wheels are unsprung weight, and you want to keep that under control. Stock 16-inch MINI alloy wheels weigh about 17 to

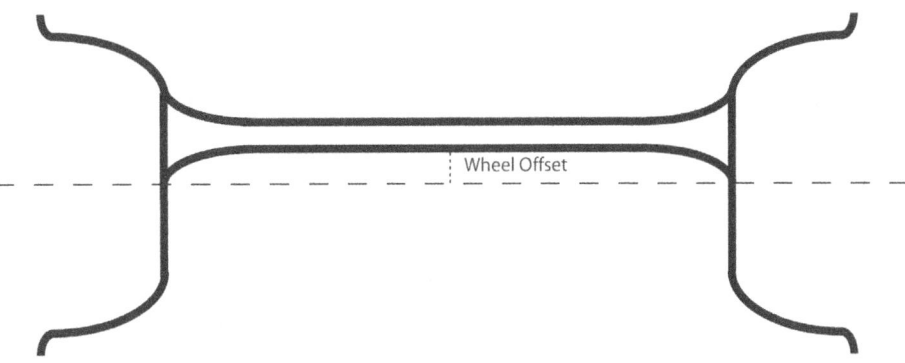

MINI wheel offsets run in a comparatively narrow range, about 3/4 inch.

20 pounds each—not bad for stock wheels from an automaker that doesn't want to have to replace broken wheels under warranty. Aftermarket wheels from 15 to 17 inches in diameter generally range from 11 to 22 pounds, and most weigh about 16 to 18 pounds. The 18-inch wheels are somewhat heavier on average, usually weighing about 20 to 25 pounds each.

Bolt Pattern

MINI bolt patterns are easy—all MINIs use a 4-on-100-mm bolt pattern. This means that from the center of one bolt hole to the center of the opposite bolt hole is 100 mm. This is a common import bolt pattern, which means there is a great variety of wheels likely to fit your car. This measurement is also known as the pitch circle diameter (PCD).

Lug Bolts versus Nuts and Studs

If you are planning for serious driving, you may also want to upgrade to wheel lug studs. The lug bolts used by the factory make changing a wheel and tire more of a pain than it needs to be, and studs are an easy installation. Of course, you may not like the look of bare studs sticking out, but you can also purchase capped lug nuts. Just make sure your studs are not too long.

Studs are also useful if you decide to use wheel spacers for a little wider track. If possible, pick studs with an unthreaded shank of the same depth as your wheel spacers. This helps guard against breaking a stud over time.

Selecting Tires

Selecting a brand and a particular model of tire is almost a religious pursuit. Each brand has its following, and people swear by their favorite tires as the best. In truth, any high-quality,

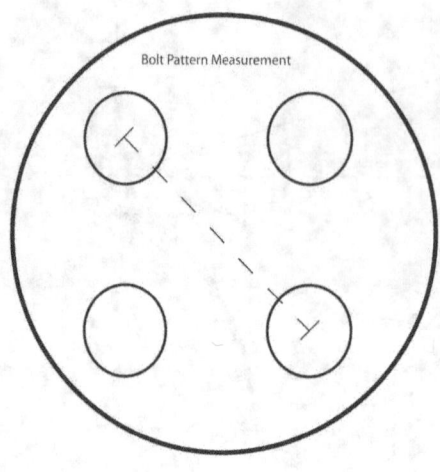

The MINI bolt pattern is one of the most common in the industry, which means that lots of wheels are available to fit your car.

well-known, name-brand tire rated for the kind of driving you're planning to do is likely to be a good choice. Street tires today have tremendous grip, and most perform well in both wet and dry environments.

Selecting a replacement tire requires some tradeoffs. The very best dry-traction tires tend to be very scary on wet pavement, and completely useless on gravel, snow, or ice. For most street cars, you'll want to get a tire with good all-around performance, since you don't want to choose between swapping shoes and going surfing every time it rains.

Dedicated autocrossers, track day competitors, and rallycrossers usually have a set of competition tires that they install on race day, and another set of good street tires for general use.

One factor in tire choice for your MINI is whether or not your car came equipped with run-flat tires. Run-flats eliminate the spare tire, so manufacturers like them. They save space in the car and money in the manufacturer's pocket. However, run-flats are

Wheel studs make changing tires a whole lot easier, and they're so easy to install that there's very little reason to keep the stock lug bolts.

noisy and harsh and not as good for performance driving as regular tires of the same size. Many Cooper S owners have elected to go to conventional tires and run the risk of a flat.

Alignment

Just as all the great engine parts in the world won't help you much if they aren't properly tuned, your suspension needs to be tuned to give you the performance you've paid for. Suspension tuning is every bit as important as engine tuning, and in some respects it's harder to do. With engine tuning, you can use a dyno and ECU readouts to measure torque, horsepower, timing, and air/fuel ratio. With suspension tuning, you have to rely more on feel and personal preference. You can (and you should) use accurate tools to set up your suspension, but it's harder to identify the optimum setup. One skill that professional racing drivers cultivate is the ability to describe a car's handling characteristics in precise terms, and to repeat a test lap the same way every time to get a valid test of new suspension settings. The rest of us just have to work at it as best we can.

Factory Alignment

The factory alignment settings are very good for most street driving. These settings are optimized to minimize NVH and maximize your fuel economy and tire wear. If you don't need a different alignment for track or autocross competition, it's best to leave things in the stock configuration.

Start by having your car aligned to the factory specifications. If you have substantial aftermarket modifications such as caster/camber plates, adjustable shock absorbers, or a coil-over suspension, you have more adjustability than with the stock components. Then from stock, make incremental changes and test your results until the car feels good to you. Don't be afraid to keep adjusting until the car no longer feels good, then work your way back to the optimum setting.

Alternately, find a credible source for good performance settings for your model and modification status. In all cases, however, let common sense and your personal comfort be your guide.

Setting Ride Height and Corner Weights

If you have changed over to a coil-over suspension, some new adjustments are available to you. Because you can change springs easily and set the total strut height and spring compression individually, you have more control over the ride height and the weight distribution to the four corners of your vehicle.

First, park on a flat, level surface. Set the basic ride height to appropriate (and legal) levels for your purposes. Measure ride height from the ground to the same point on each side of the car. When you've got the ride height set, you can make adjustments to set the corner weights and correct the alignment. Then go back and check it all again, because each change you make affects the others. Don't forget to check what your changes have done to the angle of the lower control arm and your roll center.

You need a set of wheel scales to set weights. Sometimes scales can be rented from racing shops, but a better plan is to find a tuner or racing shop with a set of scales and take your car there for corner weighting. It will take a lot less time and effort, and will probably yield better results. Be sure to bring your car in its usual configuration and sit in the driver's seat while the weights are taken. By adjusting each strut's total length and spring compression up or down a little, you can maintain a level ride (or the angle you want) and equalize weights side to side in the car. The MINI has a natural weight distribution of about 62 percent in the front to 38 percent in the back.

Aligning Your Car

Aligning your car is another part of performance tuning you can usually perform yourself with some practice and effort. However, it's generally affordable to pay a professional shop to perform this adjustment, and you end up with better results. Autocrossers often take the time to learn to align their cars on the fly so that they can change to a racing setup for competition and then return to a more relaxed alignment for street driving. But even with the aftermarket parts required to allow adjustment, setting camber accurately is hard without specialized tools, and caster changes generally require changing out parts, so the main thing you can align at home is toe.

Setting your car's toe is easy. You can make a set of toe plates or simply create two parallel lines using string. Either way, you need at least one accurate measuring tape.

Toe plates are two identical flat plates with slots created in the sides. For example, if your tires are 26 inches in diameter, make the plates about 26 inches long by 18 inches tall. Cut a slot 3 inches up on each short side of each plate. Get a friend to help stand the plates snug against the outside of the front tires and centered with respect to the axis of the wheel. Next, take two identical tape measures and slip the ends into the slots on one plate and run them under the car and through the slots in the other plate. You will be able to read each measure where it comes out of the plate. If the forward measure reads 72 inches exactly and the rear measure reads $72\frac{1}{16}$ inches, you have 1/16 inch of toe-in. Easy!

To "string" a car, you have to first find the centerline of the chassis by measuring from fixed points on the car. Then use four jack stands and two pieces of string to create two parallel lines on either side of the car. The car's centerline must be exactly parallel to the strings. It's nice if the car is exactly centered between the two lines, but not necessary. In fact, you might find that your car is not exactly the same side to side. That's interesting, but not critical. What you want to measure is the relationship of the tires to each other. Measure perpendicular (using a carpenter's square is helpful) from the string to the frontmost point of each tire and from the rearmost point of each tire. Then compare your measurements and look for the differences. For example, if the fronts of the tires are 12 and 11¾ inches from the strings, and the rears of the tires are 12 and 12¼ inches from the strings, you know that one tire is 1/4-inch toed out, and the other is parallel to the centerline of the car. Now you can adjust one or both wheels toward the desired setting and measure again.

Using toe plates is generally quicker and easier, but the advantage of stringing a car is that you can also find the relationship of the front wheels to the rears. Sometimes you discover that the rear end is consistent with itself in alignment, but is offset with respect to the front. This can indicate old crash damage, or simply that the subframes of the car are out of alignment with each other.

Centering a Steering Wheel

If you have made changes to your suspension and alignment settings, you may find that the steering wheel no longer sits straight when you drive in a straight line. You can fix this by making opposite and equal changes to the steering rods. If you shorten one rod while lengthening the other, the total distance between the tires remains the same, but the position of the steering gear changes, moving the steering wheel. Keep the car's front wheels straight and you can adjust the steering wheel back to true.

Basic Alignment Settings

Camber and caster are expressed in degrees, and toe is expressed in degrees with an approximation in inches. If you have a professional align your car, the machine reads in degrees. If you use plates or string, you measure in inches. These settings should be a reasonable place to start your tuning process.

Toe-Out

For each degree you change the front camber toward negative, you can expect to get about 1/2 degree of toe-out without separately adjusting the tie rods. So, changing both front wheels from +1.5 to -2.0 gives you about 1.75 degrees additional toe-out.

Alignment Settings

R50 / R53 STOCK SETTINGS

POSITION	ANGLE	MEASUREMENTS
Front	Camber	-.30, +/-.25 (-0.55 maximum negative)
Front	Toe	.18, +/- .05 toe-in (about 1/8 inch, +/- 1/16 inch)
Rear	Camber	-1.3 to -1.6
Rear	Toe	.24, +/- .08 toe-in (about 1/8 inch, +/-1/16 inch)

R50/R53 AUTOCROSS / TRACK SETTINGS

POSITION	ANGLE	MEASUREMENTS
Front	Camber	-2.0 to -3.0 total
Front	Toe	.06 to .13 toe-out (1/16 inch to 1/8 inch)
Rear	Camber	-1.0 to -1.6 total
Rear	Toe	0.0 to .06 toe-in (1/16 inch)

R56 STOCK SETTINGS

POSITION	ANGLE	MEASUREMENTS
Front	Camber	-.30, +/- .25 (-0.55 degree maximum negative)
Front	Toe	.12, +/- .05 toe-in (about 1/8 inch, +/- 1/16 inch)
Rear	Camber	-1.45 +/- .20
Rear	Toe	.24, +/- .08 toe-in (about 1/8 inch)

R56 AUTOCROSS / TRACK SETTINGS

POSITION	ANGLE	MEASUREMENTS
Front	Camber	-2.0 to -3.0 total
Front	Toe	10 to .20 toe-out (about 1/16 to 1/8 inch)
Rear	Camber	-1.2 to -1.6 total
Rear	Toe	0.0 to .06 toe-in (zero to 1/16 inch)

CHAPTER 4

Improving Braking

Most of the time, performance enthusiasts focus on how to make their cars go faster; they look for torque, acceleration, top speed, and grip. But it's just as important that your MINI can stop as well as it goes; maybe more important if it's a car you drive on public roads. Beyond the considerations for safety, your car will be more fun to drive with a really good brake system. Brakes don't cost much more than any other high-performance system on your car, and you really notice the results. But before you dive into your brakes, remember that the stock brakes on a MINI are very good for most purposes and only those engaging in high-performance driving really require any sort of upgrade.

MINI Stock Brake System

The MINI uses a four-wheel disc-brake system. All stock Cooper and Cooper S brakes use single-piston

Professional

If you are not confident of your ability to work on your own brakes, take your car to a professional. This is one area where a screwup can endanger others as well as yourself and your wallet.

Nothing looks more sporty and functional than a great set of brakes behind a nice lightweight wheel. But brakes are also a critical safety and handling device on your car, so you have to make sure they're done right. (Photo courtesy Stephan McKeown)

The R56 John Cooper Works edition is the first MINI to come with a fixed front caliper from the factory. Perhaps this is the shape of things to come for the Cooper S?

The R56 John Cooper Works edition comes with a traditional floating caliper in the rear, but painted red for that sporty look.

THE NEW MINI PERFORMANCE HANDBOOK

CHAPTER 4

(also known as "single-pot") floating calipers on all four wheels. That goes for the R53 John Cooper Works and GP special editions as well as regular models. Starting in 2007, all JCW editions received an OEM Brembo four-piston fixed caliper in front, but retained the single-piston floating caliper in the rear.

The table below shows the rotor sizes and caliper configuration for all North American market MINIs.

The MINI's disc-brake rotors are made from a single piece of cast iron and machined to the proper thickness. Stock front rotors are vented, while the rears are solid. All stock rotors are smooth-faced, which is to say, they aren't drilled through with holes, nor do they have grooves in the friction surface.

Many aftermarket brake rotors are grooved or cross-drilled, and the fancier brake kits use rotors made from two pieces. The friction surface is still made of machined cast iron or steel, but the center "hat" portion is made of aluminum. The two halves of each rotor are bolted together. This aids in cooling and allows you to replace the friction surface without having to replace the center.

The MINI uses a vacuum-assisted brake master cylinder, an anti-lock braking system (ABS), and hard lines throughout the chassis. The anti-lock system includes an automatic brake force distribution function that ensures that the rear brakes receive as much pressure as they can take without locking up, and modulates brake pressure when the car is cornering. This system, known as EBD (electronic brakeforce distribution), helps keep the car stable at all times under braking. Both the anti-lock system and the brake force distribution system are always on—you can't turn them off, and for most purposes you wouldn't want to.

The parking/emergency brake on all MINIs is a basic cable-actuated mechanical interface (not hydraulic) to the rear brake calipers. There are no additional pads or friction surfaces associated with the emergency brake.

When you think about upgrading the brakes in your MINI, realize that the master cylinder and ABS power-brakes in your car have plenty of power to stop the car. You don't need to upgrade these parts, and you really wouldn't want to make changes in this system for a street car. Just keep your brake master cylinder and vacuum booster in good shape and use good, fresh brake fluid as recommended and they'll last for years.

Brake Bias

Auto manufacturers must find the best compromise on brake balance; one in which the brakes always work pretty well under a

STOCK MINI BRAKES		
APPLICATION	FRONT / REAR ROTOR	CALIPERS
R50 (02-06 Cooper)	10.9/10.2 inches (276/259 mm)	Single-piston floating
R52 (04-06 Conv)	10.9/10.2 inches (276/259 mm)	Single-piston floating
R53 (02-06 Cooper S)	10.9/10.2 inches (276/259 mm)	Single-piston floating
R53 (JCW & GP)	11.57/10.2 inches (294/259 mm)	Single-piston floating (red paint)
R55 (Clubman)	11.0/10.2 inches (280/259 mm)	Single-piston floating
R55 (Clubman S)	11.57/10.2 inches (294/259 mm)	Single-piston floating
R55 (Clubman JCW)	12.4/11.0 inches (316/280 mm)	Four-piston fixed/ Single-piston floating
R56 (07+ Cooper S)	11.57/10.2 inches (294/259 mm)	Single-piston floating
R56 (07+ JCW)	12.4/11.0 inches (316/280 mm)	Four-piston fixed/ Single-piston floating
R57 (08+ Convertible)	11.0/10.2 inches (280/259 mm)	Single-piston floating
R57 (08+ Conv. S)	11.57/10.2 inches (294/259 mm)	Single-piston floating
R57 (08+ Convertible JCW)	12.4/11.0 inches (316/280 mm)	Four-piston fixed/ Single-piston floating

This two-piece rotor is both drilled and grooved. It looks great, but doesn't really do any more work than the stock rotor.

wide variety of conditions. If you change your brakes to work at maximum efficiency under any particular scenario (including how much weight is in the car, how fast is the car traveling, on what kind of road surface, and how quickly do you want to stop), you are trading off performance under other scenarios. Because you encounter so many different scenarios in real-world driving, proper brake bias and design is necessarily a compromise.

Ideally, you want the braking force on the front and rear wheels to be allocated according to the weight on each pair of wheels. But depending on how briskly you're stopping, more weight in the car shifts forward, placing more weight on the front wheels than they have when you're accelerating. Because rear wheel lockup is especially dangerous, automakers make conservative decisions on brake bias, meaning that the stock system is usually biased to the front enough to make a full panic stop without rear wheel lockup. Anti-lock brakes help maintain stability, but the system is still biased to put the most force on the front wheels.

It is possible to get more braking efficiency under dry, smooth conditions by changing the bias. However, there are other variables at work, such as the road surface and the current temperature of the brakes. So unless you have real-time cockpit-adjustable brake bias and the time and space to figure out the exact optimum balance, and the skills to handle the results when you're wrong, you should honor the design engineers' decisions about brake bias. Further, you should consider all upgrades to your brake system with an eye toward maintaining that bias.

Brake Fade

Brake fade happens when the brakes get very hot. The primary factor that contributes to brake fade is that brake pads lose their grip when they are heated past their designed range (more on that later). Just as critical is that brake fluid can boil and release compressible gases when the brakes get very hot. Since the brakes depend on pressure to work, the vaporized fluid compresses instead of the brakes squeezing the calipers. You feel this as a soft or springy brake pedal, and you don't slow down. In extreme cases, the brake pedal may go to the floor—not a good thing if you're on a race track headed into a corner!

Brake fluid is a mixture of oils and other ingredients, designed to have a very high boiling point. MINIs require a Department of Transportation (DOT) brake fluid standard called DOT4. Most brake fluids that you buy in auto parts stores are DOT3, so be sure to get the right fluid. Repeated heat cycles "cook" the fluid and reduce its effectiveness, so you should change the fluid every year or so. Always use a fresh, sealed can of fluid when you begin. Just sitting on the shelf, an opened can of brake fluid gets old fast.

When you change brake fluid, you must be extremely careful never to let the brake fluid reservoir drain completely. This introduces bubbles into the system, and once those bubbles get into your hydraulic system, they're very difficult to remove. You can get brake bleeding tools for the MINI that include a large, pressurized canister that contains a large amount of fluid. You attach this canister to your brake fluid reservoir; it ensures a constant feed of fluid to the system. This allows you to open the bleed valves on your brakes and simply let the pressure push any air bubbles out!

Another reason for brake fade is excessive accumulation of brake dust. Brake dust is simply the abraded pad material and rotor material that is generated every time you step on the brakes. If you have changed your brake pads to a compound that creates more dust than the stock pads, make sure you get in there and clean this up frequently.

Upgrading Your Brakes

The places where you can improve your MINI's braking system are at the four corners, by upgrading the flexible brake lines, calipers, pads, and rotors. Nothing currently on the market for MINIs replaces any parts outside of the wheel wells. As long as you stay away from the master cylinder and all the electro-hydraulic equipment, the MINI brake system is easy to work on and most people with reasonable mechanical aptitude and the right set of tools can get good results in a home garage. MINI service manuals call for some specialty tools, but there are commonly available tools that do a good job.

There are a few practical factors to consider when you think about upgrading your brakes. They include making sure that you upgrade things in the right order and in balance, and making sure that your brakes fit under your wheels. Then you can move on to the fun parts: braided stainless-steel lines, directionally vented front rotors, slotted or drilled rear rotors, 2-, 4-, or 6-pot calipers, and a good pad compound. (We'll look at each of these areas in turn.)

Many aftermarket shops talk about brake improvements in terms

CHAPTER 4

Expert Interview: Warren Gilliland on Brakes

Warren Gilliland has been designing and implementing brakes since the 1960s. He began his career as a designer at Hurst/Airheart, where he worked on the first drop-in brake pad calipers. He's worked on trains, planes, and automobiles, including the Autopia cars at Disneyland. Along the way, he helped build Hurst/Airheart and JFZ Brakes to prominence before founding his own company, The Brake Man, in 1993.

Q: At what point should performance enthusiasts consider upgrading their brakes?

They should upgrade at any point where they have decided that they will use the car in a different manner from which it was intended by the factory. If they're going to run hard through the canyons or mountains, that can be considered extreme use. Maybe we're just talking about changing to a better pad material to improve the aggressiveness of the brakes, but basically cars are designed for street use that doesn't encompass hard-performance-style use.

Q: We talk about stages of brake modification with the first stage as pads and fluid and the second stage being stock-size slotted replacement rotors with the pads. Do you recommend aftermarket stock-size rotors?

I don't think the aftermarket rotors are as good as the rotors you're taking off the car. They won't work as well as the factory rotors. Slotted and drilled rotors don't do anything for your performance, and they probably hurt it. The reason we drilled rotors 50 years ago was that the brake pads had no torque, so we drilled the rotors to increase the bite between the pad and rotor. The coefficient of friction of those brake pads was .3, and the coefficient of today's brake pads is .5! Just the bite of the pad alone will double the torque going into the rotor, which means the rotor has to displace much more kinetic energy. Now the limiting factor is that the rotor's getting way too hot, and those holes in the rotor stop the airflow from effectively keeping the rotor cool.

Q: But doesn't drilling and slotting help dissipate heat and remove brake dust?

The way a rotor cools is very simple. Heat is being generated on the friction surfaces between the pad and the rotor. The rotor dissipates heat in three ways. The first is radiating the heat back outward from the friction surfaces. And it doesn't help that the factory puts these dust shields on the inside that keeps the heat from moving away from the inside surface. And it forces dust back out to your wheel! The second way a rotor cools is by taking the heat that's being generated on the face and moving it to the center, because cast iron likes to be all at the same temperature. That helps heat soak the rotor to the center. The third way a rotor cools is that there's a low-pressure area at the inner diameter of the rotor, and air comes in and runs through the vanes of the rotor and keeps the center

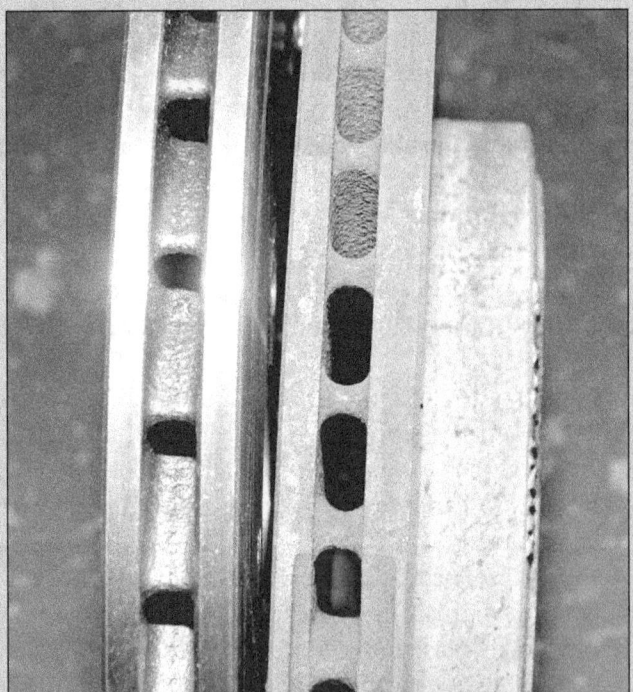

You can see the difference between a directionally vented and a straight-vented rotor by looking in from the outside diameter of the part. Just remember that as the rotor spins forward, directional vanes should be flinging air out, not scooping it in!

and the vane area of the rotor cooler than the friction surface, and the vanes expel the hot air out through the outside diameter of the rotor. So the capacity of the vanes, the surface area of the vanes, and how effectively the rotor gets air into itself determines how cool the center of the rotor will be. By keeping the center of the rotor cooler than the friction faces, the heat is pulled away from the friction faces. If the air going in the inner diameter of the rotor doesn't go up through the vanes and out the outer diameter, but instead seeps out through holes drilled in the face, then the center's going to get hot. The bottom line is this: Dyno testing proves that cross-drilling rotors does not improve the rotor's capacity to dissipate heat.

Q: And yet you sell drilled and slotted stock-size rotors. How does that work?

The drilled rotors we sell are made from steel. Steel and cast iron are very different metals. Cast iron is very brittle, while steel is very malleable. A steel rotor is not going to crack, so we can drill the rotor to lighten it up. Our front rotor is a substantial enough part for the MINI that the temperature is never going to be high enough to create a problem, so we can give people the bling they want while still supplying a rotor that will meet the needs of the thermal dynamics you're going to put through it.

Q: How about two-piece rotors? What's the advantage there?

Cast-iron rotors expand and contract with temperature. By having a flat-plate rotor mounted to an aluminum hat, you allow the rotor to expand and contract more freely, which help keep the rotor from cracking. It's also far lighter, which reduces rotating weight. And you'll note that the mounting ears on the inner diameter of the friction face are about half the overall thickness of the rotor. As the heat transfers into that thinner cross-section, it brings the temperature up more quickly. That helps the temperature differential remain constant between the rotor and the mounting ears, which helps prevent change of shape and warping.

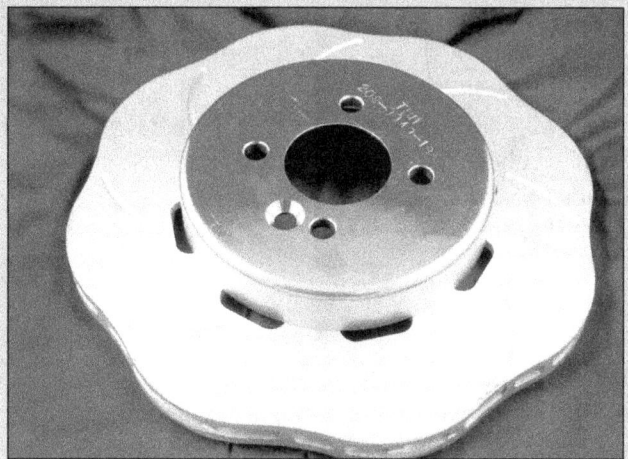

The Brake Man uses a two-piece convoluted shape with directional vanes and slots on his street rotors. It looks great and it's functional.

Q: What's the point of the wavy outer perimeter on your rotors?

That's called a convoluted design. That design changes the height-to-width ratio of the rotor down substantially. Also I put a V-groove in the outer edge of the rotor, which also reduces the height-width ratio. That helps eliminate the tendency of the rotor to want to change its shape. Then we do a four-day thermal process to stabilize the material.

Q: Do you still need to bake racing pads in a toaster oven or any of the other old rituals and tricks?

It depends. Remember that up until about 15 years ago, most pads were asbestos-based, and they outgassed. Modern pads are carbon-based, semi-metallic, or ceramic-based, and they don't outgas. So we're not talking about the same thing, although a resin-based pad still benefits from having the resins burned out of it.

Q: Tell me the difference between ceramic, semi-metallic, and other pads. How should people choose a pad?

If your only concern is how your car looks and you want to avoid dusting up your wheels, you need a ceramic-based pad. If you're going to take the car to

Expert Interview: Warren Gilliland on Brakes CONTINUED

a track or run autocross, you need semi-metallic. If you're going to go out and run the car longer than a 15–20 minute session on a race track, you need a full-out racing pad. You haven't got a choice. There's no such thing as one pad that works well under all conditions. It just doesn't happen.

Q: How about for a performance street car; what should that person use?

We make pads and replacement rotors that will take more punishment than their stock parts. We have a #82 performance street pad, and potentially people can upgrade to our stock replacement High Performance SuperBrake rotors. Then just upgrade the pads to our #82 in the rear. One thing to remember is that if you buy new pads, you do not want to put them over the top of the friction material that has already been transferred to the rotor. It's very important to remove that. If the rotor's in a good flat condition, taking a vibrating palm sander with 80-grit sandpaper will remove the material transferred from the stock pad. If you do not remove that layer, you can significantly impair the new pad from laying down the material it wants to properly give you the performance you should have. Most people who think they have warped a rotor just have material built up unevenly on the rotor.

Q: How hard should they sand the rotors?

You can see the material transfer on the rotor in most cases. You just want to put a nice crosshatch on the rotor so the surface is clean enough so the new pad can lay itself down. It comes off pretty readily; it doesn't take much effort, just 2 or 3 minutes on each side. It's more about getting the face of the sander flat on the rotor on both sides.

Q: What should be done for rear brakes on a MINI?

You have to look at what they're doing with the car overall. If they're just putting brakes on the front and trying to stop from 120 as opposed to 60 mph, they're going to be unloading the back end much more. Now it depends on whether they're doing that once or 50 times. If it's just once, then having extra brake on the front and doing nothing in the rear is probably OK. However, the pads they have on the car will determine whether they've done a good job balancing the car.

Q: Is it possible to have too much brake on your MINI?

Absolutely. The limiting factor is the limit of the tire against the surface you're on. Off-road on dirt, you can't achieve more than about .6 or .7 G before you break the tire loose. On asphalt you can see 1.2 or 1.3 G, which is twice the torque you need to stop the car. Also, it quadruples the heat you put through the rotor. What you need to remember is this formula: It's mass times velocity squared to stop the car. That means that stopping from 120 as opposed to stopping from 60 is not twice as much work, it's four times as much work. That's where people get into trouble on the street when they drive their cars too fast.

---

of "stages." Simply put, a stage is a set of upgrades that generally go together. The higher the stage number, the more complex the upgrade (and the higher the cost). You can pick the stage that works for you.

Stage 1 is the most basic upgrade. The primary upgrade is replacing your stock brake pads with high-performance pads. "We recommend good street pads, with a little more bite and less fade when they heat up. Then you can still stop on your way to work in the morning," says John Leitl of Alta Performance. An optional stage 1 brake upgrade is to change to fresh DOT4 brake fluid.

Stage 2 includes all the stage 1 upgrades, plus a set of stock-size replacement rotors. Common stock-size replacements are made by Brembo, StopTech, and Brake Man.

Stage 3 includes all the stage 2 upgrades, plus a set of fixed calipers and braided stainless-steel brake lines. Examples include Goodridge or Stoptech lines and JCW front calipers and rotors for the R56.

Stage 4 involves a full upgrade to an oversize big-brake kit with fixed calipers. There are a wide variety of these kits on the market, made by Brake Man, StopTech, Girodisc, Brembo, Wilwood, and so on.

Stage 1: Upgrading Brake Pads

High-performance brake pads are an easy upgrade for your system. The stock pads selected by any automaker are generally optimized to produce as little brake dust as possible and to last a long time, while delivering braking power according to the engineering plan for the car.

As mentioned before, when you overheat any set of brake pads past their designed range, you experience brake fade. You experience this as a mushy or springy feeling in your brake pedal, with noticeably reduced braking effect.

By choosing a set of high-performance brake pads, you can get more stopping power and more resistance to brake fade at high temperatures. But you're trading off the amount and type of brake dust that is produced, and frequently, you also trade off stopping performance when the brakes are cold. Every brake pad has a heat range where it works best. High-performance brake pads are designed to work once the brakes have been heated-up over a few laps on a race track. Stock pads are designed to work through a much lower temperature range, where the discs may never get warmer than the ambient temperature.

In normal driving, you probably won't ever reach the optimum heat range for a racing pad like the Hawk Blue or Black compound. This is one area where "racing parts" aren't necessarily better for your purposes. But Hawk, like most other high-performance brake manufacturers, also makes a line of high-performance street pads

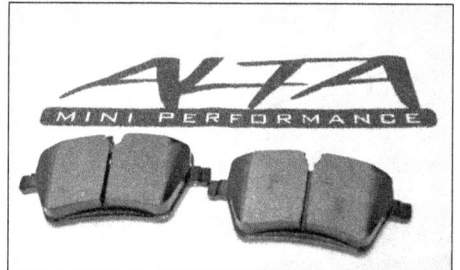

The Hawk HPS brake pad is commonly available and a good choice for street-performance driving.

designed for the MINI. If you want more braking power for your street car, choose a street-performance pad such as the Hawk HPS.

You can improve overall brake performance with a set of upgraded brake pads without worrying about cold pads, because there are so many different types and grades of pad to choose from. You can buy good, high-quality upgrade pads from AEM, Brembo, EBC, Ferodo, Axxis, Hawk, Wilwood, Carbotech, Performance Friction, and others. Each brand has its own following, usually very dedicated.

To choose a pad for your car, talk to performance experts in your area—people who drive on the same roads in the same weather in the same kind of car as you—and find out what works for them. Be prepared to try a few different brands and you'll find one that works well for you.

One thing to keep in mind is that if you go away from OEM stock pads, you might lose the brake wear sensor function in your MINI. There's a wire that attaches to the stock brake pads, and when they get thin, it triggers a light on the dashboard. You'll have to tie that wire and its connection fitting out of the way if you change to aftermarket pads that do not support the sensor, and then monitor your brake wear personally.

You can buy racing brake fluid at any good performance auto parts store. Check the packaging carefully to make sure it's at least DOT4 for your MINI.

Finally, whatever pad you choose for your driving habits, be sure to replace all the brake pads at the same time, to preserve the balance between the front and rear brakes.

To install new pads for a Stage 1 upgrade, follow the appropriate instructions in the Stage 2 Front Brake Upgrade Project on page 89 and the Rear Brake Upgrade Project on page 91.

Stage 2: Upgrading Rotors

Upgrading your rotors generally goes along with changing your calipers, and that means a full brake kit, but there are benefits to upgrading stock rotors even if you can't afford the whole big-brake kit.

There are two ways you can get more out of your brake rotors. One is to use larger rotors. Larger rotors have more friction surface (also known as swept area), more mass to absorb and disperse heat, and you're getting better leverage on the wheel with a larger rotor. But a larger rotor

Ken Jubb's 2005 Cooper S

Ken Jubb bought this Cooper S after it had been modified, which is a great way to save some money, assuming that you agree with the modifications made by the previous owner. He's added a few touches of his own to make his ride complete. In this configuration, his MINI is pushing 205 wheel hp and 184 ft-lbs of torque.

But more important is the set of brakes he's using. He's got a 14-inch kit from TCE in front and the TCE 11.75-inch rear brake kit. Both kits use Wilwood components. With these brakes, the 18-inch OZ wheels on this car are not optional!

Here's the full rundown on this 2005 R53 MINI Cooper S in Electric Blue Metallic with Panther Black Leather-Suede interior:

Engine and Drivetrain
- Alta 15-percent supercharger pulley
- Alta header with high-flow catalytic converters
- Alta 2.5-inch exhaust with custom tip
- Alta cold-air intake
- Alta classic intercooler
- Magnecor spark plug wires
- M7 ECU tuning
- Carbon-fiber air diverter
- Texas Speedwerks engine damper
- Dynamat sound-damper padding throughout

Suspension and Brakes
- Hotchkiss lowering springs
- Alta rear sway bar
- Cusco carbon-fiber front and rear strut braces
- OZ Racing Ultraleggera 18x7 wheels
- Toyo Proxes 215/40-R18 tires
- Wilwood 14-inch front-drilled, grooved two-piece rotors
- Wilwood red four-piston front calipers
- Wilwood 11.75-inch rear-drilled, grooved two-piece rotors
- Wilwood rear parking-brake calipers
- Stainless braided brake lines

Interior and Aero
- Factory Aero kit, custom-painted
- JCW rear wing
- Sparco Modena seats
- JCW steering wheel
- JCW shift-indicator lights
- Defi boost and oil-temperature gauges
- Alta short shifter
- Euro parcel shelf
- Schrader rear-seat delete kit

Ken Jubb bought this MINI mostly prepared, but added his own touches here and there.

The 18-inch OZ wheels are not optional with this brake kit. Always check to make sure your wheels will fit over your new brakes, or you could be adding a lot of money to your project budget.

This two-piece, drilled and slotted rear rotor is 11¾ inches in diameter —more than 1½ inches larger than stock.

IMPROVING BRAKING

These StopTech stock replacement rotors are easy on your budget and make a nice replacement for the stock units. The slots may not actually do anything, but they look the part.

requires an expensive aftermarket caliper, so what else is there?

You can still get a rotor upgrade by using a stock-diameter rotor with improved features. The best you can get is a directionally vented rotor. Grooved and drilled rotors are lighter than stock rotors, but not by much, and these features don't help your braking.

The main thing is to buy a rotor with better venting. Most stock-vented rotors can go on either side of the car because the vanes between the two friction surfaces are radial—they travel straight out from the center. An upgraded rotor has curved vanes, which act like a centrifugal pump, flinging air from the center of the rotor out through the perimeter continuously as the wheel turns. Such rotors are marked as left side or right side, or marked with an arrow that indicates their forward rotation. It's important to install these rotors in the proper orientation so that the pumping effect works as designed. Brembo, StopTech, Girodisc, Racing Brake, Brake Man, and Wilwood make excellent curved-vane front replacement rotors in solid, grooved, or drilled configuration.

PROJECT
A Stage 2 Front Brake Upgrade

When it's time to freshen-up your brakes, you might as well spend a couple more bucks and get a basic upgrade. You can do the job in your own garage with two people in less than an hour. This job installs a pair of StopTech slotted stock-size replacement rotors and Hawk HPS pads on the project R53 MINI Cooper S. (The procedure for the rear brakes is similar, but rear brake pads should last several times longer than front pads under normal driving conditions.)

Before you do anything to your brakes, get an official factory repair manual for your specific model and year and follow all the instructions in that manual. The basic steps in the process are:

1 Jack the car up and get your good set of jack stands underneath it, then remove the front wheels. Do one side at a time. Arrange all the replacement parts in a place where they're close by and won't get dirty. You need a 10-mm wrench for the bleed nipple, a caliper piston tool, a 7-mm Allen-head wrench, a flathead screwdriver for the spring clips, and a T-50 Torx wrench or socket. If you plan to change the fluid, you also need some clear rubber tubing, an empty bottle or can, a fresh can or two of brake fluid, and a pressurized bleeder. If you don't have that last tool, delegate one person to keep the fluid reservoir full at all times.

2 As the legendary auto repair manual author John Muir

The stock front brake is very simple and easy to work on. You can install an aftermarket replacement kit in an afternoon and still have time for a drive in the country.

used to say, consider the picture in front of you. At both the front and the rear, you have a caliper that is bolted to the hub, a captive brake rotor, and a flexible hydraulic line connecting the caliper to the rest of the brake system. You have an electric wire connected to the brake wear sensor on the left front and right rear brakes. You can see the suspension and steering and control arms as well.

3 Remove the brake-pad wear sensor wire carefully. Do not ever cut the wire or pull the sensor

Take care not to damage these pad wear sensors. Even if you don't plan to use them, they'll trigger the brake wear light on your car and they're a little difficult to replace.

THE NEW MINI PERFORMANCE HANDBOOK

from the stock pads roughly. If the sensor is damaged, the brake wear sensor light on the dashboard illuminates until you replace the sensor. The sensor unplugs from the brake pad. You may need to use a screwdriver to gently pop it free. Some aftermarket brake pads do not support the use of the wear sensor, so use a pair of zip-ties to secure the sensor and its wire out of the way if you can't reuse it.

4 A spring clip holds the pads in place within each caliper. Pry the spring clip off the caliper to allow the pads to move.

5 Feel around the back of the caliper. You're looking for two plastic plugs. You should be able to remove these plugs with your fingers, but prying them out with a screwdriver may be necessary. Behind these plugs are 7-mm Allen-head bolts that hold the caliper together. Use a 7-mm Allen-head wrench or socket to remove these bolts.

The bolts that hold the caliper to its frame are an 8-mm Allen head. They come out easily if the caps have been in place to keep them clean.

6 Once the bolts are loosened, you can pull the center of the caliper body away from the brake rotor. If the rotor is worn, there may be a lip around its perimeter, and you may have to wiggle and twist the caliper slightly to compress the piston enough to provide clearance.

7 The outboard brake pad may stay with the rotor and the caliper frame. You can lift this pad out easily. The pad next to the caliper piston has spring clips that hold it in place in the piston. You'll remove this pad shortly, but before you do, use your caliper spreader tool to press the piston back into the caliper. You need to do this to fit the new pads into the caliper. Press the piston back until the back of the brake pad is just flush with the piston seal. Don't force it.

We removed this caliper to clearly show how to use a caliper press. You can use your thumbs if you have strong hands, but a caliper press costs about $10 at any auto parts store and makes the job a snap.

8 Now pull the second pad away from the piston. You can see the spring clips. The set of four new pads should include two with spring clips designed for this position. Place a spring-clipped pad into the piston.

Each rotor is held in place with a T-50 Torx bolt. I nearly stripped one of them trying to remove a 40,000-mile rotor. If they strip, you're in for a devil of a time drilling it out—so be careful.

9 Remove the caliper frame from the hub flange. This frame is held on with two 16-mm bolts. Then undo the T-50 Torx bolt that holds the rotor to the hub. This bolt may be rusted and dusted into place, so be firm but gentle—Torx bolts are not strong and you might strip out the drive pattern. When the Torx bolt has been removed, wiggle the rotor off its hub boss. You might need to tap with a rubber hammer to get it loose.

If the rotors have been on the car a while, you might need to tap them free very gently with a lead or rubber hammer.

10 Clean up and scuff the replacement rotors. Make sure you have the correct rotor on the correct side of the car and push the rotors onto the hub boss. Line up the holes and reinstall the Torx bolt.

11 Bolt the caliper frame back to the flange. The torque spec for the 16-mm bolts is 81 ft-lbs. Reassemble the caliper with the new pads and place the caliper body in the frame. Don't forget the spring clip. Note that the assembly is likely to be loose. The caliper will come together when you first step on the brake pedal.

12 Repeat steps 1 through 9 on the opposite front brake. You can bleed the system if you think the fluid needs replacement or if you think there may be air bubbles in the calipers. However, if you did not

IMPROVING BRAKING

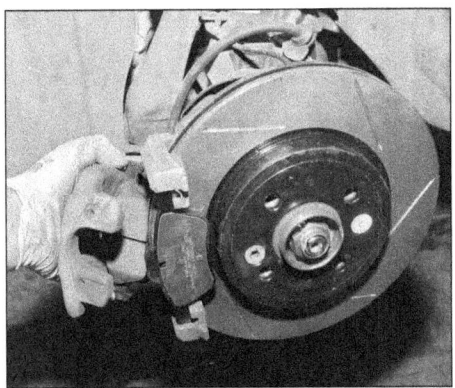

It's easiest to install the outer pad on the caliper frame first, and then install the main caliper body around it. These brakes go together very easily. If they don't fit, something is very wrong.

The new brakes don't look much different than the stock ones at this point, but you'll feel the difference with the Hawk pads and fresh racing fluid.

open the brake hydraulics, this should not be necessary unless you want to upgrade the brake fluid.

13 Step on the brakes a couple times and hold pressure while your assistant checks the front brake system for leaks. If your foot goes slowly to the floor, chances are you've got a leak. When you're satisfied that everything is snug and tight, put the wheels back on and lower the car to the floor. Take a very careful test drive and pay attention to your brakes for the next couple hundred miles to make sure it's all working correctly.

PROJECT
A Stage 2 Rear Brake Upgrade

You can do this job in your own garage with two people in about an hour. This project installs a set of StopTech 10.2-inch slotted stock-replacement rotors and Hawk HPS pads to fit the stock caliper on our project 2005 R53 MINI Cooper S. The procedure is substantially the same for any aftermarket rear brake kit that uses the stock caliper.

Special Tool

This project requires a MINI special tool to recompress the stock caliper piston. If you don't have that tool (and no one does, except for professional MINI mechanics), you can take this job to a professional or use a generic tool for this kind of brake caliper.

1 Begin by laying out all the parts you will use and make sure you have all the tools and parts to complete the job, including a supply of fresh brake fluid. You need an 8-mm wrench for the bleed screws, a 7-mm Allen-head wrench, a T-50 Torx socket or wrench, and a flat-head screwdriver for the spring clips. If you plan to replace the brake fluid, you also need some clear rubber tubing, an empty bottle or can, and a fresh can or two of brake fluid.

2 Jack the car up and get your set of good jack stands underneath it, then remove the rear wheels. You can see the entire stock

brake system clearly. Note the caliper and pads, rotor, flexible brake line, and brake wear sensor wire that is attached to the inboard brake pad on the right side.

3 There is an electric wire connected to the brake wear sensor on the right rear brake. Remove the brake-pad wear sensor wire carefully. Do not ever cut the wire or pull the sensor from the stock pads roughly. You may need to use a screwdriver to gently pop it free. Some aftermarket brake pads do not support the use of the wear sensor, so use a pair of zip-ties to secure the sensor and its wire out of the way if you can't reuse it.

4 A spring clip holds the pads in place within each caliper. Pry the spring clip off the caliper to allow the pads to move.

5 Feel around the back of the caliper. You're looking for two

The stock rear brake is very much like the front brake. Not much to look at, but it does the job quite well.

THE NEW MINI PERFORMANCE HANDBOOK

plastic plugs. You should be able to remove these plugs with your fingers, but prying them out with a screwdriver may be necessary. Behind these plugs are 7-mm Allen-head bolts that hold the caliper together. Use a 7-mm Allen-head wrench or socket to remove the top bolt, and then the bottom bolt. You can then move the caliper away from the rotor.

6 Remove the old pads from the caliper and have a look at the piston. It has four holes in its face. You need the MINI special tool to both press the piston back into the caliper and twist it in a clockwise direction to create more room for the new pads, or you can find a generic tool that turns the piston while pushing at the same time.

Here is how the factory tool works on the rear brake caliper. The correct tool costs a couple hundred dollars, or you can buy a similar generic disc brake caliper tool set at your favorite discount tool store for about $20.

7 Use the T-50 Torx socket to undo the Torx bolt holding the

When you're finished, check the tightness on the Torx bolt and make sure the wire retainer is firmly in place.

rotor to the hub. Remove the rotor and replace it with the new part. Unlike the fronts, you don't have to remove the caliper frame to replace the rear rotors. Tighten the Torx bolt down snugly but gently. Remember, those star points are weak.

8 When you've got the new rotor in place and the caliper compressed, install the new pads and reassemble the rotor. You can bleed the system if you think the fluid needs replacement or if you think there may be air bubbles in the calipers. However, if you did not open the brake hydraulics, this should not be necessary unless you want to upgrade the brake fluid.

This is the adjustment interface on the rear caliper. You either need to use the special tool or you can try a generic substitute. I cheated and borrowed the correct tool from a MINI mechanic.

As with the front brakes, you can install the outer pad on the frame for easy assembly.

Stage 3: Upgrading Brake Lines and Calipers

The stock flexible brake lines run from the ends of the hard lines in the wheel wells to the brake calipers. These lines need to be flexible in order to move with the wheels as you drive. The stock lines are made from a layered reinforced rubber, and they're pretty good, but they do inflate slightly when you press on the brakes. The older they get, the more they can balloon, and eventually crack. This expansion steals some of the braking pressure and contributes to a spongy pedal feel. You can fix this with a set of braided stainless-steel brake lines.

StopTech and Goodridge both make high-quality, braided-steel brake-line kits for many cars, including MINI. These kits come with fresh sealing washers and any other required hardware, and you should use the hardware in the kit instead of reusing your stock connections.

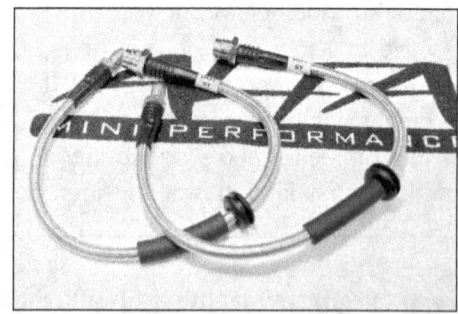

Braided-steel brake lines like these StopTech lines will really firm up your brake pedal. And they look great, which is always a plus.

Bleeding

While the system is open, go ahead and install speed bleeders. These are standard metric bleed nipples with a one-way valve built in. They prevent the system from sucking air back in during the bleed process. There's no special work required. Just take out your old bleed nipples and screw in the speed bleeders the next time you bleed your brakes. You can purchase speed bleeder nipples at any good automotive supply shop for about $10 each. These are the only things I've found in more than 25 years that really work to improve the bleeding process.

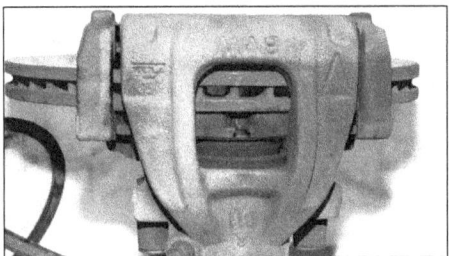

Looking in from the outside edge of a stock caliper and rotor, you can see how much (or how little) pad material remains. You can also see the installation slot for the pad wear sensor.

Using ordinary hand tools, you can install these lines in a couple of hours, and the process is included in the big-brake kit replacement procedure on page 95. You will need to bleed your brakes when you're done, so be sure you've got a friend to help, some fluid, a length of rubber hose, a receptacle for used fluid, and the 8-mm and 10-mm wrenches that fit the bleed nipples.

The stock calipers on your MINI are very good OEM parts. But like all

Aftermarket calipers like this unit from The Brake Man are well-made and use two pistons on each side of the caliper to place uniform and controllable pressure on the pads. Pad replacement is also much easier than with a floating design.

What's wrong with this picture? The bleed valve is on the bottom of the hydraulic piston of this caliper—it's on the wrong side of the car!

manufacturers, MINI tends to prefer solutions that are less expensive to manufacture, so unless you've got an R56 JCW, your MINI is designed to use "floating" calipers. This means a single hydraulic brake piston is placed on one side of the caliper, and the caliper body floats back and forth on a pair of posts. When you step on the brakes, the piston extends and not only pushes the near pad toward the rotor, it pulls the far pad toward the rotor.

With a fixed caliper, there are pistons on both sides of the caliper and each piston pushes its pad against the rotor. Because the caliper body does not move, the system gives you a firmer pedal feel and better control of the rotor under braking. Virtually all aftermarket caliper upgrades are a fixed design. Most aftermarket front calipers use four pistons, with two on either side. Most aftermarket rear calipers have two pistons, with one on either side of the rotor, though these are used far less often.

If you upgrade your calipers, be aware that you will likely have to change your brake pad format (shape and size) as well. Most aftermarket calipers use standard pad formats, but these are not necessarily compatible with the stock format.

By increasing the number of pots and using larger pads, you are improving braking efficiency by increasing the ability to squeeze the rotor, and you are also increasing the area of the rotor that is squeezed at any given time. Increasing the friction area gives you more stopping power.

When buying calipers, be sure you get both a left- and a right-side unit. Most calipers are directional because they mount in the same position, but in an opposite orientation on the left and right wheels. In all cases, the bleed nipple must be on top of the caliper for it to work. If you mount a left-side caliper on the right, it will be upside-down and the bleed nipple will be on the bottom!

You can choose from several good aftermarket calipers. Brake Man, Brembo, StopTech, Wilwood, and Girodisc all make popular and affordable high-performance calipers.

Stage 4: Big-Brake Kits

When you're ready to go all the way, it's time for a big-brake kit MINI. Depending on the kit you choose

CHAPTER 4

MINI FRONT BRAKE KIT COMPARISON		
BRAND	**ROTOR SIZE**	**CALIPERS**
Brembo Sport Grooved	10.9-inch (276-mm) one-piece grooved or drilled	Stock single-piston floating
Racing Brake	10.9-inch (276-mm) one-piece grooved and drilled	Stock single-piston floating
PowerSlot	10.9-inch (276-mm) one-piece grooved	Stock single-piston floating
Brembo R53 JCW Sport Kit	11.57-inch (294-mm) one-piece solid	Stock single-piston floating
Brake Man Basic Kit	12.19-inch two-piece convoluted slotted rotor with directional vanes	Four-piston fixed
Brake Man Big Kit	13-inch two-piece convoluted slotted rotor with directional vanes	Four-piston fixed
Brembo R56 JCW Sport Kit	12.4-inch (316-mm) one-piece solid	Four-piston fixed
AP Racing Big-Brake Kit	11.9-inch (304-mm) one-piece drilled	Four-piston fixed
Wilwood Racing	11.75-inch one-piece grooved	Four-piston fixed DynaPro (stainless pistons)
Wilwood Street	12.19-inch two-piece SRP grooved and drilled with directional vanes	Four-piston fixed DynaPro (with rubber boots)
StopTech Street (R56, R55)	11.57-inch (294-mm)	Stock single-piston floating
StopTech Racing	12.9-inch (328-mm) two-piece grooved or drilled	Four-piston fixed
Brembo GT	12.6-inch (320-mm) one-piece drilled or two-piece drilled or slotted	Four-piston fixed
TCE 13-inch Wilwood FSL	13.0-inch with directional vanes	Six-piston fixed
TCE 13.1-inch Wilwood FSL	13.1-inch with directional vanes	Six-piston fixed
TCE 14-inch Wilwood BSL4r	14.0-inch with directional vanes	Six-piston fixed

MINI REAR BRAKE KIT COMPARISON		
BRAND	**ROTOR SIZE**	**CALIPERS**
Wilwood Rear	10.2-inch (259-mm) one-piece drilled	Stock single-piston floating
StopTech SportStop	10.2-inch (259-mm) one-piece grooved	Stock single-piston floating
Brembo Drilled Rear	10.2-inch (259-mm) one-piece drilled	Stock single-piston floating
Racing Brake	10.2-inch (258-mm) one-piece	Stock single-piston floating
Brake Man	10.2-inch (259-mm) two-piece convoluted drilled and slotted	Stock single-piston floating
Brembo R55, R56, R57 JCW Sport Kit	11.0-inch (280-mm) one-piece solid	Stock single-piston floating
TCE	11.75-inch two-piece Wilwood grooved/drilled	Wilwood Combo Parking Brake Calipers

IMPROVING BRAKING

Front Brake Kits

Some factory design changes were made during 2003 that require the use of slightly different front brake kits. Be sure to check your kit application if your car was built around April/May of 2003.

There are kits available where rotors and calipers of different sizes and configurations have been adapted to the MINI. The kits listed on page 94 are commonly available.

The advantages of a big-brake kit are numerous: better leverage, more pressure on the pads, bigger pads, more swept area, directionally vented rotors, and a choice of high-performance pad compounds. Plus they look great, especially if you have some nice, open wheels to show off your kit. There aren't too many downsides to a big-brake kit, though depending on the kit, you might sacrifice a little extra unsprung weight. And, of course, there's the expense. A big-brake kit just for your front wheels can cost more than $2,000, not including installation.

The main consideration when you're thinking about a brake kit is much the same as for all the individual components—will this kit work with the kind of driving you're going to do? Even if you plan on street driving only, chances are you'll love a big-brake kit, provided you choose a good street pad and not a racing pad.

and your current wheel size, you might even need to buy new wheels and tires at the same time to clear your new binders.

PROJECT
Installing a Stage 4 Big-Brake Kit

You can do this job in your own garage with two people in just a couple of hours. This project installs a set of two-piece 13-inch Brake Man rotors, four-piston front calipers, and a set of braided-stainless brake lines on our project 2005 R53 MINI Cooper S. It also installs a pair of drilled and convoluted two-piece Brake Man Revolution rotors into the stock rear calipers. The procedure is substantially the same for any aftermarket brake kit.

With any brake kit of this size, plan on solving wheel fitment issues. The Brake Man 13-inch kit fits most 18-inch and some 17-inch wheels, but not the stock R85 S-spoke (a.k.a. LeMans or S-lite) wheels that seem to have been installed on most R53s over the years. If you have these wheels, this kit requires 15-mm spacers and possibly a stud conversion—and even then, the calipers took off

Pad and Rotor Wear

With any aftermarket big-brake kit, you lose the functionality of the stock brake-pad wear sensor. If you install aftermarket brakes, you must take responsibility for monitoring your own pad and rotor wear.

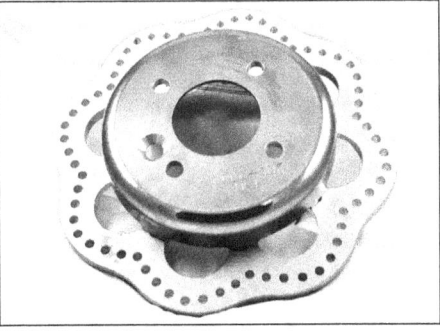

This stock replacement rear rotor from The Brake Man is a two-piece design, convoluted and drilled for lightness. It makes a good partner to a big front brake kit because it keeps the stock rear caliper and parking brake apparatus.

One of the responsibilities you take on when you install a big-brake kit is shimming and adjusting the caliper so that it's in the correct position on the rotor and evenly spaced on either side of the rotor's friction face.

THE NEW MINI PERFORMANCE HANDBOOK

the internal stick-on weights! Luckily, Brake Man also makes a 12.19-inch kit that works perfectly with stock 17-inch S-lite wheels.

Whichever kit you purchase, Brake Man's street kits use a convoluted and slotted directionally vented rotor. Convoluted means that the rotor has a wavy perimeter and looks somewhat like a flower when viewed from the side. The look is exotic and always makes an impression, but the functional aspect is to remove weight without reducing the rotor's ability to transfer heat.

In all vented rotors, the air comes in through the center of the rotor and pushes out the edge. A directionally vaned rotor can pump more air because it's built like a fan. Many people install directional rotors backward, though, because they think the air flows the opposite way—that the air is sucked in from the perimeter toward the center. But a curved-vane rotor pumps the cooling air outward from its center, instead of bringing heated air to the center and heating the hub and ruining your bearings. Brake designers want to expel heat from the rotor, and a directionally vaned rotor is the best for that purpose.

Factory Repair Manual

Before you do anything to your brakes, get an official factory repair manual for your specific model and year and follow all the detailed instructions in that manual. Furthermore, always follow the printed instructions that come with your brake kit.

1 Begin by assembling the brake rotors and "hats" according to the manufacturer's torque specifications. The torque value to affix the rotor to the hat is measured in inch-pounds—do not overtorque these! Brake Man ships the rotors and hats assembled for you, with the bolts safety-wired. Lay out the parts you will use and make sure you have all the tools and parts to complete the job, including a supply of fresh brake fluid.

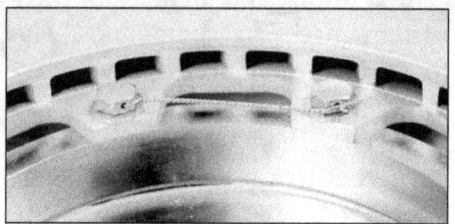

This rotor from The Brake Man has been safety-wired to keep the two pieces from coming apart. These bolts typically have a very low torque spec, so use thread locker if you don't have the tools to safety wire the bolts.

2 Jack the car up and get your set of good jack stands underneath it, then remove the front wheels. You can see the entire stock brake system clearly. Note the caliper and pads, rotor, flexible brake line, and the brake-wear sensor wire attached to the inboard brake pad on the left side.

3 Take a moment now to undo the retaining screw that holds the stock brake rotor to the hub. This screw uses a 6-point Torx T-50 fitting. If the Torx screw is stuck, place a screwdriver into the perimeter of the rotor, using the vanes to hold it tightly against the caliper. It may require some effort to loosen the Torx screw.

4 A spring clip holds the pads in place within each caliper. Pry the spring clip off the caliper to allow the pads to move.

5 Use a 16-mm wrench to remove the two bolts that hold the caliper frame to the hub.

Note that the mechanic has inserted a screwdriver in the vents of this front rotor to hold it against the caliper as he breaks the Torx bolt loose. If you have a rusty or stock Torx bolt, be careful!

The bolts are located out of sight behind the caliper. Remove the caliper from the rotor. If the rotor has significant wear, you may need to twist the caliper slightly to recompress the hydraulic piston to clear the lip on the perimeter of the rotor.

6 Remove the brake-pad wear sensor wire carefully. Do not ever cut the wire or pull the sensor from the stock pads roughly. If the sensor is damaged, the brake-wear sensor light on the dashboard will illuminate permanently. The sensor unplugs from the brake pad. You may need to use a screwdriver to gently pop it free. Aftermarket brake kits do not support the use of the wear sensor, so use a pair of zip-ties to secure the sensor and its wire out of the way.

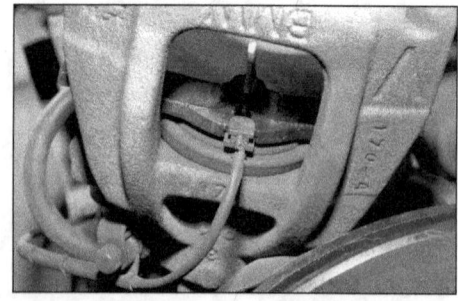

You can see the pad wear sensor wire installed on this stock front caliper. Pry that sensor out of its slot carefully with a screwdriver.

IMPROVING BRAKING

If your pad wear sensor is damaged or the wire gets cut, this is what you see on your dash.

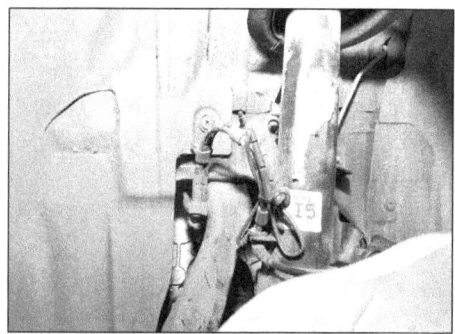

If your new brakes do not accommodate the pad wear sensor, just zip-tie it out of the way.

wrench to loosen the hard line connection. It is critical that you do not damage the connection or twist or crimp the hard line in any way. This area may require some cleaning, as dirt and road debris tends to collect at this fitting.

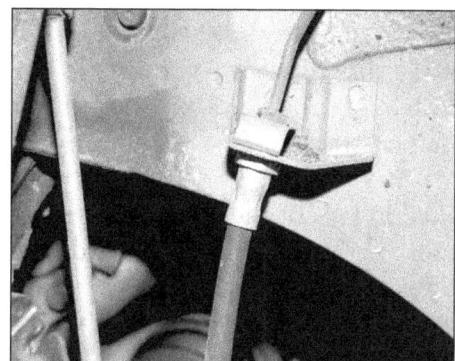

The hard-line connection uses an 11-mm wrench on top and a 17-mm wrench on the flex-hose side. The 11-mm side turns and unthreads from the flex line, then you can pull the flex line down and out.

8 A rubber grommet on the flexible line fits into a holder on the hub body. Use a set of diagonal-cutting pliers to cut the grommet and remove it from the flexible line. You will reuse this grommet with the new flexible lines.

Clip this grommet to fit around the new flex line and reinstall the grommet and the new line in the stock location.

7 Remove the flexible brake fluid line from its fixed mount point in the wheel well. There is usually a spring clip that helps hold this assembly in place. You can remove the spring clip with needle-nose pliers. Then spray the connection with penetrating oil to help loosen the threads. Use a 17-mm wrench on the flexible line and an 11-mm line

Brake Fluid

When you remove the flexible line, some brake fluid will run out of the open end of the hard line. Have rags or a receptacle ready to catch that fluid so it doesn't end up on your suspension or brake components.

9 Remove the stock rotor from the hub. You may need to gently tap the rotor loose with a soft-faced mallet, as it is a tight fit on the hub, and some rust and dust may be holding it in place.

10 You are now looking at the bare hub, and you can see the Torx T-25 mounting screws for the dust shield. Remove the dust shield, as it will not fit an aftermarket big-brake kit.

The caliper and rotor are gone from the hub, and you can see the small T-25 Torx bolts that hold the dust shield to the hub carrier.

11 With some aftermarket flexible lines, you must use a drill to increase the size of the hole in the fixed mount to the hydraulic hard line, but the Brake Man stainless hose end fits the stock hole. Carefully protect the hard line and fitting if you need to drill.

12 Now you can begin installing the replacement kit. Before you start, take a moment to scuff-up the friction faces of the rotors with 80-grit sandpaper. Use a vibrating palm sander if you have one. Get a good crosshatch pattern into the friction surfaces. This helps them bite and wear-in correctly. Then begin by installing the rotor. Brake Man aftermarket rotors are directional. If you

CHAPTER 4

There is some manufacturing tolerance between the hub and the hub bearing carrier. This does not affect the stock brakes, but can result in interference with an aftermarket kit. You must either shim the rotor outward, risking interference between the wheel spokes and the caliper body, or grind away some material from the bearing carrier.

This casting has been ground away just a few millimeters to clear the aftermarket rotor face.

have a two-piece rotor, make sure that all the fasteners holding the rotor to the hat have been installed according to the manufacturer's directions. Now install the rotor onto the hub. Use the same Torx T-50 screw and at least two lug bolts to affix the new rotor and center it on the hub. Pay special attention to make sure that the rotor assembly is seated properly around the central hub boss.

You may find that the inboard friction face of the rotor touches the hub carrier casting at the bottom side. There's enough manufacturing variance tolerance in this part to hit some rotors. The good news is that this part of the bearing carrier is not a critical stressed part, so you can simply grind it away until there is about 2 mm of clearance.

 One of the main reasons to choose an aftermarket brake kit is to obtain a fixed caliper, but with a fixed caliper you must set the spacing to make sure the caliper fits evenly around the rotor. There are wide manufacturing tolerances that affect the precise placement of the caliper mounting flange relative to the rotor face. A floating caliper can accommodate those tolerances because it self-centers on the rotor. However, a fixed caliper has to be centered with shims. Your brake kit should come with a set of bolts, spacer shims, sleeves, and washers to position the caliper relative to the mounting bracket.

Use the stock 16-mm bolts to fasten the caliper mounting bracket to the hub flange. Then snugly mount the caliper on the bracket with no shims. Insert the brake pads and rotate the rotor. You might be able to feel one pad or the other touching the rotor, but the pads should not drag. If one pad is significantly tighter than the other, it is usually the outer pad. You can insert shims between the caliper and the bracket to move the caliper outward until the pads are evenly loose around the rotor. In the event that the inner pad is too tight, note that the bracket is not the same from side to side and you can reverse the bracket on the flange to change the spacing.

> **TECH TIP** **Brake Fluid**
>
> Do not assume that the two sides of your car require the same thickness of shims. Each side must be measured and shimmed separately.

14 The caliper should also be adjusted so that the brake pad friction material comes almost to the perimeter of the rotor. Do not finalize your setup until the rotor perimeter is set properly and you have the correct number of shims in place.

Finally, before you torque down the caliper on the bracket, make sure your caliper is oriented correctly. Some aftermarket calipers have bleed valves at both the top and the bottom of the caliper body so that they can be used on either side of the car. Other aftermarket calipers have one or two bleed valves that must be positioned at the upper end. If you install the caliper with the bleed valve pointing down, you can never get the air out of the caliper. So examine your calipers and understand their proper orientation before you install.

15 The brake fluid inlet hole on each Brake Man caliper is covered with a removable cap. Remove the cap and install the flexible line.

Always use the sealing hardware that comes with the flexible-line kit. Install the fitting so that the line leaves the caliper pointing out and up when the caliper is in its installed position.

16 When you have the shims set up correctly, torque the caliper to the mounting bracket. The 3/8-inch bolts must be tightened to 31 ft-lbs. Use a good torque wrench and some Loctite or other thread sealant.

17 Route the flexible line through the stock retainer and use the grommet you removed in step 8 to pad and protect the line. Use a zip-tie to secure the line and grommet to the stock installation location.

18 Feed the flexible line to the hard line and once again use an 11-mm line wrench to snug the hard line connection to the flexible line. Use the stock spring clip to secure the connection.

19 Perform the same steps on the opposite side of the car. Then, when all the new components are installed, refill the fluid reservoir and bleed the front brakes until there are no air bubbles in the system.

20 Put the wheels back on your car and carefully check for clearance. You may find that stick-on balancing weights hit the caliper. Just pull them off and take your car in and have the wheels balanced with the weights elsewhere on the interior face of the wheel.

21 To complete the package, a pair of 10.2-inch Brake Man Revolution rotors were installed on the stock rear package with corresponding pads on the front brakes and stainless-steel flexible lines. (For specific instructions, see the Stage 2 Rear Brake upgrade Project on page 91.)

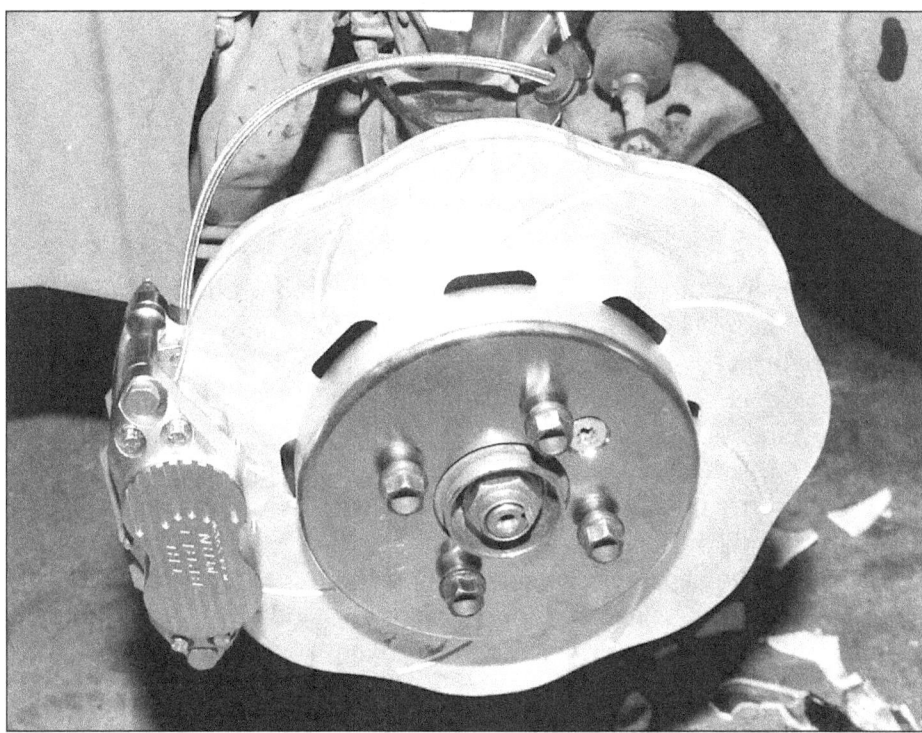

When this project is finished, you'll have an oversized, directionally vaned, slotted, and convoluted two-piece front brake rotor; fixed four-piston caliper; braided-stainless brake lines; high-performance brake pads; and upgraded brake fluid. Not bad for an afternoon's work.

The Brake Man's Revolution rotors are a drop-in replacement for the stock units, and look fantastic. They do make more noise than the stock units, and you might have to grind a bit on the caliper frame to get precise fitment, however. This rotor is shown with a 15-mm spacer installed.

Again, there are minor fitment issues you may have to address with aftermarket products. The manufacturing variation on the MINI parts means that the bolts that hold the caliper frames to the hub assembly protruded through the caliper frame, and they rubbed on the connecting bolts of the two-piece rotors. Placing a washer behind each bolt maintained the thread penetration but made the inside edge flush. It was also necessary to grind away a small casting boss on the caliper frame to fit these rotors to the rear of the car.

When you're all done, take it easy on your new brakes for a while. Even the best brakes need a couple hundred miles to really bed-in and work their best.

CHAPTER 5

UPGRADING TRANSMISSION AND DRIVELINE

With a MINI, you've got very few choices to make in regard to transmissions. There are two minor variations of the five-speed manual transmission, each with its own set of gear ratios. The first 5-speed was a Rover "Midlands" design, used in North American Coopers from the 2002 to 2004 model years. This transmission has a tendency to lose its bearings around 100,000 miles. The second, an improved 5-speed, was a Getrag unit used in Coopers in 2005 and 2006 and in the Convertible R52 Cooper until 2008.

There are four different models of the Getrag 6-speed manual transmission: the original 2002–2004 Cooper S transmission, the 2005–2006 transmission with revised ratios, the 2007+ R56 Cooper, and the 2007+ R56 Cooper S.

From 2002–2006 (and up to 2008 with the R52 convertibles), you also had the option of getting your Cooper with a Variomatic continuously variable transmission (CVT). The Cooper S was never offered with this unit. The CVT is a two-pedal transmission that uses a different design from a conventional automatic. There are no set gear ratios in this transmission, but rather a set of two adjustable pulleys that drive a steel linked-belt. By changing the working diameter of the pulleys, the CVT changes the drive ratio.

If the CVT used in the Cooper had been a better unit, it could have worked well with the Cooper's small-displacement, rev-happy engine, but the sad fact is that these transmissions are weak and there's nothing you can do about it. You should avoid any Cooper with the CVT option.

Starting in 2005 with the Cooper S, and then in 2007 with all R56-based cars, MINI went to a conventional 6-speed automatic with paddle shifters on the steering wheel for all two-pedal applications. There's not much you can do with this unit, either, but it's a good automatic. In the "MINI Spotter's Guide" in Chapter 1, you can see that top speed, acceleration, and fuel economy are all slightly negatively affected by an automatic. But if your MINI has an automatic, that's not cause to despair. You still have a great car, and every other performance enhancement still works fine.

Electronic Traction Control

MINIs come equipped with some combination of Acceleration Stability Control (ASC), Dynamic Stability Control (DSC), Anti-lock Brake System (ABS), Dynamic Traction Control (DTC), and Electronic Differential Lock Control (EDLC). All of these systems operate by reading the rotation speed of all four wheels and comparing that information and other sensor readings.

Disconnecting or otherwise disabling any of these systems, except by using the switch that MINI put on the dash, is a very bad idea.

Many autocrossers or racers

 Gearboxes

Many owners of R50 Coopers who have worn out their 5-speed Midlands gearboxes have replaced them with a Getrag 6-speed from the Cooper S. The 6-speed is a little "shorter," which is to say that you turn higher RPM to drive the same speed, but you also get a little better acceleration as a tradeoff.

disable all traction control while on the race track, but even Porsche is now delivering its top-of-the-line factory-built race cars with active traction control and ABS. Unless you're a professional race driver, chances are that you're not as good at car control as your MINI's DSC is. Swallow your pride and leave it on.

PROJECT
Installing Lower Transmission Mount Bushings

Poly bushings insert into the open spaces in a stock-rubber engine and transmission-mount bushings. With the poly bushings in place, the drivetrain is less flexible than the stock unit, and holds the transmission firmly in place where drivetrain torque can twist the stock bushings. The firmer mount gives you better power transfer and a more solid feel to the powertrain. The tradeoff of this modification is that more vibration is transferred from the drivetrain to the chassis and its occupants.

Follow these steps to install the Madness poly engine bushings in any MINI:

1. Raise the car and support it on a lift or jack stands.
2. Locate the lower engine mount at the rear of the engine area on the passenger side of the car. It's a teardrop-shaped aluminum casting held in place with two bolts.
3. For the R56-based cars, remove the big-end bolt and loosen the little-end bolt and rotate the mount down. Insert the form-fitted poly supports into the gaps in the big-end bushing. Rotate the mount back up and refit the bolt. Tighten everything down. You're done!

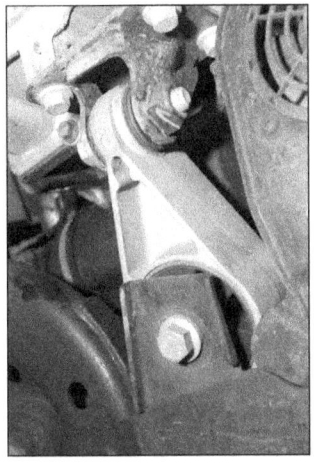

The R53 engine mount is also located behind the oil pan on the passenger side, but requires more work to remove from the car.

4. For the R50, R52, or R53, remove both the big-end and little-end bolts and remove the mount from the car. The little end fits into a bracket that is bolted to the engine block by four 13-mm bolts. It's easier to reinstall the mount if you remove this bracket.
5. Take your engine mount to a hydraulic press or bench vise and press out the stock rubber bushing from the little end. Do not press or damage the big-end bushing. Place the replacement poly little-end bushing in the little-end hole. Insert the form-fitted poly supports into the gaps in the big-end bushing.

You can find the R56 lower engine bushing just behind the oil pan on the passenger side of the car. You need only undo the big-end bolt and loosen the little end to swing this down and install the bushing supports.

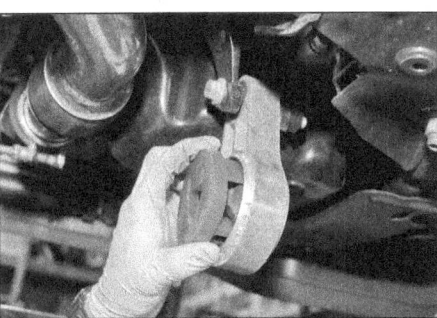

Line up the gaps in the stock bushing with the flanges of the poly insert and push the insert into either side of the bushing.

Once the inserts are in place, simply swing the assembly back into position and tighten it down. This is probably the easiest performance bushing installation you will find.

With the R53 unit, you need to remove the little-end bushing. This is easy with a hydraulic press, or you could do it by hand with a bit more effort.

CHAPTER 5

Insert the little-end bushings and their sleeve, and place the big-end bushings into the gaps in the stock bushing. When the mount looks like this, you're ready to reinstall.

6 Work the little end into its bracket and line up the bolt hole. Replace the bolt. Mate the assembly to the engine. You might have to push the engine to get it to fit. The engine moves easily. Work the big end into its fitting and replace that bolt. Then refit the four 13-mm bolts that attach the little-end bracket to the engine block. When all the bolts are started, tighten everything down and you're done.

The stock shifter is replaced with this bump stick. You select gears by moving the stick forward or back. The gear you've selected is displayed on a gauge on your steering column. (Photo courtesy M7 Tuning)

MINI Gear Ratios

The table below lists the effective gear ratios that have appeared in the MINI Cooper and Cooper S lines. The R55 Clubman and R57 Convertibles are the same as their respective R56 Cooper and Cooper S models. Ratios are not applicable to the CVT because of its continuously variable design.

In the Getrag 6-speed manual transmission, there are two final drives of 2.74:1 and 4.05:1. First, second, fifth, and sixth gear use the 2.74:1 ratio, while third, fourth, and reverse gears use the 4.05:1 ratio. The effect is that third and fifth gears are the same size, as are fourth and sixth gears. The final-drive-ratio difference changes the overall gearing when you shift.

For this reason, MINI and many information resources list radically different ratios than those published here. For example, 11.43:1 or 12.79:1 for first gear, and so on through the gears. Those ratios include the final-drive reduction. However, the ratios in the table at right are normalized to provide a sense of the relative gear ratios you are experiencing, compared to other years and models.

Changing Your Gearing

The gears in your car—both transmission and final drive—control the speed at which your wheels turn at a given engine RPM. You can buy aftermarket gear sets for your MINI, but they are both difficult and expensive to replace. However, there's one other gearing factor that affects your car's speed and acceleration that is easy to change: your wheel/tire combination. By far, your car's shoes are the easiest place to make changes to the overall drive ratio.

By changing to a larger-diameter wheel/tire combo, the increased circumference effectively makes the final drive ratio taller, which is to say, every time that wheel turns around, you're bound to cover just a little more ground. Conversely, choosing a smaller-diameter combination shortens the gearing. Racing teams that cannot change transmission gears or final-drive gears frequently carry several different diameters of tires to fine-tune their gearing for track conditions.

Just keep in mind that while bigger rims may look good, they can make your final-drive ratio taller than you want it to be. Also bear in mind that your wheels must be large enough to clear your brakes and any aftermarket suspension products you may be using.

Manual Transmissions

Most, but not all, cars used for performance driving are equipped with manual transmissions. Manual transmissions allow you to use the clutch and select your own shift points based on everything that is happening, or is about to happen, to you and your car. But manual transmissions aren't for everyone; those who commute through long stretches of stop-and-go traffic quickly grow tired of three-pedal driving. Still, almost anyone can learn to manage a clutch, and most people with an interest in performance driving will do so.

The 2005-and-later 5- and 6-speed transmissions are a big improvement over the 2002–2004 units. The ratios are better-suited to

 Ratios

For the 2009 JCW, the ratios are the same as the Cooper S, but the gear clusters are heavy-duty versions of the same parts.

UPGRADING TRANSMISSION AND DRIVELINE

2002–2009 MINI TRANSMISSION EFFECTIVE GEAR RATIOS

MODEL YEAR	MODEL	TRANSMISSION	1ST	2ND	3RD	4TH	5TH	6TH	FINAL DRIVE
2002–2004	R50 Cooper	5MT	3.42	1.95	1.33	1.05	0.85	N/A	3.94
2005–2008	R50/R52 Cooper	5MT	4.10	2.37	1.56	1.17	1.00	N/A	3.51
2007–2009	R56 Cooper	6MT	3.21	1.79	1.19	0.91	0.78	0.68	4.35
2002–2004	R53 Cooper S	6MT	4.17	2.62	1.33	1.09	1.33	1.09	3.13
2005–2008	R53/R52 Cooper S	6MT	4.09	2.49	1.81	1.42	1.22	1.00	3.13
2007–2009	R56 Cooper S	6MT	3.31	2.13	1.48	1.14	0.95	0.82	3.65
2007–2009	R56 Cooper	6AT	4.15	2.37	1.56	1.16	0.86	0.69	4.10
2005–2009	R53/R56 Cooper S	6AT	4.04	2.37	1.56	1.16	0.85	0.67	3.68

American driving and the transmissions are simply stronger. The 2007-and-later transmissions are also strong, but they are made for the R56 chassis, and cannot be easily retrofit onto an earlier MINI.

How Not To Drive Your Transmission To Death

The most common reason that transmissions break is bad driving. Your transmission is made of steel and aluminum, but it's not indestructible. Smooth shifts rely on a set of synchronizers that gently press against each other to encourage the gear shafts to spin together as you select gears. As the gears come together and you release the clutch, torsional and shear forces are applied to the various bearings, gear teeth, and axle joints throughout the drivetrain.

If you think about it, being rough with your gears makes no sense at all. Abusing the gearbox does not help you go faster. Slamming the car into gear at full throttle at the moment the clutch is engaging makes the car jump, upsetting traction as well as applying a hammer blow throughout the engine, drivetrain, and suspension. I have watched in horror as a driver destroyed the transmission on his brand-new Audi during the course of a single, 30-minute open-track practice session. He did it by hammering each shift until the third- and fourth-gear synchros just gave up and died.

Conversely, the best racing drivers in the world are silky smooth with their shifts. They hold the shift lever lightly in their hands, and they touch it only when selecting a gear. Their shifts are not slow, but not faster than the machinery can handle, either. You may hear race drivers making lightning shifts when you watch a race, but remember that those are exotic dog-ring gearboxes, which are built for that kind of treatment, and they get rebuilt after every race.

When you drive, treat your clutch and shift lever like they're made of thin glass. You can learn to shift your car both quickly and smoothly. If the car jerks or the gears don't want to engage smoothly, back off, slow down, and make sure you're doing it right. You will be rewarded with years of reliable service from your clutch and gearbox.

Whole Transmission Upgrades

There aren't a lot of options for upgrading manual transmissions. By far the most popular upgrade is to place the 6-speed 2005–2008 R52/R53 Cooper S transmission into a 5-speed R50/R52 Cooper. This is almost a direct-replacement part, and with the lower power output of a Cooper, the Getrag 6-speed is reasonably bulletproof once installed.

Limited Slip Differentials

Differentials ("diffs") are the devices that allow the drive wheels to turn at slightly different speeds during cornering. This is achieved by a set of four bevel (also called "spider") gears that come together in the axle housing.

Expert Interview: Peter Horvath of M7 Tuning

Peter Horvath is the man behind M7 Tuning in Los Angeles. He has developed a sequential shifter for the R53 and R56 MINI Cooper S 6-speed manual transmissions. The system allows the driver to preselect a gear using paddles on the steering wheel, and then the gear is automatically engaged as the driver steps on the clutch. The advantage of a system like this is that the driver never needs to remove his hands from the steering wheel to manage gears on a race track. The system is expensive at nearly $7,000, but it's the ultimate aftermarket modification for a manual-transmission MINI.

Q: What led you to develop a paddle shifter for the manual transmission?

I was looking for something out of the ordinary and exciting. There's a company that already had the technology to do it, but they hadn't done much with it. So they gave me a box and told me to go at it. I was left to my own devices to make it work. It took about six months to make it work on the MINI. Now the system's been so successful on the MINI, we took that knowledge and we're making the system for the Porsche 996 and 997.

Q: The stock system relies on moving two cables with the bottom of the shift lever. How does this sequential shifter work?

It's a very sophisticated computer-controlled setup. We can control the stroke, we can control the speed of the shift, and we can jump gears and control reverse and neutral. We can set it up with paddles or a bump stick. The paddles actually use an RF wireless module to send a signal to the system, so there are no wires to the steering wheel. Then there's a box in the back of the car with solenoids and shift cables.

Q: How does a driver use the system?

There are two ways to use it. You can select the next gear, then step on the clutch, and it goes into gear. Or, if you're coming to a very slow corner, you can hit the paddles several times to select any gear,

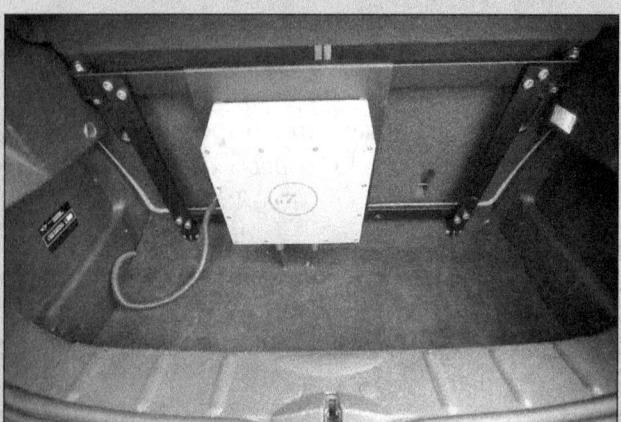

This box sits behind the rear seats and houses the solenoids that actuate the shift cables in the M7 sequential shifter. This product allows you to preselect any gear, and the system automatically selects the gear for you when you step on the clutch.

It's often easier to undo the mounting bracket at the little-end side and then put it all back together and tighten everything down. This is still an easy project.

step on the clutch, and it goes into that gear. To select neutral, you have to hold the paddle down for a quarter-second or a second—that's configurable on each system. I found that a quarter-second is long enough that you won't bump it in by mistake. Then neutral to reverse or first is instantaneous.

Q: It looks as if the system can use paddles or a bump stick. If you use the paddles, you gain an extra cup holder where the shifter used to be, right?

That's right. The system includes the bump shifter. Paddles are an option. The reason for that is because when you drive around town, when you do a three-point turn or something, you might hit the paddles and shift to a higher gear, so for a street car the bump shifter makes a lot of sense.

Here is the gear selection indicator gauge and the optional upshift paddle. The paddles use radio to communicate with the shifting system, eliminating extra wires going to the steering wheel. (Photo courtesy M7 Tuning)

As the axles rotate, the bevel gears can counter-rotate relative to each other to allow for different axle speeds.

With an open diff, a slipping wheel always spins freely, while the wheel with grip just sits there. Inside the axle housing, the little bevel gears are spinning madly to allow power to go down the path of least resistance. This is great for smooth cornering on dry pavement and very frustrating when you're stuck in snow or mud or trying to power out of a corner.

A limited slip differential (LSD) is designed to bind up when a certain amount of slip is reached. Generally this is accomplished through some kind of friction device—either conical or flat plates rubbing together. There are many other designs as well, each with its own strengths and weaknesses. A fully locked differential that forces all drive wheels to turn at the same speed at all times is not a differential at all, but instead is called a "live axle."

Planetary gears like these are the basis for most differentials because they can rotate as a unit while allowing axles to rotate at different speeds. But they do not limit slip.

The Quaife limited slip differential comes as an assembled unit. But it's not as easy as just dropping it into place.

CHAPTER 5

PROJECT
Installing the Quaife Limited Slip Differential

If your MINI was built in model year 2005 or later, an LSD was an option from the factory. The option cost just $400 to $500 over the years, yet many MINIs have been ordered without the option. If your car lacks a limited slip, you're missing out on some traction in corners. Recall that lateral load transfer takes weight off the inside wheels as you corner. A standard differential sends engine torque through the path of least resistance and spins the inside front wheel while the outside wheel—the one with all the traction—just sits there. A limited slip differential fixes that.

RT Quaife Engineering, Ltd., is one of the world's leading manufacturers of LSDs. Its products are used in race cars and street cars at all levels. This project installs the Quaife LSD into a 2006 R52 convertible Cooper S JCW.

WARNING: *Be aware that this is a major disassembly, and this level of work is generally the exclusive domain of professionals. Do not attempt this project if you need to drive the car in the next day or week, and make sure you have a complete set of tools before you begin. Make sure you have a good shop manual for your year and model before you begin. MINI recommends you use a set of front-end supports—threaded rods that screw into the chassis to allow you to pull the radiator core and support forward to clear the way to remove the transmission. If you don't have these tools (and who does, apart from professional MINI mechanics?), you can use a pair of 4- to 5-inch M8 13-mm bolts in their place. What is harder to substitute is the engine support—a device that mounts to the strut towers and bridges the engine bay. There is a threaded rod with a hook to support the engine when the transmission is removed, and a bracket that must be installed on the back of the head to hang from the support bridge. If you have (or can make) a bracket, you can substitute a traditional engine hoist for this support.*

Keep your official MINI shop manual close by when performing this project. There are photos, diagrams, and descriptions in that manual that will help you understand what you are seeing. The steps listed here are slightly different from the shop manual and reflect the knowledge of expert MINI mechanics, but you will want to refer to the shop manual to complete the picture. However, the shop manual does not cover the interior of the transmission, and for that portion of the project, this book is the only reference. Follow these steps:

1. Disconnect the battery and raise the car to a comfortable working level. A lift makes this project much easier, but it can be done on jack stands. Do not drain the transmission. The fluid in the transmission is designed to be used for the life of the unit. If you don't spill it, and then reseal the transmission, you won't lose any of it. Remove the splash shield, front bumper skin, and front bumper subassembly. When the skin is removed, disconnect the foglights, turn signals, and ambient temperature sensor.

A slider tool is simply a rod that screw into your chassis and allow your radiator to move out without being disconnected.

Remove the bumper and all the underbody fascia first. You're going to disassemble most of the front end of the car.

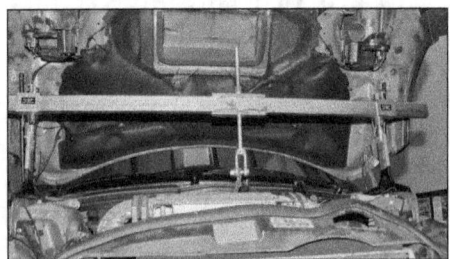

This engine support is a specialized tool. If you're handy with a welder you can make your own. If not, you might be able to rent or borrow one like this or a traditional engine hoist.

2. In the engine bay, disconnect the ECU and remove it and the entire air intake to provide access to the top of the transmission. Then loosen the strap that holds the power steering reservoir and move that part out of the way. Finally, use a pry bar to pop the shifter cables off their lever arms on top of the transmission and out of their plastic retainer clips.

UPGRADING TRANSMISSION AND DRIVELINE

You need access to the top of the transmission. Removing the air intake reveals many of the connections you need to remove.

The shift cables are on ball joints that pop off with a little effort from a pry bar. Be careful, but firm, with these and they'll come off easily

3 Install the MINI special tools for supporting the radiator. Remove the bolts that hold the bumper to the radiator core support. Then look for the crush tubes that support the bumper frame and remove them at their connection with the bumper. Remove the bumper assembly carefully—it's

Four bolts hold the throttle body to the air intake to the supercharger. It must all be removed to gain access to the transmission-to-engine bolts.

heavy! Then remove the crush tubes from their connection to the front undercarriage. Finally, undo the four plastic clips that hold the fog lights and horns to the chassis, and remove those components.

4 Remove the throttle body and air-intake pipe by unscrewing the four bolts that hold the throttle to the intake. There is also a crankcase vent hose that attaches to the air pipe. Undo the bolt that holds the plastic tube between the throttle body and the supercharger on the front of the engine. There are two brake master cylinder vacuum tubes that install into small, red, lock fittings on this intake tube. Press the red lock fittings away from the engine block, and the vacuum tubes release.

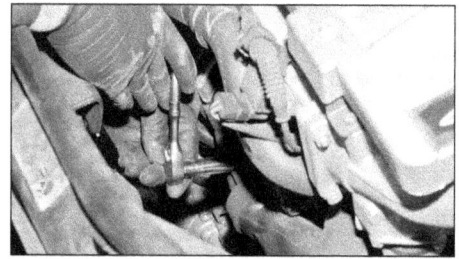

Look carefully at this picture so you can find the bolt that releases the supercharger intake tube.

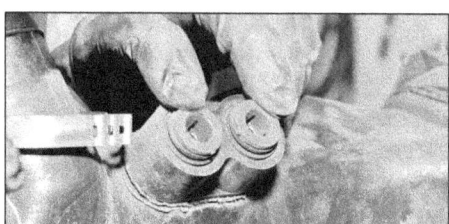

Press in on these red fittings to release the vacuum tubes from the supercharger inlet tube. The tubes will press back in when you reassemble the car.

5 Disconnect the forward wiring harness at the driver's-side strut tower. This is a barrel-shaped connector that twists apart. Also you must disconnect a plug to the fuse box (as shown) and a wiring plug near the engine block to gain clearance to the transmission perimeter bolts.

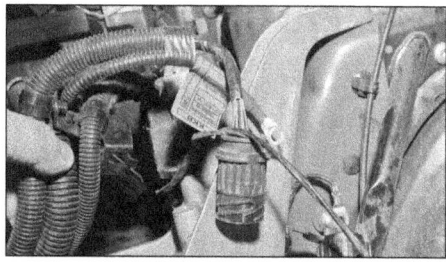

Look for this barrel connector on the driver's side of the car. Also, note the ground wire on the sheetmetal behind it, which needs to come loose, too.

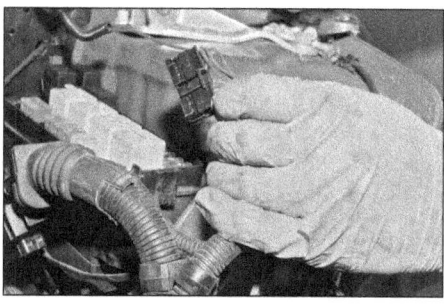

Look for this connector at the fuse block and undo it.

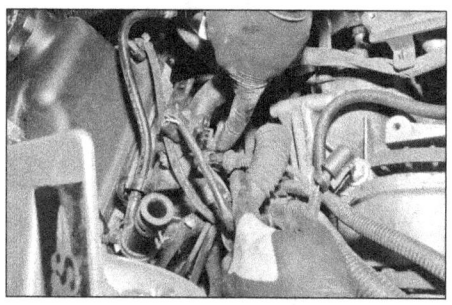

Look for the small red plug on the side of the engine block. That has to come undone to remove more parts.

6 Remove the cooling line from the back of the head, just to the passenger side of the shift linkage. This allows access to the bolt holes to install the engine hanger bracket. Install the bracket and then remove the two bolts (as shown) under the driver's-side end of the

THE NEW MINI PERFORMANCE HANDBOOK

intercooler to remove the large octopuslike wiring harness gang plug from the engine.

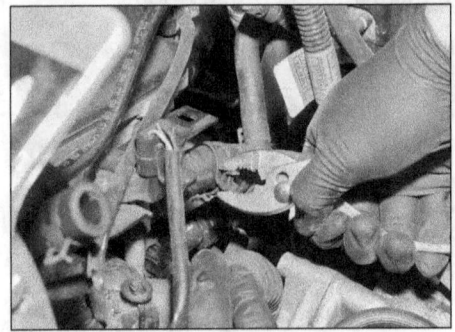

Use pliers to release the clip that holds this coolant line to the engine. You must remove this line to install the engine lifting bracket.

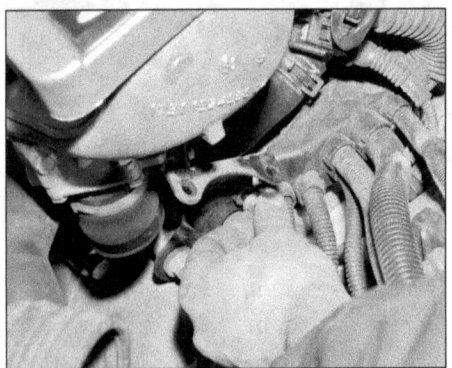

Two bolts under the driver's side of the supercharger have to come out to release the main wiring bundles for the engine.

With all that wiring disconnected, you can bolt the engine lifting bracket to the side of the engine. Some threaded holes are already there to receive the bracket.

7 Remove the clutch slave cylinder from the transmission. On the 6-speed Getrag transmission, this part is underneath the transmission. On the R50 Midlands 5-speed transmission, the clutch slave is on top of the transmission.

Working from the top, release the power steering reservoir. Then from below, remove the power steering fan and disconnect the steering column.

Look on the underside of an R53 or the top side of an R50 for the clutch slave. It has to be disconnected before you can remove the transmission.

8 Disconnect the small end of the lower engine mount and remove the cooling fan for the power steering. There are several power plugs in this area that must also be unplugged. Undo the steering column from the steering rack. Next, disconnect the end links from the front sway bar and remove the lower ball joints from the hubs. Also disconnect the steering arms at this time so that the front brakes and hubs hang from the struts. Then undo the inner end of the lower control arms from the car.

The sway bar comes out with the front subframe. It's easiest to disconnect it at the end links.

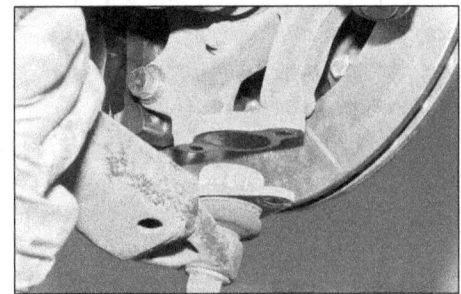

The ball joint on each side comes loose with just two bolts. The control arms come out of the car with the subframe.

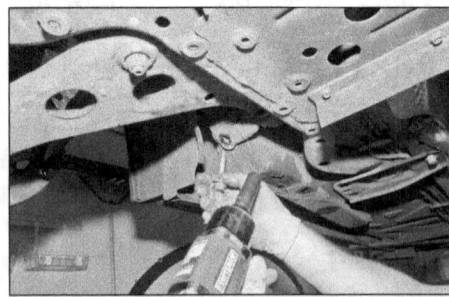

The lower control arm is connected to the chassis at the rear and to the subframe in the middle. This is a good time to think about upgrading that chassis-mount bushing.

UPGRADING TRANSMISSION AND DRIVELINE

> **TECH TIP**
> **Control Arm Bushings**
>
> If you are planning to replace the lower control arm bushings, this is a good time to do it.

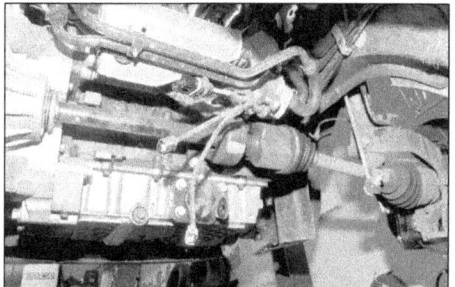

The passenger-side driveshaft is in two parts, with a supporting mount in the middle. Remove the whole assembly from the engine and transmission, but leave it connected at the hub.

The driver's-side driveshaft is easier to remove. With everything disconnected it should come right out of the transmission. Leave it connected at the hub end.

9 Pull the driveshafts from the transmission carefully. You can use a pry bar to gently lever the splined ends out of the transmission case. The passenger-side (right) shaft has a central section with a support bearing that bolts to the engine block. Unbolt the three 13-mm bolts that hold the support to the engine and you can remove that side of the axle assembly from the transmission.

You can undo these six bolts at the rear to release the subframe, but get a jack or support under there first—this is a heavy part!

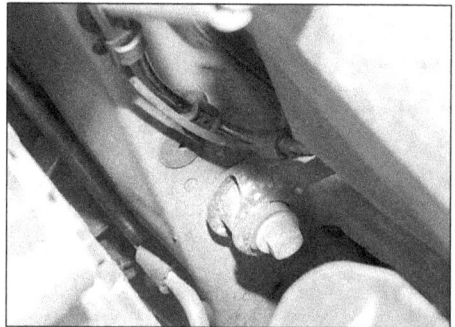

These two bolts are positioned high at the front, near the bumper crush tubes. Release these and the subframe is ready to be removed.

10 Mount the engine support and hook it up to the bracket you installed on the engine in Step 6. Place a strong jack under the transmission—if you're using a lift, it must be strong enough to support the whole weight of the transmission. Undo the bolts that hold the front subframe cradle to the bottom of the car. Six 16-mm bolts go through the two plates on either side of the chassis, and two more are located at the front, on the inner wheel arch above the bumper horns. The subframe will come loose and two people can lower it to the ground. When the subframe comes out, it brings the lower control arms, power steering unit, power steering reservoir, tie rods, and the front sway bar with it.

With the front subframe out, you can see how the MINI is put together. If you want to replace the front sway bar, there's never a better time than right now.

11 Tighten the engine support and then remove the four bolts that hold the transmission to the large support casting on the driver's side.

Support the transmission and undo the driver's-side top mount. The transmission is still supported by its perimeter bolts, but you'll want to support the engine/transmission assembly against tipping while you work.

12 Slide the radiator and its support structure forward onto the special tools. Remove the nine 15-mm bolts that hold the starter to the transmission and let the starter hang with the engine. Then begin to remove the 15-mm perimeter bolts that hold the transmission to the engine. You will need to get at some from the underside of the engine and some from above. You can lower the engine support to tip the driver's side

CHAPTER 5

of the assembly down to obtain more clearance on some of these bolts. Leave the last two perimeter bolts on the bottom of the transmission and under the starter motor for last.

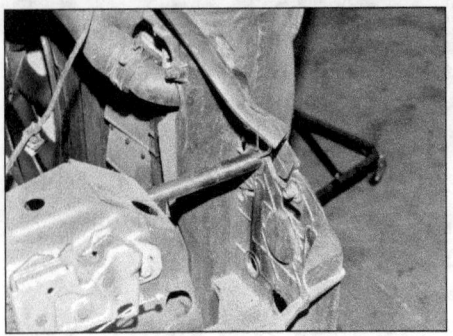

Slide the radiator assembly forward on the slider tool you installed before. This allows room to get at the radiator perimeter bolts.

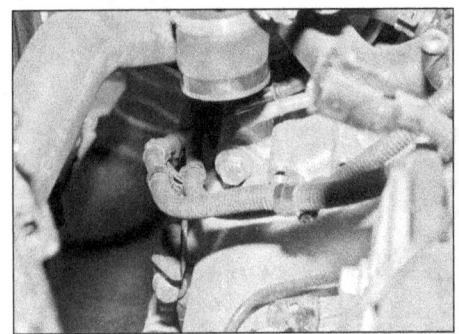

This photo shows two of the perimeter bolts. Loosen them and then remove them at the same time you remove the starter motor.

13 You might need to pry a bit to break the transmission loose, but don't pry hard; you might still have a bolt connecting the transmission to the engine. You might also need to move some wires or undo some retaining clips to remove the

Control Arm Bushings

If you're thinking about replacing your clutch, this is a good time to do it.

transmission. Use your jack, because the transmission's quite heavy.

Carefully lower the transmission to the ground with the bell housing facing up so you can work on it.

14 With the transmission on the ground, look into the bell housing and around the perimeter of the unit. There are 19 T-40 Torx bolts. Some are inside the bell housing and some are around the perimeter. One of these bolts has a hole in the perimeter of the bell housing that allows you to stick a socket extension through to get at one particularly inconvenient bolt. You must also remove the shift-cable braket, which is held on by three T-40 Torx bolts. There are small spring clips in the shift cable bracket—don't lose them.

There are 19 Torx bolts that hold the transmission case together. Work carefully and methodically, and don't force anything.

15 With all the bolts removed, look for the tabs near the axle holes that allow you to lever apart the two halves of the transmission case. There are two locating dowels along the perimeter of the case. Work the case halves apart gently until the dowels are loose. Leaving the bottom of the case flat on the ground, lift the bell housing off the gearbox. You see the differential right on top, attached to a large ring gear.

When all the bolts are out, use the tabs to pry open the transmission case.

With the case apart, the differential and ring gear can be found sitting right on top of everything. If you don't tip the transmission over, you can reuse the special MINI gear oil.

16 Using an air impact wrench, undo the ten 15-mm bolts that hold the differential to the ring gear. Remove the differential and ring gear together. Separate the ring gear from the differential; you might need to tap it a few times with the rubber hammer. Place the new differential

THE NEW MINI PERFORMANCE HANDBOOK

into the bearing race with the small side down. Then place the ring gear on top of the differential bolt flange and line up the bolt holes. The holes are equidistant, so any orientation will work. Bolt the ring gear to the new differential. There is no published torque spec for the transmission internals, but the torque spec for comparable bolts that hold the flywheel to the crank is 66 ft-lbs. Tighten the bolts in the usual criss-crossing mechanic's pattern, working up to your final torque spec. For example, tighten a bolt at 2 o'clock, then 7, then 10, 4, 12, 6, 9, and 3 o'clock. Go around several times to bring the torque to 66 ft-lbs.

17 Near the ring gear along the perimeter of the case, there is a slot and in that slot is a large O-shaped magnet. That magnet picks up all the metal dust generated by the gears. Take the magnet out and clean it while you've got the case apart, and then replace it in its slot. That's just a good thing to do.

18 Wipe the perimeter of the transmission case clean and place a line of blue flange sealant around the entire mating face. Replace the bell housing half of the

It's easiest to remove the ring gear from the differential with a light-impact wrench and the differential still in place in the transmission.

Position the Quaife differential in its place with the small end down. It should fit perfectly, with no fiddling.

Replace the ring gear and torque down the 10 bolts. You can see if the gear is meshing evenly with the drive gear.

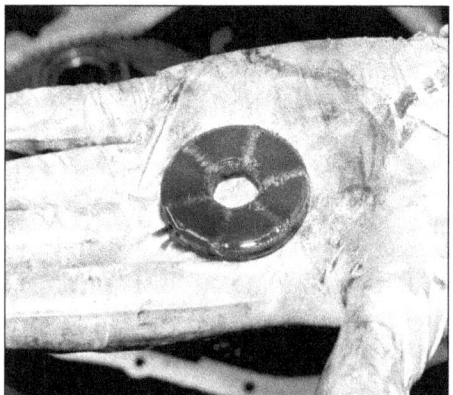

While you're in there, you might as well clean the magnet that attracts all the little metal shavings and dust that come off the gears as they wear.

When you're done cleaning the magnet, don't forget to put it back in its slot. You'd hate to get the car all buttoned up and then find this on the workbench!

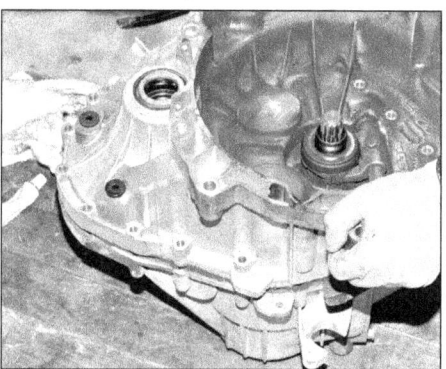

Use some blue hylomar to reseal the transmission case against leaks. It has locating dowels to help you line things up perfectly. Make sure it is lined up—don't force it.

You can see the Torx bolt that requires a long extension through a hole in the bell housing. The transmission should go back together easily.

case and gently tap it into place on the locating dowels with a rubber hammer. Do not force anything or start any bolts until the two halves are snug together. No torque spec is published, but the standard torque spec for a T-40 Torx bolt is 40 ft-lbs. Remember, that case is aluminum, so don't over-tighten!

When you're putting everything back in place, note that there is a stub on both front attachment points for the subframe. This will help you get it lined up right the first time.

 Replace the transmission and reverse the procedure you used to disassemble your car to this point. Your factory shop manual is an extremely valuable resource in this process. When you replace the lower subframe, note that there are locating stubs for the front mounts. Get the jack under your subframe and line up those dowels and then put some bolts in loosely to hold things in place. When you're reinserting the axle stub ends, be careful and make sure that they go in smoothly. Don't force them.

Clutch and Flywheel

MINI's manual-transmission cars all use the industry-standard clutch design. The standard clutch disc is a round plate faced with an organic asbestos-like surface material. The disc has a splined hole in its center and it slides onto the splined transmission input shaft. The pressure plate and flywheel are connected to the engine's crankshaft. The clutch disc is like the meat in a sandwich made by the pressure plate and flywheel. The pressure plate is spring-loaded and squeezes the clutch disc when the clutch is not engaged. As you step on the clutch, the pressure plate levers pull the pressure plate face away from the clutch disc, thereby disconnecting the transmission input shaft from the engine's crankshaft.

The most common upgrades available to improve your clutch and flywheel system are lighter flywheels and stronger clutches with improved clutch discs. An engine with a lighter flywheel spins-up faster because it has less mass to accelerate. The tradeoff here is that the mass of the flywheel helps you get the car moving smoothly. Lighter flywheels can tend to judder on takeoff and make the engine easier to stall, but the advantage in throttle response is dramatic.

As you increase the torque output of your engine, you can overwhelm the ability of the clutch sandwich to hold together. When this happens, the clutch begins to slip and very rapidly wears out altogether. Your stock clutch should be able to handle anything your MINI engine can dish out, but you can kill any clutch quickly with abuse.

Clutch Components

The clutch disc (also known as a driven disc), pressure plate, and throw-out bearing are a team, and they should always be replaced together. Since you have to do all the work to separate the engine and transmission to replace any of these components, it just makes sense to do them all at the same time. You should also resurface your flywheel when you replace your clutch components, or at least scuff up the mating surface with emery cloth or a Scotch-Brite pad while you're in there.

The ACT clutch kit includes a lightened flywheel, light high-grip clutch disc, and stronger pressure plate than stock. Not shown is the throw-out bearing, which you have to buy separately in most cases.

If you're in danger of overpowering your clutch, the solution is to get a stronger pressure plate and a better clutch disc. An improved pressure plate is designed to squeeze the clutch disc with greater force, and the clutch plate is made of tougher stuff to better grip the pressure plate and stand up to the torsional forces that are exerted when you release the clutch under power. Most clutch upgrade kits don't look (or behave) much different from a stock unit, but you may notice that the clutch pedal takes more effort to engage, and the new system may feel more "grabby" than the stock clutch.

There are several kinds of clutch discs. On some, all the organic material has been replaced with kevlar, iron, bronze, ceramic, or carbon-fiber composite materials. Each of these materials has different friction characteristics; ceramic clutches, for example, are designed to handle high heat, while metal clutches offer the most friction.

There are clutches with and without springs between the splined mounting hole and the friction material. The stock flywheel on the MINI is made of several pieces with rubber bushings that help smooth out some of the rotational force when you let out the clutch. They damp the shock as the clutch disc starts moving. In the aftermarket, the flywheel is one piece and the clutch disc is made of several pieces, with springs to smooth out the shock. A racing clutch disc is made without those springs, and can thus be noisy and grabby.

The friction surfaces of various clutch disks are different. "Full face" clutches have a full surface of material with grooves. These are commonly used in OEM designs because they engage smoothly. "Segmented" or "partial" clutches have several pads of material with gaps in between. "Puck" or "button" clutches use ceramic or bronze buttons as the mating surface.

The thing to remember is that the smaller the surface area on a clutch, the more pounds of pressure are applied by the pressure plate to the surface area. This is why button clutches can be grabby, whereas OEM clutches are smooth.

You can also get racing clutch systems that are smaller in diameter than the stock unit. These clutches are designed to work with lightweight flywheels to further reduce mass and polar moment of inertia to allow the engine to rev up faster. These units are much more jumpy than stock and you really don't want one for street driving.

PROJECT
Installing a Lightened Flywheel and Performance Clutch

This project installs a lightweight ACT clutch kit on a 2006 R52 Cooper S JCW. The ACT clutch pack weighs 26 pounds, including flywheel, pressure plate, driven disc, and throw-out bearing. The stock Cooper S unit weighs 37 pounds—a full 30 percent more! You will get better clamping and quicker spin-up on your engine with a lighter clutch kit, and ACT makes some of the world's best clutches. As you will see, exposing the clutch is a big job, so if you've got the transmission off for any reason, it's a good time to replace the clutch. Follow these steps:

 Read the warnings and follow steps 1 through 13 of the procedure for installing a Quaife limited slip differential (on page 106). This gets you to the point where your transmission is free of the engine and you're looking at your stock flywheel and clutch pack.

TECH TIP — Limited Slip Differential

This project involves 90 percent of the work of installing a limited slip differential. You might as well do both while you're in there.

Remove the six T-8 reverse Torx bolts that hold the pressure plate to the flywheel. You must have the proper socket to do this—no other tool will do the job. Use a pry bar wedged between one of the perimeter bolts and the teeth of the ring gear if you do not own the tools required for a proper flywheel lock.

The stock clutch is a good unit; if treated well, it will last well over 100,000 miles. But for high performance, we're going to replace it. If you've got the car apart anyway, it makes sense to invest in all these upgrades at once.

CHAPTER 5

The stock flywheel is held on with eight bolts. It installs in only one orientation, so pay attention when you fit up the new one. All eight bolts must line up.

The new flywheel comes with new Allen-head bolts. Always install a new flywheel with fresh fasteners. These bolts are subjected to tremendous shear forces.

3 Remove the eight 13-mm bolts that hold the flywheel to the crankshaft. Loosen them in stages, following a mechanic's criss-cross pattern. Continue using a pry bar as a flywheel lock.

4 Line up the new flywheel on the end of the crankshaft. The holes are not equidistant from each other, so the flywheel lines up all the holes in only one orientation. The ACT kit comes with eight new 8-mm Allen-head flywheel bolts because these are critical stressed components. Place a dab of blue Loctite on the new flywheel bolts and install them in the same criss-cross tightening pattern. The torque spec is 66 ft-lbs.

Make sure you have a clutch alignment tool as you install the new clutch disc and pressure plate. Move the tool around as you tighten things down to keep everything centered or you'll have a tough time getting the transmission back on.

5 Bring the drive disc, clutch alignment tool, and pressure plate to the flywheel. The pressure plate lines up in only one orientation on the flywheel, and the driven disc has a sticker that indicates the flywheel (FW) side. Place the driven disc on the flywheel, then the pressure plate, and loosely start the reverse Torx bolts, then insert the alignment tool to keep the components in place.

6 Work your way around in a criss-cross pattern to torque down the pressure plate, and rotate the alignment tool in the clutch as you go. If you do not rotate the alignment tool, it can become wedged in the assembly and you'll have to loosen the clutch to free it. The final torque spec on the pressure plate is 17 ft-lbs.

7. Replace the throw-out bearing in your transmission's bell housing every time you've got the clutch exposed. It's an inexpensive part, and it would be a real drag to have to do this job again soon just to replace a cheap part.

8. Reassemble your car in a reverse of steps 1 through 13 of the procedure for installing a Quaife limited slip differential (on page 106). Your factory shop manual is an extremely valuable resource in this process.

Agitronic Automatic Transmission

Automatic transmissions and performance enhancement are generally mutually exclusive. Upgrade parts are not widely made for automatics, and the assumption is that if you want performance, you have a manual transmission. Automatics also cost you in 0–60 time, top speed, and fuel economy. Transmission conversions are more work than they're worth. So if you like your automatic, go ahead and perform the engine enhancements and enjoy driving your car. If you're shopping for a MINI to modify, avoid automatics unless you really want one and you understand the tradeoffs for two-pedal convenience.

The MINI 6-speed Agitronic automatic transmission is a technologically advanced unit compared to most automatics. The Agitronic uses a TCM (transmission control module) computer that MINI calls EGS. The EGS works in concert with the ECU to control shift points and increase fuel economy and transmission lifespan. The MINI EGS also has the ability to "learn" your driving style and make shifting decisions based on those inputs.

The Agitronic uses a torque converter to perform the same function that a clutch performs for a manual trasmission. The torque converter is attached on one side to the engine and on the other side to the transmission. A torque converter has two internal turbine fans, like propellers facing each other, and the unit is filled with transmission fluid. There is an input turbine connected to the engine and an output turbine connected to the transmission. When the engine side of the converter begins to spin, the turbine moves the fluid around in the converter. Hydraulic motion forces the transmission turbine to spin as well, passing power to the gearbox. There's more that happens inside a torque converter than this describes, but suffice it to say that they get the job done and you can't work on them.

A key thing to know about torque converters is that at low speeds, the fluid allows the system to slip somewhat, which is why you can hold an automatic transmission in gear at a stop by keeping your foot on the brake. As you increase engine revs, the engine propeller begins to move the fluid faster, which forces the transmission propeller to move as well, transferring motion to the transmission.

In the racing world, automatic transmissions are most popular with drag racers. Drag racers use custom torque converters that allow them to rev the engine into the power band without moving the car, then lock up quickly to deliver maximum power to the wheels. These are called "stall" converters, and unless you're building a dedicated drag racing car, you won't need or want one.

Here's a sight you don't often see. Torque converters are not user-serviceable, so it's rare to see one opened up. The "fan" in the center is matched with another one so that the hydraulic action, when the engine side turns, forces the transmission side to turn as well.

CHAPTER 6

INTERIOR AND EXTERIOR UPGRADES

Sooner or later, every MINI owner does something to modify the interior and exterior of his or her car. Maybe it's as basic as a sticker package—MINI occasionally sends them to you—or maybe it's as radical as a body kit. Most owners fall somewhere in the middle, toward the mild end.

This chapter provides some ideas and a few simple projects to customize your MINI's interior and exterior. Some of these are simply dress-up items, but most have an emphasis on performance.

Adding Lights

Aftermarket lights are a great addition to any car and nothing says Rally Sport like a big bank of lights on the front of a MINI. The factory offers fog lights on most cars as part of the Sport Package, and a pair of small dealer-installed rally lights has been a popular option from the beginning of the line.

In addition to the factory options, there are many aftermarket light kits. Each kit has its own installation plan, but most involve a set of tabs that install in your MINI's upper or lower grille. All rally light kits require either a connection to a 12-volt positive power source and a switch in the car, or tapping directly into the car's wiring. Be careful about cutting the wiring, as that can lead to innumerable problems. Consider

 Check Local Laws

Check your local laws for limitations on the installation of things like high-intensity-discharge (xenon) lights, extra fog lights, and rally/driving lights.

There's nothing like a bank of driving lights to dress up the front end of your MINI. The look evokes the classic rally cars of the 1960s. But check first to make sure it's legal in your area to run four additional forward-facing lights.

If you want the real rally item, you need a removable light pod for the front of your car. Good luck finding one in the United States, however. You may have to adapt a pod meant for another type of car. (Photo courtesy Doug Berger)

INTERIOR AND EXTERIOR UPGRADES

You can add up to four gauges alongside your tachometer with ease. If you have navigation or the factory gauge package, your aftermarket options are limited.

any lighting upgrade carefully before you proceed.

For the serious enthusiast or rallyist, a light pod is a major custom piece. The advantage of a pod is that it can be removed when it's not needed. Of course, the installation hardware will still be on the hood or front bumper. For nighttime driving in areas without streetlights, you can't beat a pod. For a fitted MINI pod, you really have to shop the European providers, or be prepared to modify a pod made for a different make of car. Check your local laws, as some municipalities limit the number and intensity of lights that can be used.

Gauges and Indicators

One of the first interior areas you may want to consider for improvement is the selection of gauges and indicators. In stock form, your MINI offers little information. Just a water-temperature gauge, a tach, and a bunch of "idiot lights" to tell you when things are outside of normal operating ranges. MINI did offer a gauge pack that included ammeter, water temperature, and oil temperature, but not boost or oil pressure, which are much more important.

Most performance enthusiasts want the information that gauges can provide, plus there's the fact that a bunch of gauges looks pretty cool. You can upgrade as little or as much as you like in this area. Gauges and sensors exist for oil temperature and pressure, turbo boost, air/fuel mixture, exhaust gas temperature, and even tire pressure.

You can buy gauge pods (some made of carbon fiber) that fit on your dashboard or steering column. These typically allow you to install up to four gauges of a standard size.

Hooking up aftermarket gauges can be tricky—many of the locations to sense status for the gauge are inconvenient and require special tools to access. Also, note that in general, critical sensors such as exhaust-gas temperature should be calibrated to the gauge being used. Consult an experienced shop for help with gauge selection and installation.

PROJECT
Installing the PROMINI R53 Oil Pressure and Boost Gauge Kit

This project installs a set of PROMINI gauges for supercharger boost and oil pressure in our project R53. There are complete instructions provided with the kit, so these steps should be considered commentary to those instructions.

1. Disconnect the battery for the duration of this project.
2. Remove the tachometer from the steering column. It is held on with two T-25 Torx screws. There is also a cover plate that comes off with the tach. You'll need to modify both of these a bit. Next, remove the kick-plate from under the steering column. This piece just pulls loose at the top, and the bottom clips act like a hinge. Wiggle it a bit and it will come loose.

Two Torx screws right behind the tachometer must be removed to mount the gauge pod.

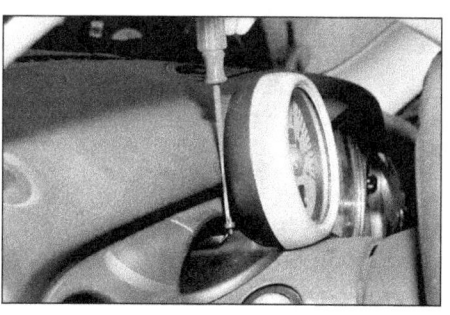

3 The kit includes a pair of plastic spacers and long screws. Remove the standard screws, install the spacers, and screw the gauge pod to the back of the tach. Next, you must trim the cover plate to accommodate the cables from the gauges. Just clip the corners of the plate, and the cables will fit conveniently.

The kit comes with longer screws and spacers to fit the gauge pod without buzzes or rattles.

Just use a pair of wire cutters to trim this plate to accommodate the wires from the new gauges.

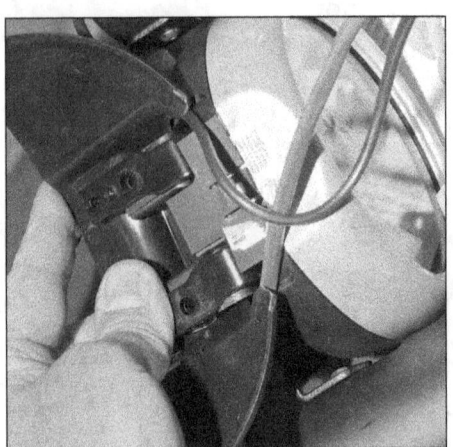

Test-fit the cables and be sure you understand how they need to run before you reinstall the tach.

4 Reinstall the tach, routing the cables forward through the cutouts you made and then into the steering column. It's easiest to feed the wiring plug through the column first, then line everything up and screw the assembly down. You should end up with the gauge wiring plug down around the brake pedal area.

5 Now you have some under-car work to do. You may find that you need some professional help with this step. The good news is that you can complete the boost gauge hookup now and come back to this step later. Get the car on a lift or jack stands. Remove the oil-pressure warning-light sender. The best access to this is from under the car, just to the passenger side of the header. Reach up and you'll feel a wire going to a large plug just below and to the left of the oil filter. To undo the wire, there's a red tab that must be pushed to the driver's side to release the clip. You might find it easiest to go in through the right front wheel well to press that clip over with a screwdriver. Once the clip is released, slide the wiring plug off the sender.

6 Working from under the car again, you need a BMW special tool to unscrew the oil-pressure

The intercooler is removed for the vacuum/boost tube installation. You'll find the factory boost port on the left (passenger) side as you face the engine, under the intercooler plenum.

sender. The instructions suggest a 12-point 27-mm deep socket, and this may work for some models, but not our project 2005 R53. (A 6-point 27-mm socket may work on some models.) We took the car to a MINI mechanic to have this part removed and the new hardware installed. The new hardware includes a brass extension with several threaded ports. The original warning-light sender installs in one port, and the oil-pressure-gauge sender in another.

7 Next, mount the MAP sender. This part mounts to the plastic firewall on the passenger side of the car. There's a flat place to stick it on the bracket. The mounting location overlooks the anti-lock brake system's distribution block. Drill a 1/4-inch hole through the plastic—be careful not to damage anything—to bring through the boost pressure tube.

8 Remove the intercooler to find the vacuum/boost port on the passenger side of the intake manifold. The kit includes a Tee fitting that you splice into the line to the fuel-pressure regulator, a pair of plug ends, and a nylon tube to bring boost pressure to the MAP sensor you installed in step 7. Plug the boost line into the port on the MAP sensor. When the pressure lines are connected, reinstall the intercooler.

9 Run wires from the cabin to the engine bay. There is a wiring harness provided in the kit. With an X-acto knife, reach above the brake pedal and find the rubber grommet through which the main harness passes from the cabin to the engine bay. The harness "rope" is not centered in the grommet, and you can find a safe location to poke the knife through and make a hole for the new wires.

10 The kit instructions say to use a clothes hanger as a guide for

INTERIOR AND EXTERIOR UPGRADES

the wires, but we used a piece of welding rod for the same effect. There is a plug on one end of the provided harness—that end stays in the cabin. On the other end are three wires with needle-like fittings, and a thin purple wire. Wrap these in tape around the end of your hanger or welding rod and push them through the hole you made in the grommet. Your wire bundle will appear just to the left of the brake-fluid reservoir. Pull the wires through far enough to pass them to the passenger side of the car and reach the MAP sensor. Be sure the purple wire is long enough to reach the oil pressure sender.

The instructions say to use a wire coat hanger, but we had some welding rod lying around, and it works just as well.

11 The kit contains a wiring plug designed to fit in the MAP sensor. Plug the needle-like fittings into this plug and then put the plug into the MAP sensor and bolt the MAP sensor (with the vacuum/boost fitting pointed downward) on the bracket you installed in step 7. This is a tough bit of bolting, using small 10-mm nuts on the underside of the bracket.

12 Back under your dash, find the purple wire with a black stripe and yellow bands down at the brake light switch. This provides power to the gauges whenever the car is turned on. The kit provides a tapping clamp that cuts the wire

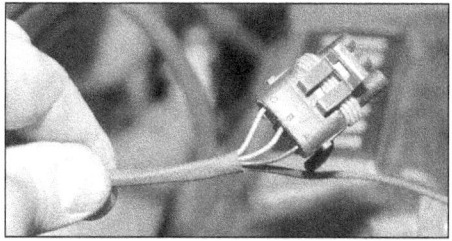

You must assemble this plug and then connect it to the MAP sensor you installed. Then bring the vacuum/boost hose to the MAP sensor and plug it in.

Nuts

To avoid losing your nuts, put a small piece of tape on the back of a 10-mm box-end wrench and stick the nut into the wrench. The nut will stick to the tape long enough for you to thread it onto the bolt.

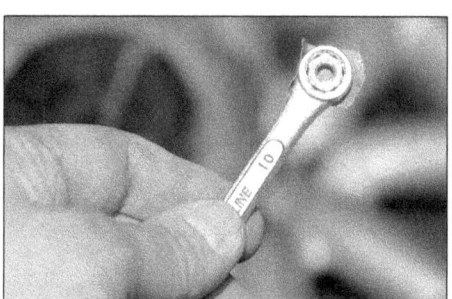

This works well under almost all circumstances. You can use a piece of blue masking tape to hold the nut in the wrench while you get the threads started.

The power wire for the gauges taps into the purple/black/yellow wire to the brake light switch.

insulation and makes the connection. Close the clamp with pliers and you can plug in the black wire on the kit harness.

13 Find the 10-mm bolt just above and to the left of the steering column. This bolt connects to a good ground, so mount the ground wire (with the ring connector) there. Also find the gray wire with a red stripe in the main harness bundle, and tap into that wire to provide power to the gauge lights. They'll work fine without this, but they won't illuminate at night. This wire gets panel voltage, so the gauges light up and dim with the rest of the dash lights.

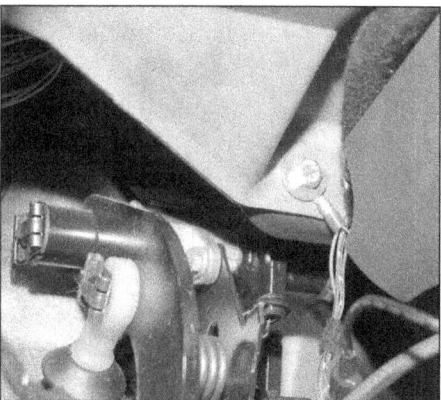

This ground location is easy to find and easy to use for the gauge ground wire.

14 Before the gauges will work, you must insert the provided blade-type fuse into the power line. Make sure all wires are safely tucked out of the way and close up the kick panel. Reconnect the battery and start the car. You should see oil pressure immediately, and vacuum showing at idle on the boost gauge. The boost gauge is set up to show a warning light when the boost exceeds the level you specify. If you have the stock pulley, you should see up to about 10 psi of boost. A 15-percent-reduction pulley can raise that to 15 psi.

THE NEW MINI PERFORMANCE HANDBOOK

Steering Wheels

Your car's steering wheel is another safety component, because it houses the driver's air bag. Aftermarket steering wheels look and feel great, but you don't generally get to keep your car's original air bag. It can also be difficult to get your horn and automatic turn-signal cancelers to work with an aftermarket wheel. R56-based MINIs have a telescoping steering column, which makes changing the wheel that much more problematic.

Among manufacturers of steering wheels, Momo is the leader in import fitments. Grant also makes a wide variety of aftermarket wheels, but some are much less appropriate than others for performance applications. In any case, the main advantage of an aftermarket wheel is in the ability to custom-select the diameter and configuration of the wheel and the thickness of the outer ring. Select a wheel that is comfortable to hold. Remember that a larger-diameter wheel gives you more steering leverage, and even with power steering you may find turning a small wheel to be more of a chore than you expected.

You can also purchase a quick-release kit for your wheel. Many racers use them because they allow you to bring the wheel closer to you, but you can pop the wheel off the steering column for easy entry and exit from the driver's seat.

SCCA National Champion Pete Taylor has this nice racing Momo wheel installed in his racing R53.

Short Shifters, Shift Knobs and Brake Handles

The other places you put your hand while driving are the shift knob and the e-brake handle. The stock shift knob MINI gives you is good, but it's an item many folks like to replace. Carbon-fiber and wooden knobs are popular and stylish, but for true high-performance applications, you can't beat a leather-covered knob for positive grip.

If you select an aftermarket knob, make sure it's got the right threads to attach to your shift lever and that the threaded part of the knob is well-attached. You wouldn't want the knob to come off in your hand!

Programming the PROMINI Boost Gauge

There are two buttons on the face of the PROMINI boost gauge by Autometer. One is labeled "Warn" and the other is labeled "Peak." To program the gauge, turn the car on, but do not start the engine. Press and hold the Peak button while the gauge needle climbs through the range. Stop the gauge needle anywhere past your maximum boost. (For a stock R53, this is 10 pounds positive. For a car with a 15-percent-reduction pulley, it is 15 pounds. For a car with a 19-percent-reduction pulley, it is about 17 pounds.) Then press the Warn button for a second or two until the warning light blinks. The needle will travel to the Peak point you just set. Press the Warn button repeatedly to set the point where the warning light illuminates. Each time you press the button, the warning boost level drops by 1 pound. Using this technique, you can set the warning light to

The new boost and oil pressure gauges work well, and the boost gauge has a handy light you can program to warn you about overboost conditions.

INTERIOR AND EXTERIOR UPGRADES

PROJECT
Installing The Craven Speed Short Shifter

Several aftermarket houses make short shifter units for performance enthusiasts. There are different designs, but they all work on the same principle: By changing the relative lengths of the ends of the shift lever on either side of a fulcrum, you can reduce the throw length between gears. This allows you to shift gears more quickly, but you must first know how to shift smoothly, or you'll damage the transmission over time. The Craven Speed short shifter is a nice unit, and the project R53 shifts more smoothly and precisely with this product than it did with the stock shifter.

> **TECH TIP**
> ### Aftermarket Exhaust
> Most short shifters require you to disconnect or remove the exhaust and heat shielding to install the product. If you're going to do that, isn't this a good time to install an aftermarket cat-back exhaust?

This project installs the Craven Speed adjustable shifter and boot replacement cup in our project R53. Follow these steps:

1 Remove the stock shift knob by pulling it off the shift lever. This is not easy, but it will come off. Then squeeze and remove the shift boot and its mounting ring from the console. Looking down, you can see into the shift linkage box.

2 Raise the car and support it on a lift. You can use jack stands, but a lift makes this job a lot easier. Disconnect the exhaust from the header and catalyst and disconnect the center support from the car and move the exhaust out of the way.

3 Remove the central piece of heat shielding. This thin metal piece is held in place by several 10-mm washer/nuts, screwed onto threaded studs. Note that there is a single 8-mm screw above the catalyst where several pieces of heat shielding come together. Also remove the wire to the O₂ sensor from a clip on the piece of heat shield. Wiggle the heat shield free and set it aside. Do not damage it. This shield is critical and must be reinstalled.

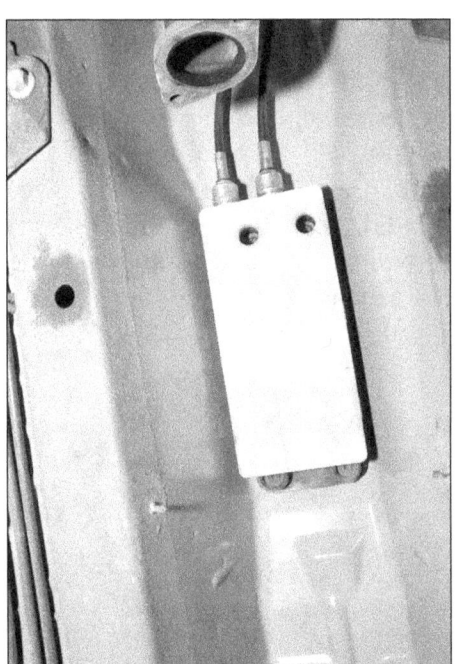

With the exhaust and the heat shield removed, you can see the shift box at the top of the exhaust tunnel. You'll remove this box to work on the internals.

4 You are now looking at the underside of the shifter box. Four T-30 Torx bolts hold the box to the underside of the car. Remove these bolts from below, and then from above, release the several plastic clips that also hold the box to the chassis of the car.

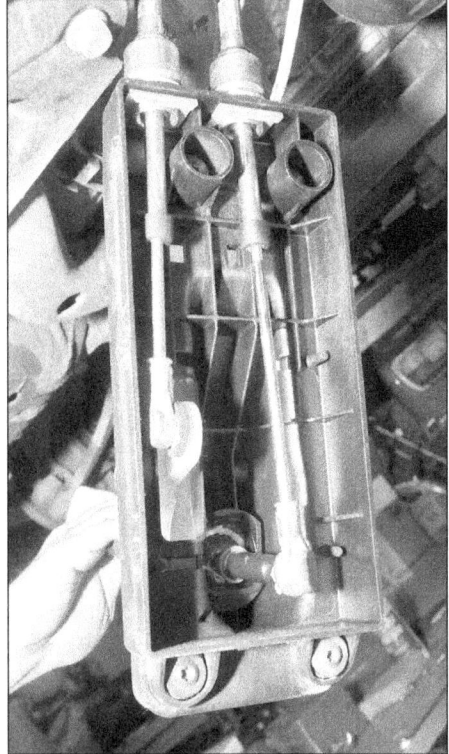

Here you can see the shift cables and their ball-and-socket joints on the shifter. By moving the shifter, you push and pull these cables, transferring the motion to the transmission.

5 Pry the bottom of the shift linkage box off its several clips to expose the two ball-and-socket joints that connect the shift cables to the shift lever. Then carefully pop the socket joint off the bottom ball of the shift lever. One convenient way to do this is to place an open-end 12-mm wrench around the narrowed neck where the ball end of the shift lever meets the socket. You can then place a flat-head screwdriver between the wrench and the socket, and pop it loose.

THE NEW MINI PERFORMANCE HANDBOOK

The stock shifter has been removed. You need the little red O-ring, the white cap on the side ball, and the large white sleeve around the main pivot ball.

6 There is a bell crank attached to the side ball joint of the shift lever. The fulcrum of this bell crank is held to the shift box by a circlip. Remove the circlip by inserting a small screwdriver and gently prying it off its shaft. Under the circlip there is a wavy spring washer, a thicker flat washer, and plastic sleeves. Keep them in order. You can now remove the bell crank from the shift lever. The shift cable stays attached to the bell crank. Remove the small white sleeve from the side ball of the lever.

7 There are three tabs in the white plastic cylinder that fit into the shift box. To remove the shift lever from its housing, carefully pry those tabs inward and pull on the shift lever to remove it from the shift box entirely. Take care not to damage the white plastic cylinder.

8 Liberally grease the central ball on the short shifter lever, and fit it into the white plastic cylinder. There is a groove in the shift box and a tab on the cylinder that allows it to slide into the box in only one orientation. Click the cylinder into place.

9 Next remove the O-ring (the one on our project car is red) from the shaft of the old shift lever and place it on the new shift lever. Then grease the two ball ends of the new shift lever and pop the small white sleeve on the side ball. Reassemble the bell crank onto the shift lever and replace the sleeves, spring washer, flat washer, and circlip. Be careful to ensure that the circlip rides in its groove on the bell crank shaft. Finally, pop the socket of the shift cable onto the bottom ball end.

10 Now you have a decision to make. The Craven Speed unit is adjustable from the driver's seat, so you can select the length of your throw. Shortening the throw means extending the bottom end of the shift lever and shortening the upper end in the cabin. If you replace the bottom of the shift box, you will not be able to fully extend the bottom end to shorten the shifter throw. We elected to replace the bottom of the box to help keep things clean and cool inside. If you do not replace that lid, only the heat shield stands between your greased shifter and the hot exhaust.

This cup replaces the stock shift boot for a nice dress-up. It's not a performance enhancement, but it looks good, and not everyone has one.

11 Before you replace the shifter box, get out your boot replacement. This is an anodized aluminum cup with a sliding plastic plate, rubber grommet, and spring. Line up the cup so that its hole is as close to the right-front corner of the driver's seat as possible. The small holes in its underside line up with holes in the console. From below, install the small screws that hold the cup to the console. Just snug—not too tight!

12 Insert the grommet into the hole in the plastic plate. Place the spring and then the grommeted plastic plate over the shift lever, and thread the shift lever through the hole in the cup as you replace the shift box. The clips on the shift box engage the chassis sheetmetal and you can replace the four Torx bolts that hold the box in place. When you're done, the plastic plate should be held snugly up against the bottom of the cup for a nice effect.

The Craven Speed unit, like several others on the market, allows you to change your shift lever length for a shorter throw. It's easily adjustable at any time after you install it, which is nice.

13 Replace the heat shield and the exhaust.

14 The Craven Speed short shift lever is threaded to accept an aftermarket shift knob. The threaded shaft is 7/16 inch, which matches many available knobs. However, the

INTERIOR AND EXTERIOR UPGRADES

kit includes a plastic sleeve that you can thread over the shaft to accept your stock MINI shift knob or any knob made to fit the stock shift lever. For this project, we installed a classic wooden knob. The threading surface on many of these knobs is soft plastic, designed to be drilled to the size of the shift lever shaft. The knob creates its own threads in the soft plastic as you screw it onto the lever. The feel of a wooden shift knob is nice, and it's a unique interior dress-up item.

I opted for a classic wooden knob with a MINI Cooper badge. It's light and fits my hand better than the stock ball.

three set screws that lock the handle in place. Rotate the handle so that the set screws are conveniently aligned and placed over solid metal on the brake handle body. Insert and snug-down the set screws, but not too tight.

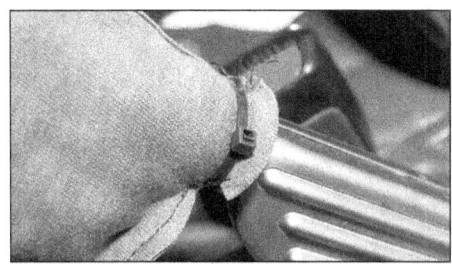

You have to clip this zip-tie to remove the boot. You'll replace it in just a moment as you reassemble.

PROJECT
Installing the Craven Speed E-Brake Handle

This project installs the Craven Speed CNC-machined e-brake handle in our project R53. There's no performance advantage here, but it's a fun dress-up part. Follow these steps:

1 Squeeze the middle of the boot mounting around the base of the handbrake lever to release the clips that hold the boot in place. Invert the boot around the brake lever to expose the zip-tie that holds the boot around the brake handle. Then clip the zip-tie and remove the brake handle boot.

2 Remove the end cap from the brake lever. In the area exposed, find the clip at the outer end of the handbrake lever. Pry up the clip to release the body of the brake handle.

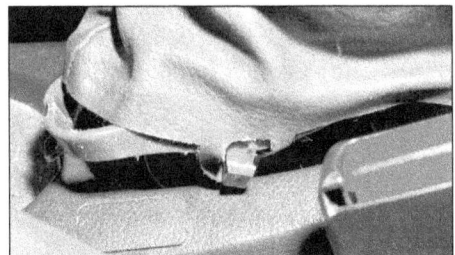

Pinch in the middle to unhook the e-brake boot retainer ring. After just four years, this brake boot is already torn!

3 Slide the new brake handle over the lever. You might need to gently tap it into place. There are

> **Custom Boot**
>
> If you're handy with leather-working, you can use the stock vinyl boot as a pattern to make yourself a custom suede or leather e-brake boot in any color.

4 Replace the boot in its inverted state and tighten a new zip-tie around the brake handle. Then pull the boot over the handle and reinstall the mounting lip into the e-brake base. Finally, roll the rubber O-rings into place on the new brake handle.

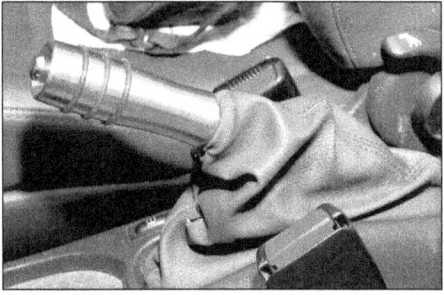

This new brake handle is CNC-machined for a nice feel. It's held in place with set screws under the O-rings.

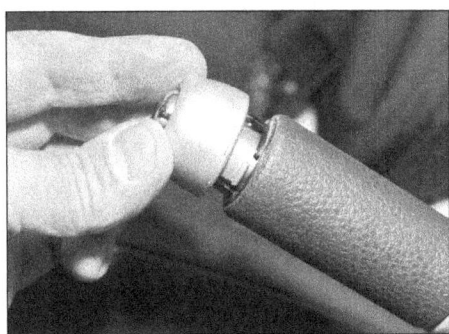

To begin the e-brake handle replacement, pinch the end cap and remove it to expose the tab that releases the rest of the handle.

A modern racing seat has head supports to restrain the driver's head in an accident. It has a fixed back angle and is generally hard-bolted to the floor or roll-cage structure.

If your race car is shared among several drivers, you can install a sliding mount. This mount bolts to the floor of the car, and allows you to move the seat forward and back.

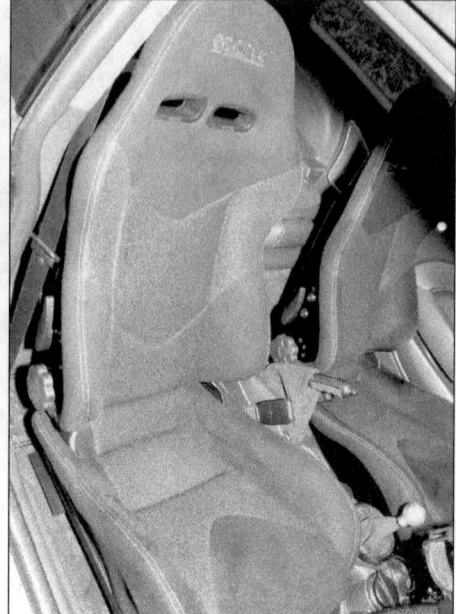

An aftermarket sport seat can usually be installed right on your stock seat rails with an adapter kit. Aftermarket seats, however, are not likely to be a lot better than MINI sport seats.

Seats

Your MINI's seats are a vital safety component. Together with the seat belts, air bags, and the body construction, the seats help keep you safe in an accident. Some aftermarket seats are very very good, and some are not as good as the stock seats in a crash. Look for an FIA rating on a motorsports seat to indicate that it has passed stress testing. The FIA rating is the European/international equivalent to the SFI rating.

But perhaps the area where people compromise the safety of their seats most is in the mounting. For street cars we like to be able to adjust the seat for different drivers, while in a race car people usually bolt the seat right to a welded-in brace for a fixed position. There are many aftermarket seat-mounting kits, and look carefully at any kit and choose one that is solid and well-made. Because your seats are so critical to safety, you should have any aftermarket seats installed by a professional.

Grab the back of a seat and shake it back and forth. The stock seat will move some, and an old and worn seat may move quite a bit. An aftermarket performance seat, properly installed, should move very little. A hard-mounted FIA-rated racing seat should flex a little, but not move.

One more thing to note about seats is that most FIA-rated racing seats have a fixed position; you can't adjust the angle of the seatback. The hinges and stops that allow you to adjust the rake of the seat back are a weak point, and have been known to break or give way in an accident. There are some adjustable racing seats, but these are the exception rather than the rule. Also, because of the high side bolsters and shoulder supports, most racing seats do not work correctly with your stock seat belts and require a racing harness to properly hold you in the car.

Safety Equipment

As you modify your car for performance, one area where you don't want to cut corners is in your safety gear. If you move out of street performance and into racing, many of these decisions are written into the preparation rules. You must have a certified racing seat, racing harness, fire extinguisher, and so on, or you won't be racing.

For each of the modifications you make, ask yourself if what you're doing will compromise the basic safety margins built into your car from the factory. If it's going to put you in danger to make a modification, reconsider whether you really want to take that risk.

INTERIOR AND EXTERIOR UPGRADES

Apart from the expensive gear you put into a performance car, consider carrying a fire extinguisher and a good first-aid or winter-weather kit. It never hurts to be ready to help others or yourself in an emergency. One great place to find all kinds of safety gear for your car is www.safedrives.com.

Safety Belts and Harness Bars

As you increase your performance level, think about increasing your safety gear as well. As mentioned before, a good racing seat helps hold you in place not just in an accident, but as you drive. The second half of that equation is the driver and passenger harness. A good 5- or 6-point racing harness, well-attached, keeps you planted in the seat, so you're not expending energy or mindshare on keeping your body under control while you drive. Leading manufacturers of quality harnesses include Simpson, G-Force, Willans, Sabelt, and others. Look for a harness that is SFI or FIA-rated.

The 4-point "sport" belts on the market are not real racing harnesses, and suffer from a tendency to ride up on your midsection if you tighten the shoulder belts. In an accident, you want the lap belts low across your hips and your shoulder belts tight. You need a 5- or 6-point harness for that, and a proper racing harness costs no more than a 4-point, although you will need a seat that accommodates the anti-submarine strap between your legs.

If you do decide to put a 5-point racing harness in your street car, chances are still good that you do not want to weld in a full roll bar with an integrated harness bar. For a racing harness to work properly, it must be installed to a lateral bar running behind the driver's shoulders. Therefore, aftermarket manufacturers have created bolt-in harness bars. These provide mounting locations at the correct height and distance for a racing harness. You bolt these bars to the floor of your MINI behind the driver and passenger seats. They pretty well make the back seats useless, so consider a rear seat delete kit if you plan to install harness bars. Follow the instructions on both the harness bar and on the harness carefully.

Sound-Deadening Materials

Some people enjoy the sound of their car's engine and the rumble of the road, but others want a quiet ride. If you're a fanatic for quiet, you can improve on the stock sound deadening. Products like Dynamat or Second Skin really cut down on road and engine noise in the cabin.

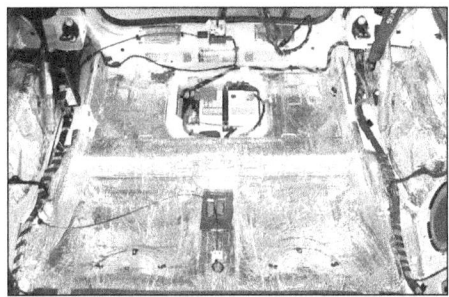

If you want to go all-out for sound damping, you have to remove the whole interior and pad the entire cabin. (Photo courtesy Stephan McKeown)

If you want more than the stock 3-point belts, go ahead and mount a real racing 5-point harness. Street-use 4-point harnesses do not let you tighten the shoulder straps without pulling the lap belt too high on your middle.

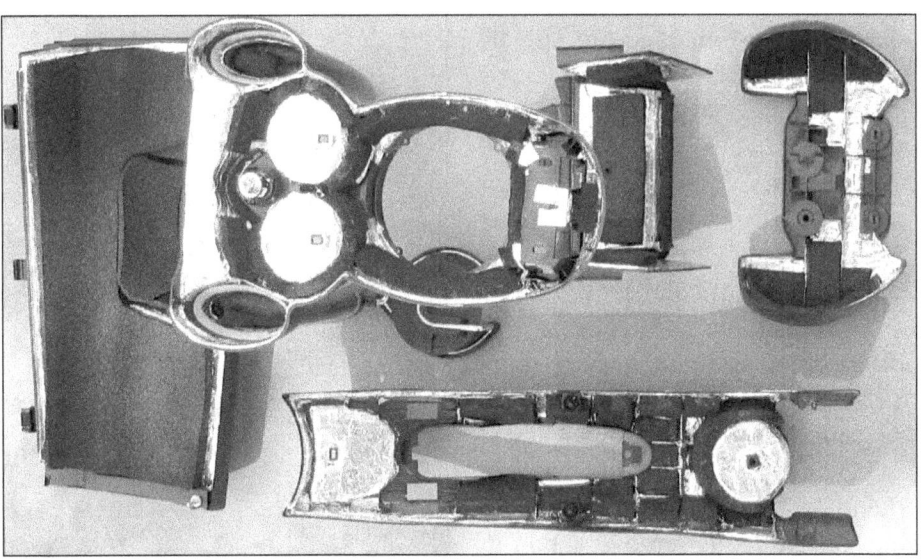

An often neglected area for sound deadening is in the trim pieces of the cabin. (Photo courtesy Stephan McKeown)

CHAPTER 6

For an easy project, you can pull out your console and other trim pieces and insert the padding behind them. If your goal is much more quiet, you can pull the entire interior and line your entire cabin with sound deadening pads.

Roll Bars and Roll Cages

A good roll cage is a necessity for a car that you plan on driving on a race track more than a couple times each year, and if you plan on driving to the limit of the car's potential. Besides holding the driver's compartment open in a rollover, a roll cage helps stiffen the chassis.

Your choices with roll cages are essentially unlimited because a custom cage can include anything you want. You can also buy a premade "bolt-in" cage kit and install it yourself.

Of the two, custom work costs a little more, but it's worth it. A custom cage is generally (but not always) welded into the chassis of your car. It fits your car better and you can have the builder make the cage as complete or as unobtrusive as you like. A custom cage can also tie into your strut towers and potentially extend from bumper to bumper. Be sure to choose a good cage builder. Someone with experience in the local motorsports business is best, especially if you're building to a particular set of rules.

Bear in mind that if you choose a bolt-in cage, you'll be drilling some holes through your floorpan and various panels. If you choose a custom cage, you'll be welding plates and potentially penetrating bulkheads in your car. You can remove a bolt-in cage and fill the holes and walk that modification back, but a weld-in cage is forever and limits the resale market of your car to other racing enthusiasts.

Aerodynamic Devices

There are quite a few different kinds of aerodynamic devices in use on cars today, and any of them can be installed on a MINI. The following is a review of the major components—what they're called and what they're supposed to do.

Wings

Wing is a term generally given to an aerodynamically shaped device

This wing actually produces some downforce, but not very much at typical highway speeds.

The GP Edition R53 is the only MINI to carry a real wing from the factory. All the rest are spoilers.

that is mounted on braces at the rear of the car (also known as an airfoil). Purpose-built race cars such as Indy cars also have wings on the front end of the car, but sedans do not generally use those.

Airfoils work because of their shape: convex on one side and slightly concave on the other. Air flows faster past the convex side than the concave side. This creates lower pressure on the convex side, and higher pressure on the concave side; the difference in pressure is felt as lift or downforce. The end plates keep air from spilling off the side of the wing, increasing the effect.

A wing on your car is fundamentally the same as a wing on an airplane, but where an airplane uses a wing to generate lift so it can fly, on a car we turn the airfoil upside down to generate downforce. Downforce is nice on a car because it adds road grip, but not mass. If you were to put a scale under a moving Indy car, you'd find that at 220 mph, it's got something like 5,000 pounds of downforce on a 1,500-pound car.

In order for a wing to do any good, it has to sit in the airflow over the car. The only MINI to carry a real wing from the factory is the GP edition. The GP wing is high enough in the airflow to do some good.

Aftermarket wing makers generally don't have access to the kind of development and testing facilities that the automakers do. If you want to see the result of serious downforce requirements and the budget to figure out the best possible solution, take a look at the wings that professional racers use on their cars.

Realistically, until you're going well in excess of reasonable street and highway speeds, no wing is going to do a whole lot more than gravity is already doing to pin down

This is the stock R53 Cooper S rear spoiler. It looks great, but apart from churning up the airflow a little, it doesn't really do much.

This is the stock R53 Cooper S spoiler again, but with an add-on piece that kicks up a bit more at the rear. This increases the spoiler effect, but doesn't offer significant downforce.

the rear end of a 2,700-pound car. So the bottom line is that you should regard your wing as an aesthetic decoration until you're ready for serious racing—then your wing will likely be specified for you in the racing rules.

Spoilers

Spoilers are often confused with wings because so many spoilers are mounted on the back of a car in same place as a wing. But if you look closely, a spoiler is not designed to produce downforce.

Rear spoilers improve a car's stability by creating turbulence in the airflow going over the back of the car, negating lift that your car is generating. If you stand back and look at a car from the side, it looks a little like a wing with the roofline as the convex side and the underside as the concave side. Moving that shape through the air can create lift.

CHAPTER 6

By disrupting the airflow over the top of the car, you eliminate the wing effect and reduce the amount of lift naturally generated by the shape of the body. Some people also use "chin" or "lip" spoilers on the front of a car to disrupt the air trying to pass underneath the body.

Air Dam

An air dam is a specific kind of spoiler. You see these frequently on track racing cars. They are flexible walls at the front of the car that brush the ground (or come close to it). As the car moves forward, the air dam prevents air from flowing under the car and generates low pressure under the body, sucking the car to the ground. At various times, racers have put skirts along the sides of a car in addition to the air dam to enhance the vacuum. These are called "ground effects" and they are usually not allowed in formal racing. The most famous case was the Chapparal 2 "sucker car," which used skirts and then added a large fan that sucked the air out from under the car. It was so effective at sticking the car to the ground that it was banned from Can-Am racing.

Splitters

A splitter is another implementation of the wing idea. With a splitter, you place a flat surface parallel to the ground at the bottom of the front bodywork. By sticking this plane out in front of your car, you create a high-pressure area on top of the plane because the air is running into your car's nose and "piling up" there; it cannot deflect downward and under the car. With lower-pressure air flowing below the splitter, the nose of the car gains some downforce.

You can see the splitter on the front of Stephan McKeown's R53. This does more than a spoiler to provide some downforce on the front end. (Photo courtesy Stephan McKeown)

You can see what a diffuser is all about. The channels direct air out from under the car in a smooth manner, helping the MINI maintain low pressure under the car. Augment this M7 diffuser with an air dam or splitter on the front and a wing on the back to provide some downforce. (Photo courtesy M7 Tuning)

Canards

Canard is the French word for "duck." It also means to tell a lie, so how it came to describe little winglets on the front of a car is a mystery. But for our purposes, canards are small airfoils installed in front of the front wheels on the lower fenders. They are designed to add a little downforce, like the diving planes on a submarine.

This M7 wing sits up in the airflow where it needs to be. It's made of carbon fiber for bling factor and to be as light as possible. Use this in concert with a diffuser and some front-end aero to stick your MINI to the ground. (Photo courtesy M7 Tuning)

Diffusers

A diffuser is a special kind of spoiler. In this case, it's designed as an anti-spoiler. A diffuser sits underneath the rear bumper area of a car and directs airflow out from beneath the car smoothly into the low-pressure area that the car leaves behind as it moves forward. This helps stabilize the car in the airflow and allows the other aerodynamic devices to work to their best effect.

CHAPTER 7

MINIs in Competition

What does it mean to take your MINI into competition?

Competition cars are fundamentally different from street cars, even if you still drive them on public roads. They are different because, if you've built them right, you have subordinated every other consideration to building the car as best you can within the limits of the rules for that kind of racing (or showing).

Before you head for the garage to tear the carpet out of your daily driver, you need to understand that racing is a harsh and unforgiving sport. There's an ironclad rule that is reinforced every weekend on race tracks and rally roads all over the world. The first rule of racing is: *If you can't walk away from a total loss, walk away from racing.*

Every weekend of the year, someone somewhere completely wrecks a race car. It happens rarely at autocrosses, but it happens. If you race long enough it will happen to you, sometimes on your first day. That's why everyone wears a helmet, not just the fast guys. If you're not ready to walk away from a total loss of your investment, don't even take it to the races.

That being said, racing a MINI is the most fun you can have in a car with your clothes on. And there are lots of opportunities to compete in your daily driver. Here is a quick look

Every weekend at race tracks around the world, the first rule of racing is enforced: Don't take it to the track unless you're prepared to walk away from a wreck. (Photo courtesy George Mehallick)

Taking your MINI racing means deep commitment. Here, Michele Milder drives a 2006 R53 JCW to a fourth-place finish in the D Street Prepared Ladies class. (Photo courtesy Dan Bryant)

THE NEW MINI PERFORMANCE HANDBOOK

at each of the most common race formats and the Coopers that are beating the competition.

Autocross

Autocross is among the most popular amateur motorsports in North America, and it's the safest form of racing you can find outside of a video game. The sport demands a car that is nimble, quick off the line and out of a corner, and stable in a turn. That's a description of your MINI, and that's why so many people have chosen a MINI as their ride for autocross.

Autocrossing a MINI is a good way to win whether you're at the SCCA nationals or just tearing up the back lot of the local Wal-Mart on a Sunday. Serious competitors choose the MINI for its competition potential, but the soul of the machine makes it more than just a winning ride—it's a joy to partner up with your MINI for the win.

"MINI's the best-handling car in two classes, and with their exceptional resale value and good gas mileage they are very good cars to have. One of the great things about the MINI is that there aren't really any other cars on the road like them. When you come across another MINI on the road, every one waves. It's a good feeling," says two-time national champion Ron Williams of Topeka, Kansas.

Autocross is a timed, single-car race through a tight course set up with cones. A parking lot is the usual venue, with each competitor taking a maximum of three timed runs through the course. Each run takes between 30 and 90 seconds, depending on the course, and the fastest time wins. There's no practice, no warmup; just pull up to the line and do your best. But there's a 2-second penalty for every cone you knock over, so be careful.

Autocross is a great way to race if you have only one car. Some autocrossers go on to compete in other forms of racing, but many find a permanent racing home in the sport. Experienced autocross drivers are both fast and smooth—masters of fine-tuned car placement and control.

This is Anthony Savini, who finished second at the SCCA Solo Nationals but first in the 2008 SCCA Pro-Solo series. (Photo courtesy Craig Wilcox)

Greg Reno finished third in G Stock in 2008. The top three finishers at the SCCA Solo Nationals were all driving Pepper White R53 models with black bonnet stripes. That settles the question about which paint scheme is fastest. (Photo courtesy Craig Wilcox)

National Autocross Champions Choose MINI

Ron Williams won an H Stock national championship in his 2005 R50 Cooper. Driving the same car, Ron's wife Tina finished third in H Stock Ladies.

"I won the G stock title last year in a 2007 Cooper S, but the turbo car likes to eat the front tires quite quickly. I decided late in this year to run an '05 Cooper in H stock. We just switched the expensive struts and wheels over. We didn't start racing the car until the very end of June so we only had around seven events prior to Nationals. In the end it worked out well and I got my second championship," Williams says.

Up in G Stock, Craig Wilcox of Blue Springs, Missouri, won a championship running a 2007 R56 Cooper S. But before you read too much into the competition potential of the turbocharged R56 against the supercharged R53 model, know that second and third in the class went to 2005 and 2006 R53 Cooper S drivers. Kristi Brown of Des Moines, Washington, won the G Stock Ladies national championship in a 2007 R56 Cooper S.

This H Stock R50 Cooper carried Ron Williams to the 2008 national championship. His friend, Tom Dupler of Derby, Kansas, also drove the car in the Nationals to help keep the tires warm. (Photo courtesy Dan Bryant)

Craig Wilcox has won multiple national championships in the R53 Cooper S. Here he demonstrates the precision and speed it takes to win. (Photo courtesy Joe Silva)

A good autocross driver can make a transition to any other form of racing with ease.

Autocross requires a helmet, and that's about all the special equipment you need. An autocross should cost about $20 to $30 to enter, and you should expect three to five runs through the course for your money. A typical autocross is a half-day or full-day affair and you typically work the course (picking up cones) when you're not driving.

MINI-specific and general-purpose sports car clubs all over the world hold autocrosses. The Sports Car Club of America (SCCA) sanctions local, regional, and national championships with a consistent set of rules and classes. In SCCA's car classing system, all normally aspirated MINI Coopers run in a class called H Stock, while both R53 and R56 Cooper S variants run in the faster G Stock class. For each of these classes, there is a Ladies Division that is restricted to female competitors. However, women are welcome to enter the open competition for each class as well.

Autocross competition classes vary a bit depending on the club organizing the event, but there are usually categories for factory-stock cars, Street Prepared or Street Touring vehicles, and all-out unlimited cars. Within a preparation category, there are different classes according to the performance potential of the car. Get

CHAPTER 7

> ## The Winning Combination
>
> All of the MINI champions at the 2008 SCCA Solo Nationals ran on Hoosier tires. Here are the specs on two of the four:
>
> **Craig Wilcox, G Stock Champion, 2007 MINI Cooper S**
> - QuickSilver exhaust
> - SSR competition wheels, 16x6.5 44-mm offset
> - Koni double-adjustable shock/struts F/R
> - Schroth quick-fit harness
> - Hoosier tires, 205/45-16 A6
>
> **Ron Williams, H Stock Champion, 2005 MINI Cooper**
> - Sport Package front sway bar
> - Magnaflow straight-through exhaust
> - Koni sport front struts
> - Koni double-adjustable rear struts
> - Hoosier tires

ahold of the rules for the events you plan to enter and you can see where your car fits in. Typically, an aftermarket suspension means that you compete in the Street Prepared category, while adding a turbo or other exotic modifications may well put you into unlimited territory.

Autocross Setup For Your MINI

As the class names imply, stock classification cars are kept very close to factory-equipment specs. But as with all forms of racing, the rules are written to let you pump up the performance just a little bit.

"Stock isn't always 'stock,' but we aren't far off. Some of the modifications that are allowed are strut changes, sway bars, and aftermarket wheels, but wheels must be the same size as stock and virtually the same offset. We can also replace the exhaust from the catalytic converter back, the air filter, and the coil, spark plugs and plug wires," Williams says.

The most un-stock allowance in the stock rules allows competitors to choose any DOT-approved tires that meet the size and rim requirements. These tires are generally about as close to a racing slick as you can find. Competitors at the Solo Nationals can easily burn through an entire set of tires at the event. "Good tires alone are worth 3 seconds each run over the stock tires," Williams says.

Anyone can purchase go-fast goodies and put them on the car. If you want to go fast, you have to be able to drive fast. But the drivers at the Solo Nationals can all do that, too, so each racer has to look at the details to gain an advantage.

Each racer develops a particular alignment setup that he or she prefers for the car. Competitors generally don't like to share that information, but Williams decided to let us in on his secrets.

"With the alignment, you try to extract the most camber out of the front, which is virtually nothing: 0.3 to 0.5 degrees negative with a toe-out of 1/8 of an inch. On the rear, I try to get rid of the negative camber. I can usually get it down to 0.6 degrees negative and 1/8 of an inch toe-out," Williams says.

The camber settings he describes help maximize the front-end grip when the car is in a turn, and encourage the rear end of the MINI to be lively, helping the car rotate around corners. Setting a little bit of toe-out both front and rear also helps an autocross car turn in a corner, but would cause a street car to "wander" somewhat.

Track Days

If your goal is to go a little faster, but you still need to keep your car street-legal, consider participating in track day events. These events go by a lot of different names: High Performance Driver Education (HPDE), Street School, Driver Training Day, or Open Track Day, but they all mean the same thing: a dedicated race track with no stoplights, no police radar, and no RVs in the way. You can run these events in a bone-stock Clubman or any MINI on up to a modified JCW GP.

A track day isn't a competition. Because a track day is not competitive, no one cares much what you have or have not done to your car, or how fast you drive. However, a friend of mine likes to say, "You can't win a track day, but you sure can lose." Race tracks have walls and curbs and gravel traps. If you lose control, you can wreck your car and the greater speeds you can achieve on a track mean you might also hurt yourself. Be careful and remember the first rule of racing.

WARNING: *Your car insurance will not cover you if you crash your car on a race track. In fact, many will not cover any accident that happens on the grounds of a race track, even in the parking lot. However, you can buy special*

MINIS IN COMPETITION

A bone-stock street R50 Cooper makes a great track day car. On the track is where you really feel the difference between a stock MINI and one that you've upgraded for performance. (Photo courtesy Dan Bryant)

As you get better at track days, you'll probably find that you want to take the next step to time attack or club racing.

insurance for track days. Give it strong consideration.

Most track days have different groups that are organized by driver experience or level of car prep. Don't be insulted if you're placed in the beginner group your first few times on the track. Typically you get a chalk-talk from the lead instructor and have an instructor assigned to you. Instructors are typically amateur race drivers or experienced track day drivers. You can learn a lot from these people, so pay attention. Track days are the cheapest training you'll ever get in performance driving.

Track days cost anywhere from $100 on up. You'll need a helmet and your car must generally pass a basic technical inspection that includes a check for fluid leaks. Many marque-specific sports car clubs put on track days, but most allow any brand of car to enter.

If you build a MINI for track days, there are generally no limits on what you're allowed to do, but what you should do is focus on handling and brakes as well as on your engine.

Time Attack

Time attack (also called time trial) is similar to an autocross in that you race by yourself against the clock, but in this form of competition you're not dodging pylons, you're on the race track at full speed. In this competition, cars may be more or less street legal, or may be required to have full racing safety gear.

Luke Russell of Fort Myers, Florida, is a successful time attack racer. He competes in the challenging One Lap of America time trials, driving from track to track over eight consecutive days, looking for the fastest lap at each track.

CHAPTER 7

Over The Top: Stephan McKeown's 2006 R53 Cooper S

"I wanted both a street and track car, with an emphasis on handling and stopping over raw power," says Stephan McKeown.

McKeown bought a stock 2006 Cooper S, and to prep his MINI for both track days and street performance, he had all work planned and performed by Al Megenity at A&E Performance. Megenity sold A&E to his former employee, Steve Dinan, in 2008. Dinan has produced many performance parts for the MINI under his own name before and since.

"After listening to me ramble on about what I was looking for in a MINI, Al offered me a drive in a Cooper S prepared at A&E Performance, his shop in Campbell, California. Al's been tuning and racing BMWs and MINIs from day one," McKeown says.

McKeown's Cooper S came from the factory in pepper white, with a 6-speed manual transmission, Sport Package, Cold Weather Package, and elements of the Premium Package without the heavy sunroof option. Then Megenity went to work, primarily focusing on the suspension, but also addressing every aspect of a performance car.

"Everything works together seamlessly, creating a whole definitely greater than the sum of its parts. Al thinks in entire systems: suspension, brakes, wheels, and tires are all interrelated. By selecting and tweaking high-quality, compatible components, he puts together a great-handling MINI," McKeown says.

Here are just the highlights of Stephan's extensive aftermarket mod list. In this configuration, McKeown's Cooper S generates dyno pulls at 224 hp and 180 ft-lbs of torque at the wheels:

Exterior
- Strassentech front chin spoiler
- Rennline stainless-steel folding tow hooks
- JCW black carbon-fiber rear wing
- Alta 2-inch stubby antenna
- Texas Speedwerks aluminum jack points

Interior
- JCW leather dash with black/red stitching
- Greddy Version II 52-mm oil pressure and water temperature gauges
- Craven Speed flexpod
- B & M short shifter
- Whalen shift knob
- Schroth red harnesses

This car received extensive modification from the shop that later became Dinan BMW. Stephan McKeown wanted great track performance in a car that was also a pleasure to drive on the street. (Photo courtesy Jim Williams)

You can see how McKeown's car corners flat with the outside wheel straight up and down. That's good suspension geometry. The car doesn't even look like it's working! (Photo courtesy Jim Williams)

- Minspeed black leather autocross kneepad
- 30-percent-tint side and rear windows
- Second Skin sound damping

Wheels and Tires
- Street: 17x7.5 SSR GT2 semi-solid forged at 14.6 pounds per wheel, with 3-mm spacers and Michelin PS2 235/40ZR-17 tires
- Track: 17x7.5 SSR Comp R semi-solid forged at 13.2 pounds per wheel, with Dinan wheel nuts and Toyo RA1S 235/40ZR-17 tires

Brakes
- Stoptech 328-mm slotted front rotors with red anodized four-piston calipers
- Pagid racing pads in front
- Porterfield racing pads in the rear
- ATE racing blue brake fluid
- Stoptech braided stainless-steel lines

Suspension and Handling
- Bilstein PSS9 corner-weighted coil-over suspension system
- Camber: front -1.7 degrees; rear -2.7 degrees
- H-Sport 27-mm front and 19-mm rear anti-roll bars
- Texas Speedwerks adjustable sway-bar droplinks
- SPC camber plates
- Powerflex front control arm bushings
- MINI Mania precision steering amplifiers
- SPC billet aluminum lower rear control arms
- Moss upper rear control arms
- Powerflex rear trailing arm bushings
- M7 underbody strut system
- Dinan aluminum and carbon fiber strut tower brace

Engine Performance
- GRS intercooler
- Dinan high-flow cowl induction intake and high-flow air filter
- Dinan 15-percent supercharger pulley and belt
- Dinan 59.75-mm high-flow throttle body
- Dinan fuel pressure regulator and fuel tank pressure regulator assembly
- Dinan Stage 5 software
- Revolution MINI head: stainless nitrided valves, titanium retainers, custom locks, keepers, and dual valve springs
- Revolution MINI header and center pipe, coated with jet-hot 2000 black
- Borla sport exhaust
- GTT resistance fit steel/hard anodized lightened crank pulley (stock size)
- GTT twin-bearing idler pulley and tensioner pulley
- Minspeed tensioner pulley stop bar
- MSD coil pack
- MSD 8.5-mm red plug wires
- NGK Iridium spark plugs (IK-22)
- Quaife ATB differential
- Clutchmaster FX300 Clutch
- Texas Speedwerks Version 2 improved engine damper
- M7 air plate diverter

The good thing about time attack is that you can compete on a track without completely making your car over as a race car. The down side is that you won't have full racing protection if you crash.

"The idea is to do racing time trials at one, or sometimes two, motorsports facilities each day. After the day's activities, you pack up all your things and drive your race car all night to the next day's event. No support vehicles are allowed. All tools, luggage, tents, spare tire, and food must be loaded into or on top of your race car," Russell says.

A related sport is tougé (*tow-gay*) racing. Tougé was invented in Japan, and is similar to time attack except there's a lead car and a follow car, and the two do not race side by side through the corners, but rather the lead car attempts to run away from the follow car. If the lead car extends his lead, he wins. If the follow car can keep up or pass the lead car, he wins.

Hill Climb

Hill climbing is a specialized form of time trials or tarmac rally. In a hill climb, the organizers shut down a length of public road and contestants make a series of individual timed runs up the road. The direction is almost always up, because it's safer and easier to drive fast up a hill than down.

Depending on the club organizing the event, cars may be classed according to autocross, rally, or amateur racing preparation rules. In addition to your helmet, most hill climbs require you to carry fire extinguishers, and may require a flame-retardant driver's suit. Some hill climbs require roll bars or cages depending on the kind of car you've got.

MINIs do very well in hill climbs. Engine power is typically a greater concern in hill climb racing, but don't neglect handling and braking. The consequences for losing control and leaving the road in a hill climb can be a long trip down a hillside or a short trip into a tree. Remember the first rule of racing.

Andy Howe is the author of *How To Autocross*, from S-A Design. He describes the value differences between setting a car up for autocross and for hill climb like this: "For autocross, we set our cars up to run right on the ragged edge of control. Such a setup might be great for 55 mph surrounded by cones. But the penalties for leaving the course when hill climbing are significantly greater than autocrossing. Consequently, a car that I'm driving at a hill climb will be more stable than one that I am autocrossing. Basically, the car will be less prone to oversteer, or put another way, it will understeer more. It is much easier to recover a car that is understeering and if I go off the road while understeering I can choose what I hit. The biggest change when hill climbing is the driver's mentality. A successful hill climber will recognize that it's not always prudent to drive 10/10ths—an error at 10/10ths is an off."

Amateur Racing

The first MINI entered amateur track racing almost as soon as the cars arrived in America, and moved rapidly to the front of the pack. The leading sanctioning bodies for amateur "club" racing in the United States are the Sports Car Club of America (www.scca.com) and the National Auto Sport Association (www.nasaproracing.com). Both accept the Cooper S into at least one class.

Track racing is a fundamentally different game from other forms of racing. In this environment, you're not racing the clock for a fast time, you're racing door-handle to door-handle against other people. Your track racing car may not be street-legal, and it certainly is not set up to be comfortable on the highway, which means you bring it to the track on a trailer you purchased or rented, pulled by a truck or van you purchased or rented. It's not uncommon to spend much more on your tow rig than on your race car.

A track racing car requires a roll cage, racing seat, racing harness, and fire system, and typically runs on racing tires. Track racing a MINI is an

Hill climb is a lot like time attack, except you're running up a real road somewhere. Hill climb classes are usually pretty close to autocross classes since most hill climb cars are pretty close to stock.

MINIS IN COMPETITION

Jill Urso and Ralph Porter (obscured) lead a group of cars through the curves at Heartland Park Topeka during the SCCA Runoffs.

James Place schools a pair of Mazda Miatas at the SCCA Runoffs. The cost to play at this level can easily mount to tens of thousands of dollars.

Pete Taylor won two consecutive SCCA national championships in his R53. Ask him and he'll tell you the exact setup he uses at the track.

expensive proposition, but where else can you battle side by side with your competition?

Most MINIs still race in Showroom Stock classes. These classes are for late-model cars with extremely limited modifications. Factors such as tires, brake pads, and weight distribution are allowed limited improvement, but the core engine must stay stock. If you want to get really crazy, there are also unlimited classes where you can test your wildest ideas against the best others have to offer, but as yet, MINIs have not made a significant mark in those classes.

Costs to run a competitive amateur racing program in a MINI can easily top $40,000 to build a car and $20,000 annually to campaign it. If this is within your budget, talk to your preferred sanctioning body about class rules and safety requirements.

Pete Taylor of Ortonville, Michigan, drove his 2005 Cooper S to two consecutive national Showroom Stock C championships in 2005 and 2006 at the SCCA Runoffs.

"I bought this car two weeks before the Runoffs. I got to the track, sat on the pole, and won the national championship. People said it was just the car that won. Maybe after the second year they'll give me a little more credit," Taylor says.

Showroom Stock means just what it sounds like. The cars must be raced as they were sold to the public—almost. "In Showroom Stock racing, all you're really allowed to add is safety equipment. So it's got a 6-point roll cage, racing seat, removable steering wheel, and a fire extinguisher in the car. But that's about it, almost everything else is stock," Taylor says.

There are a few exceptions to the stock rule. Brake pads are free, all fluids are free, any DOT-approved

THE NEW MINI PERFORMANCE HANDBOOK

rubber on the market is fair game, the air filter is free, and drivers can run any cat-back exhaust they choose. Most, including Taylor, choose a straight pipe. But engines, gearboxes, wheels, shocks, sway bars, and suspension and brake hardware must remain part-number stock for the car's year, make, and model. And the 2005 model year introduction of the optional limited slip differential didn't make it through the rules committee, either. "We're not even allowed to update to the current year," Taylor says.

The thinking behind the rule is to keep racing affordable and to truly showcase the basic performance potential of the car and the driver—not the team's budget. So performance enhancements for the MINI are incremental, and razor-thin.

"I run Red Line Oil," Taylor says, and goes on to explain: "The synthetics help by making the motor that much more free. But most of what put me on the podium is preparation. I spend a lot of time at the track trying different alignments and tire pressures."

Unlike many racers, Taylor is free with his setup information. "I give it to anybody that asks. I'd rather beat them by driving. I run the Hoosier tires and Carbotech brake pads. We have to run stock 16-inch wheels, and we have to keep the alignment within the MINI specs. So I run zero toe in the front, and a little toe-out in the rear to get the car to rotate in the corners. For camber we can't do anything to the front, but I stand up the rears as much as I can. We're running 1.3 degrees negative camber in the back on both sides," he says.

After each race, the Cooper S (with driver) must weigh in at a hefty 3,050 pounds—almost 400 pounds over stock weight. "I'm the biggest guy in the smallest car," Taylor jokes. Under the SCCA's somewhat arcane competition formula, the 6-foot-4-inch, 260-pound Taylor has to add 150 pounds of ballast in the passenger footwell to keep his car legal. On top of that, MINI pilots are forced to run a 17-percent inlet restrictor just to give the competition a fighting chance.

"I've turned my size into an advantage. I've got the seat as far down and back as I can, which helps balance the weight. As heavy as these cars are in the front, your front tires heat up and start going away fast," Taylor says.

With close competition assured by the rules and drivers with decades of experience, how do you make it to the top of the podium? The winning edge is in the details, and discovered by lots of testing and practice.

"I've been around racing all my life. I started autocrossing when I was 14 in Birmingham, Alabama. I used to go to Salina, Kansas, to compete in the SCCA Solo national championships. I finished second a couple times, but never won a Solo championship," Taylor says.

Taylor's testing regimen starts early in the year, and continues through to the morning of the race. He tests different tires, alignment settings, and driving styles; always looking for the next fraction of a second. "I have an AIM lap timer and an AIM data system as well, so that once I make a lap I can see the times I'm turning, and I'm collecting data to see where I can pick up some time. For qualifying on Thursday, I was running some softer autocross tires because the weather was so cold. So I ran a little toe out in the front and a little less toe out in the rear," Taylor says.

To improve driver comfort and stamina, Taylor uses a device called a Cool Shirt. This is a special undershirt that is worn beneath the driver's fire suit. A pump circulates cool water through tubes sewn into the shirt from a reservoir behind the driver's seat. "I run the cool suit on the hot days. When it's 100 degrees out, for all the money you spend on a race car, it's worth the money."

But for all the preparation, all the testing, and all the data collection that goes on before the green flag

Here's the high point of amateur racing. You get to take your spouse and crew on a victory lap, waving the checkered flag. Some of the finest racing drivers in the world compete at this level, just for the fun of it.

drops, Taylor had a simple strategy for the race: "I told my crew chief and my wife that I had a plan. If I could get through turn one on the first lap and turn out some good laps, I knew I'd be OK. So I just put my head down and dug for all I had."

After the race, the winners have to get through the tech shed before SCCA officially awards the title of national champion. Before the drivers even get through the champagne spray and the hat dance, the top six cars are impounded and minutely inspected for compliance with SCCA rules. "We had to pull an axle out to prove we didn't have limited slip. Then we had to pull the head off and give the inspectors the head and the cams. They put the cams on the cam doctor and test them against the stock profile. They CC the heads to make sure we haven't done any work there, and they inspect all the ports to make sure we haven't touched them," Taylor says. Tech inspectors also examine each car's fuel for illegal additives, and they check ECU programming to make sure no one has attempted a technological advantage.

MINIs are also eligible to race in SCCA's Touring 3 class—Showroom Stock's faster brother. Touring 3 is the home of the John Cooper Works cars. In addition to the upgrades provided with the JCW package, drivers are allowed free rein to upgrade the ECU programming, they are allowed suspension modifications such as front camber plates, and several other significant performance upgrades. In exchange, they have to compete against fast cars such as the Mazda RX-8 and the Audi TT.

When the racing season starts up in the spring, you can head to your nearest SCCA national race to check out the action. If you've never seen a MINI in full racing trim, it's a sight to behold. And the thrill of cheering on your fellow Cooper S pilots is doubled when you find out that at most amateur races, you're welcome in the team paddock. Ask nicely and you might just find yourself sitting in the racing seat, or even joining a pit crew for the weekend. But be careful—racing is known to be addictive.

Road Rally

Imagine a perfectly crisp fall afternoon. You're flinging your MINI along a gently winding country road. The fall color is glorious, with the sun peeking out from behind the clouds that presage the arrival of winter. As you cruise past yet another picture-perfect pumpkin patch, your passenger calls out, "Ooh! There's the road we want!" and you execute a brisk right onto the new heading. Your passenger intones, "Your new speed is 35, and we're now looking for Firdale Road."

What I'm describing is a road rally, sometimes known as a time-speed-distance (TSD) rally. The sport has been in hibernation for decades, but is now enjoying a resurgence in popularity. Much of the new interest in the sport stems from the arrival of driver's cars like the MINI and the growth of new clubs made up of people looking for a reason to get out and enjoy their rides.

The premise of road rally is simple: Each car carries a team consisting of a driver and a navigator. Each team is given a set of printed instructions that describe a route, usually about 40 to 50 miles, and usually away from heavy traffic and stoplights. In addition to the route, the instructions also specify average speeds that the teams must maintain along the route. Those speeds are always set a bit below the posted legal speeds on the rally roads—no reputable rally club will ask you to break the law.

Armed with the instructions and an accurate clock or stopwatch, the teams set out at 1-minute intervals to drive the instructed route. The game is to see which team can stay closest to the specified average speeds. The rally is scored by timing each team at certain predefined places along the route called "checkpoints." The rally organizers carefully measure the route before the

Amateur Champion

You might wonder what you get when you're an amateur racing national champion. There are no photos on a box of Wheaties. Champions get a nice trophy, a bag of baseball caps, maybe a few cases of free motor oil, and a checkered flag for their efforts and investment. But they also get the knowledge that they have what it takes to win in some of the toughest racing anywhere.

TSD rally is well-suited to MINIs because you don't have to make any modifications to your car to participate. Rally gives you a great excuse to spend a Saturday touring the best country roads in your area.

CHAPTER 7

Brian Waters' All-Out MINI

With the help of Rasmussen MINI and Loyning's Engine Service in Portland, Oregon, and MINI USA, Brian Waters built what may be the ultimate racing MINI. Starting with an R50 Cooper chassis, Waters went over every inch of the car, throwing away excess weight and building an all-out race car. He was well on his way when MINI USA asked for their car back! Here's how it ended up:

Engine and Transmission
- Oversize JE pistons
- Carrillo rods
- Aluminum flywheel
- Competition clutch
- Highly modified head and valvetrain
- Custom high-lift camshaft
- 15-percent supercharger pulley
- Custom prototype front-mount intercooler
- Oversize throttle body
- Electromotive TEC-3 standalone ECU
- Accusump
- Getrag 6-speed transmission
- Quaife limited slip differential

Bodywork and Chassis
- Full roll cage
- Composite side and back windows
- Custom fuel cell enclosure
- Racing seat
- Custom gauge panel
- Hard mounted all subframes

Suspension
- Hard mounted all suspension arms
- H&R adjustable coil-overs
- H&R competiton sway bars
- Camber plates

Brakes and Wheels
- Front Brembo big-brake kit
- Steel-braided lines
- Rear brake bias control
- 17x7 PIAA wheels

"The car weighed 2,100 pounds and the engine made 260 hp at the front wheels. This was very early in the new MINI tuning days and we anticipated making further improvements to the engine. The suspension was not even fully sorted when we had to crush the car," Waters says.

Brian Waters built this car for a class with wide-open rules. By the time he was done, this MINI laid down 260 hp at the wheels. (Photo courtesy Brian Waters)

As you learn more about TSD rally, you might invest in a specialized rally clock, a GPS unit, or even a rally computer to tell you your average speed.

event and use a little basic math to determine the exact time it should take to arrive at each checkpoint.

Sounds completely easy, doesn't it? Well, it's not. Maintaining an average speed while obeying basic traffic laws like stop signs is harder than it sounds. And to top it all off, some rallies include "traps," tricky challenges that are designed to make teams early or late to the checkpoints. When you get into it, road rally is a logic puzzle played out on a board the size of a county. Like the MINI ads say, it's all actual size.

There are any number of good reasons your MINI is the perfect car for road rally. Tops on the list is that the MINI is fun to drive—and rally is all about great roads and fun driving. The quick steering and nimble handling of the MINI make it a fun car capable of maintaining even the most optimistic average speeds. Another bonus is that the odometer and speedometer are conveniently located in the center of the dash where the navigator can get at them easily.

Conversely, road rally is perfect for all MINI owners because you don't need sticky tires, coil-over suspension, or anything other than a reliable ride to participate. Cooper owners can do just as well as those

From time to time in a rally, there is a checkpoint where the organizers check your time. Teams receive penalty points for being early or late to a checkpoint, and everyone's trying to get the elusive "zero" score.

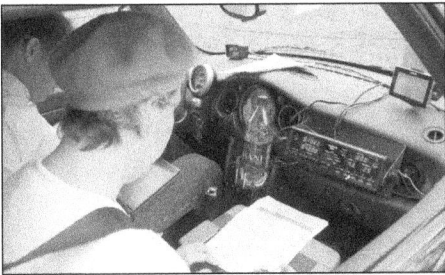

Here Renee and Marinus are working through a set of TSD rally instructions so they understand the route. You can see the rally computer and GPS that tells them how they're doing with their average speeds.

Renee and Marinus Damm drive their 2006 JCW on a rally through the Oregon countryside. Rally is a great couples activity, provided you can disagree without fighting!

with a JCW or Cooper S, because the goal is not to be fast, but rather to be accurate. The other benefit to working with a completely factory-stock car in rally is that you don't have to spend a dime beyond the cost of gasoline for the drive and about $20 for the entry fee.

Marinus and Renee Damm have rallied their 2006 Cooper S JCW all over the Pacific Northwest. "Rallying calls for all of the MINI's best skills: quick throttle response, precise steering, reassuring braking, and cheerfulness," says Marinus.

The Damms recently took part in their first SCCA national championship road rally event, driving their MINI to a respectable finish. "Our MINI keeps to the average speed better than any other vehicle we've rallied in. A big part of that is the Cooper S cornering ability; you just don't need to drop as much speed for a corner, so in turn you don't have to compensate on the straights," Marinus says.

Virtually any club can organize a rally. The rules are mostly the same wherever you go, so finding a set of basic rules to work from is easy. For a good first event, adopt some basic rally rules, then take the club's favorite backroads tour and measure it carefully. Your rally crew won't need more than some synchronized stopwatches and paper to make it work.

Alternately, you can find another local club that already organizes rallies. Older established marque clubs such as Alfa Romeo or MG clubs are good bets. Many SCCA chapters and local, generalsports car clubs also put on rallies. Most rallying clubs will be more than happy to share their events and their expertise to help grow the sport. The Internet is your friend when searching for rally events to enter or experienced rallyists to help you get started.

If the idea of timed events seems like more complication than you want to tackle, many clubs hold "Gimmick" rallies. In this type of event, you can challenge contestants to correctly identify signs, collect playing cards as in a poker run, or just follow an especially difficult route.

Last, consider starting a rally event at your local MINI dealer or aftermarket shop. They'll be happy to help out. But make sure you end it at a fun restaurant. After a rally, your club will be noisy—overflowing with tall tales and enthusiastic laughter. And that's really the best part of a good rally.

Rallycross

A rallycross takes place on a large grass or dirt field, with a course set up using traffic cones. Cars are timed as they drive the course as fast as possible, as in an autocross. In the limited-traction environment, especially after the first few cars have torn up the dirt some, you can get a taste of performance rally in your street car. The MINI is not a tremendously popular car in rallycross, but it can be competitive.

Paul Eklund owns Primitive Racing Enterprises, which makes rally-oriented aftermarket parts, and he runs the West Coast's only performance rally school. "The typical rallycrosser should be looking at underbody protection first—suspension strengthening, safety harnesses, helmets, and possibly tires for their first modifications, depending on what class they plan to run in," Eklund says.

Your first investment in rallycross should be a skidplate. Most courses are not perfectly smooth and ruts can develop in tight corners, so something other than a flimsy bit of plastic is recommended under the oil pan and exhaust headers. The only known manufacturers of MINI skid plates are in Europe, so you'll likely have to fabricate your own plate or pay shipping costs.

Another good choice for an early modification is a front strut tower bar. This bolt-on piece adds rigidity to the front of the car and helps keep the front suspension in its place over rough terrain and jumps. Competitors may also choose to combine a set of upgraded braided-stainless brake lines with a good brake fluid such as Motul or Wilwood 600+, and brake pads like the PBR Delux. Brake pads that heat quickly (organic and delux compounds) are considered better than full metallic or ceramic on short but intense rallycross courses.

"For serious competitors, I recommend changing struts to coil-over adjustable struts with some slightly taller/stiffer springs. This allows the car to be tuned for each rallycross course. I usually recommend setting full soft in the front and then dialing up the rear adjustment until the desired oversteer is generated," Eklund says.

Tires and wheels are as important in rallycross as in any other form of competition. "If you stay with stock 16-inch wheels, then Cooper Tire has a 205/55-16 WeatherMaster that fits well," Eklund says.

The attraction of rallycross is similar to autocross: You can start with your street-stock car, and add performance as your budget and your desires dictate.

Stage Rally

Stage rally is also known as Pro-Rally, ClubRally, Performance Rally, and Rally Racing. By any name, stage rally is the world's oldest motor sport.

In the most basic sense, a stage rally is a race from one place to another—not around a race track in circles, but over real roads with real hazards. In stage rally, the object is to drive the fastest time on a closed road, usually a gravel or dirt road. Over the course of a rally, 10 to 20 timed racing "stages" are raced, and the team with the lowest cumulative time wins.

Unlike any other type of car racing, rally teams must face a "track" that is not known in advance, and which consists of rugged unpaved roads of gravel, mud, or snow. Because of the unpredictable nature of the race, two people are needed to drive a rally car. The driver focuses on keeping the car on the road and going fast, while the co-driver reads the road ahead from a route book. Frequently, the co-driver doubles as a riding mechanic.

Stage rally attracts some of the best drivers in the world, because the challenge of rally is not simply to drive fast, but to do so on unknown roads with limited traction. Racing full speed on gravel roads requires courage, teamwork, an incredibly tough vehicle, and a sideways-through-the-corners driving style that is thrilling to watch.

The MINI has a great history in stage rally, notably winning the 1964, 1965, and 1967 runnings of the Monte Carlo Rally. The 2004 MC40 special edition commemorates this history. The hardy little car finished first in 1966 as well, but FIA

When you're ready for the ultimate motorsport, watch rally racing. Driving all-out on gravel roads takes skill and courage. The MINI's short wheelbase makes it eager to turn, and it's a popular rally car in Europe. (Photo courtesy of Doug Berger)

officials disqualified the MINIs based on their headlights in one of the most controversial decisions in the history of motorsports.

Car Show Competition

On the other side of the universe from racing is the car show circuit. Building up your car and then showing it can be fun—if you're proud of your work and you want to share it with others. A judged show can also be humiliating, so toughen-up your ego before you enter.

Building a car for show is more art than science, and while performance counts, it's not the whole game by a long mile. Aesthetics and style count just as much, if not more—you're completely free to express your vision and put it out there for everyone to see.

But don't make the mistake of thinking that building a show car is easier or cheaper than building a race car; it's neither. You have to please some of the toughest critics in the

You can go wild with your interior—an awesome overkill stereo is just the beginning.

business, not just go faster than some other guy.

Car show competition is about imagination, style, and execution. Unless the show has a live racing component, your car's real-world performance is measured by what's on the little sign you put in front of your display. That being said, judges like to see a balanced, well-planned car that is likely to be as good as your dyno sheet says it is.

"What wins the most points with judges, besides cleanliness, is uniqueness and completeness," says show car expert Armin Ausejo. "A car that simply has the most expensive parts that money can buy is not going to win by default."

Winning show cars have tasteful modifications in all areas: engine, suspension, wheels, brakes, bodywork, and interior. And the touches that put a car out in front of the others are always in the details. When you've attended carefully to the back side of your wheels, the inside of your exhaust tip, and the underside of your dashboard, you'll have a car that can compete.

"A car that may not have the most expensive parts, but that has a unique look and a complete package will easily win most, if not all, of the time," Ausejo says.

Approach a car show as a chance to display what you've done and get ideas for what to do next. If you leave your ego at home, you can have a good time no matter what the judges think. Some people who come to the show will like your car best, and they'll be thrilled to talk to you about your car just because it's there.

What's a MINI trunk without two television screens, several subwoofers, and custom fiberglass enclosures? He may win awards, but where does he put his groceries?

Finally, add extreme touches to really put your show car over the top with the judges. Believe it or not, those lambo-style door kits are not all that hard to install.

Rallying the MINI Cooper

In Europe, the new MINI is a popular rally vehicle, but in North America, there's been only one MINI in rally racing. Twin brothers Eugene and Felix Wong rallied a 2002 Cooper for several years in the Production class.

Production rally cars are not allowed to make any major performance modifications to the engine, but all rally cars are allowed a full replacement suspension for strength. The Wongs' rally MINI was sponsored by MINI Mania and Cascade Autosport, and outfitted as follows:
- Bilstein rally suspension
- MINI Mania cat-back exhaust
- MINI Mania braided-steel brake lines
- Michelin L81 gravel tires
- Terratrip rally computer
- Custom roll cage
- 3/8-inch aluminum skid plate

Twin brothers Felix and Eugene Wong raced this R50 MINI Cooper in performance rally for a few years. Doesn't it look like a blast? (Photo courtesy Doug Berger)

FINAL BUILD SHEETS

Project R53

- Alta R53 Cold-Air Intake
- Madness 15-Percent-Reduction Supercharger Pulley
- Magnaflow Cat-Back Exhaust
- MSD Coil and Ignition Wires
- Craven Speed Short Shifter & Cup
- Craven Speed E-Brake Handle
- PROMINI Boost and Oil Pressure Gauges
- Alta 19-mm Rear Sway Bar
- Mania Precision Steering Amplifier
- Texas Speedwerks Springs
- Madness Strut Tower Reinforcements
- Madness Poly Suspension Bushings
- PROMINI 15-mm Wheel Spacers
- PROMINI Extra-Long Lug Studs
- Brake Man 12.19-inch Front Brake Kit
- Brake Man Revolution Rear Brake Rotors
- Brake Man Stainless Brake Lines
- Brake Man #82 Pads

Project R56

- DDM Works Cold-Air Intake
- Madness JCW Challenge-Spec Turbo
- Madness ECU Reflash
- Borla Cat-Back Exhaust
- Madness Springs
- Madness 22-mm Rear Sway Bar
- PIAA Wheels

SOURCE GUIDE

MINI Parts Retailers

www.mini-madness.com
Mini-Madness

www.minimania.com
Mini Mania (parts for both original and new Minis)

www.altaperformance.com
Alta Performance

www.promini.com
PROMINI

www.m7tuning.com
M7 Tuning

www.ddmworks.com
DDMWorks

www.cravenspeed.com
Craven Speed

www.dinancars.com
Dinan BMW and MINI

www.revolutionmini.com
Revolution MINI Works

www.magnaflow.com
Magnaflow Exhaust Products

www.txwerks.com
Texas Speedwerks

www.quaife.co.uk
Quaife Engineering, limited slip differentials

www.safedrives.com
SafeDrives driving safety equipment

MINI Owner Forums

www.northamericanmotoring.com
U.S. MINI forum

www.mini2.com
European MINI forum

www.miniforum.com
MINI forum

www.totalmini.com
European MINI forum

Other Useful Sites

www.realoem.com
This site has a complete catalog of all available MINI parts. Just select your specific model and date of manufacture for a complete parts list, with diagrams.

www.gomotoring.com
The official site of MC2 Magazine

www.motoringfile.com
MINI Cooper News and Opinion

www.forcedperformance.com
Great information on turbochargers

www.tsdroadrally.com
Everything about Time-Speed-Distance Rally

More great titles available from CarTech®...

S-A DESIGN

Super Tuning & Modifying Holley Carburetors — Perf, street and off-road applications. *(SA08)*

Custom Painting — Gives you an overview of the broad spectrum of custom painting types and techniques. *(SA10)*

Street Supercharging, A Complete Guide to — Bolt-on buying, installing and tuning blowers. *(SA17)*

Engine Blueprinting — Using tools, block selection & prep, crank mods, pistons, heads, cams & more! *(SA21)*

David Vizard's How to Build Horsepower — Building horsepower in any engine. *(SA24)*

Chevrolet Small-Block Parts Interchange Manual — Selecting & swapping high-perf. small-block parts. *(SA55)*

High-Performance Ford Engine Parts Interchange — Selecting & swapping big- and small-block Ford parts. *(SA56)*

How To Build Max Perf Chevy Small-Blocks on a Budget — Would you believe 600 hp for $3000? *(SA57)*

How To Build Max Performance Ford V-8s on a Budget — Dyno-tested engine builds for big- & small-blocks. *(SA69)*

How To Build Max-Perf Pontiac V8s — Mild perf apps to all-out performance build-ups. *(SA78)*

How To Build High-Performance Ignition Systems — Guide to understanding auto ignition systems. *(SA79)*

How To Build Max Perf 4.6 Liter Ford Engines — Building & modifying Ford's 2- & 4-valve 4.6/5.4 liter engines. *(SA82)*

How To Build Big-Inch Ford Small-Blocks — Add cubic inches without the hassle of switching to a big-block. *(SA85)*

How To Build High-Perf Chevy LS1/LS6 Engines — Modifying and tuning Gen-III engines for GM cars and trucks. *(SA86)*

How To Build Big-Inch Chevy Small-Blocks — Get the additional torque & horsepower of a big-block. *(SA87)*

Honda Engine Swaps — Step-by-step instructions for all major tasks involved in engine swapping. *(SA93)*

How to Build High-Performance Chevy Small-Block Cams/Valvetrains — Camshaft & valvetrain function, selection, performance, and design. *(SA105)*

High-Performance Jeep Cherokee XJ Builder's Guide 1984–2001 — Build a useful Cherokee for mountains, the mud, the desert, the street, and more. *(SA109)*

How to Build and Modify Rochester Quadrajet Carburetors — Selecting, rebuilding, and modifying the Quadrajet Carburetors. *(SA113)*

Rebuilding the Small-Block Chevy: Step-by-Step Videobook — 160-pg book plus 2-hour DVD show you how to build a street or racing small-block Chevy. *(SA116)*

How to Paint Your Car on a Budget — Everything you need to know to get a great-looking coat of paint and save money. *(SA117)*

How to Drift: The Art of Oversteer — This comprehensive guide to drifting covers both driving techniques and car setup. *(SA118)*

Turbo: Real World High-Performance Turbocharger Systems — Turbo is the most practical book for enthusiasts who want to make more horsepower. Foreword by Gale Banks. *(SA123)*

High-Performance Chevy Small-Block Cylinder Heads — Learn how to make the most power with this popular modification on your small-block Chevy. *(SA125)*

High Performance Brake Systems — Design, selection, and installation of brake systems for Musclecars, Hot Rods, Imports, Modern Era cars and more. *(SA126)*

High Performance C5 Corvette Builder's Guide — Improve the looks, handling and performance of your Corvette C5. *(SA127)*

High Performance Diesel Builder's Guide — The definitive guide to getting maximum performance out of your diesel engine. *(SA129)*

How to Rebuild & Modify Carter/Edelbrock Carbs — The only source for information on rebuilding and tuning these popular carburetors. *(SA130)*

Building Honda K-Series Engine Performance — The first book on the market dedicated exclusively to the Honda K series engine. *(SA134)*

Engine Management-Advanced Tuning — Take your fuel injection and tuning knowledge to the next level. *(SA135)*

How to Drag Race — Car setup, beginning and advanced techniques for bracket racing and pro classes, racing science and math, and more. *(SA136)*

4x4 Suspension Handbook — Includes suspension basics & theory, advanced/high-performance suspension and lift systems, axles, how-to installations, and more. *(SA137)*

GM Automatic Overdrive Transmission Builder's and Swapper's Guide — Learn to build a bulletproof tranny and how to swap it into an older chassis as well. *(SA140)*

High-Performance Subaru Builder's Guide — Subarus are the hottest compacts on the street. Make yours even hotter. *(SA141)*

How to Build Max-Performance Mitsubishi 4G63t Engines — Covers every system and component of the engine, including a complete history. *(SA148)*

How to Swap GM LS-Series Engines Into Almost Anything — Includes a historical review and detailed information so you can select and fit the best LS engine. *(SA156)*

How to Autocross — Covers basic to more advanced modifications that go beyond the stock classes. *(SA158)*

Designing & Tuning High-Performance Fuel Injection Systems — Complete guide to tuning aftermarket standalone systems. *(SA161)*

Design & Install In Car Entertainment Systems — The latest and greatest electronic systems, both audio and video. *(SA163)*

How to Build Max-Performance Hemi Engines — Build the biggest baddest vintage Hemi. *(SA164)*

How to Digitally Photograph Cars — Learn all the modern techniques and post processing too. *(SA168)*

High-Performance Differentials, Axles, & Drivelines — Must have book for anyone thinking about setting up a performance differential. *(SA170)*

How To Build Max-Performance Mopar Big Blocks — Build the baddest wedge Mopar on the block. *(SA171)*

How to Build Max-Performance Oldsmobile V-8s — Make your Oldsmobile keep up with the pack. *(SA172)*

Automotive Diagnostic Systems: Understanding OBD-I & OBD II — Learn how modern diagnostic systems work. *(SA174)*

How to Make Your Muscle Car Handle — Upgrade your muscle car suspension to modern standards. *(SA175)*

Full-Size Fords 1955–1970 — A complete color history of full-sized fords. *(SA176)*

Rebuilding Any Automotive Engine: Step-by-Step Videobook — Rebuild any engine with this book DVD combo. DVD is over 3 hours long! *(SA179)*

How to Supercharge & Turbocharge GM LS-Series Engines — Boost the power of today's most popular engine. *(SA180)*

The New Mini Performance Handbook — All the performance tricks for your new Mini. *(SA182)*

How to Build Max-Performance Ford FE Engines — Finally, performance tricks for the FE junkie. *(SA183)*

Builder's Guide to Hot Rod Chassis & Suspension — Ultimate guide to Hot Rod Suspensions. *(SA185)*

How to Build Altered Wheelbase Cars — Build a wild altered car. Complete history too! *(SA189)*

How to Build Period Correct Hot Rods — Build a hot rod true to your favorite period. *(SA192)*

Automotive Sheet Metal Forming & Fabrication — Create and fabricate your own metalwork. *(SA196)*

How to Build Max-Performance Chevy Big Block on a Budget — New big-block book from the master, David Vizard. *(SA198)*

How to Build Big-Inch GM LS-Series Engines — Get more power through displacement from your LS. *(SA203)*

Performance Automotive Engine Math — All the formulas and facts you will ever need. *(SA204)*

How to Design, Build & Equip Your Automotive Workshop on a Budget — Working man's guide to building a great work space. *(SA207)*

Automotive Electrical Performance Projects — Featuring the most popular electrical mods today. *(SA209)*

How to Port Cylinder Heads — Vizard shares his cylinder head secrets. *(SA215)*

S-A DESIGN RESTORATION SERIES

How to Restore Your Mustang 1964 1/2–1973 — Step-by-step restoration for your classic Mustang. *(SA165)*

Muscle Car Interior Restoration Guide — Make your interior look and smell new again. Includes dash restoration. *(SA167)*

How to Restore Your Camaro 1967–1969 — Step-by-step restoration of your 1st gen Camaro. *(SA178)*

S-A DESIGN WORKBENCH® SERIES

Workbench® Series books feature step by step instruction with hundreds of color photos for stock rebuilds and automotive repair.

How To Rebuild the Small-Block Chevrolet — *(SA26)*
How to Rebuild the Small-Block Ford — *(SA102)*
How to Rebuild & Modify High-Performance Manual Transmissions — *(SA103)*
How to Rebuild the Big-Block Chevrolet — *(SA142)*
How to Rebuild the Small-Block Mopar — *(SA143)*
How to Rebuild GM LS-Series Engines — *(SA147)*
How to Rebuild Any Automotive Engine — *(SA151)*
How to Rebuild Honda B-Series Engines — *(SA154)*
How to Rebuild the 4.6/5.4 Liter Ford — *(SA155)*
Automotive Welding: A Practical Guide — *(SA159)*
Automotive Wiring and Electrical Systems — *(SA160)*
How to Rebuild Big-Block Ford Engines — *(SA162)*
Automotive Bodywork & Rust Repair — *(SA166)*
How To Rebuild & Modify GM Turbo 400 Transmissions — *(SA186)*
How to Rebuild Pontiac V-8s — *(SA200)*

HISTORIES AND PERSONALITIES

Quarter-Mile Chaos — Rare & stunning photos of terrifying fires, explosions, and crashes in drag racing's golden age. *(CT425)*

Fuelies: Fuel Injected Corvettes 1957–1965 — The first Corvette book to focus specifically on the fuel injected cars, which are among the most collectible. *(CT452)*

Slingshot Spectacular: Front-Engine Dragster Era — Relive the golden age of front engine dragsters in this photo packed trip down memory lane. *(CT464)*

Chrysler Concept Cars 1940–1970 — Fascinating look at the concept cars created by Chrysler during this golden age of the automotive industry. *(CT470)*

Fuel Altereds Forever — Includes more than 250 photos of the most popular drivers and racecars from the Fuel Altered class. *(CT475)*

Yenko — Complete and thorough story of the man, his business and his legendary cars. *(CT485)*

Lost Hot Rods — Great Hot Rods from the past rediscovered. *(CT487)*

Grumpy's Toys — A collection of Grumpy's greats. *(CT489)*

Woodward Avenue: Cruising the Legendary — Revisit the glory days of Woodward! *(CT491)*

Rusted Muscle — A collection of junkyard muscle cars. *(CT492)*

America's Coolest Station Wagons — Wagons are cooler than they ever have been. *(CT493)*

Super Stock — A paperback version of a classic best seller. *(CT495)*

Rusty Pickups: American Workhorses Put to Pasture — Cool collection of old trucks and ads too! *(CT496)*

Jerry Heasley's Rare Finds — Great collection of Heasley's best finds. *(CT497)*

Street Sleepers: The Art of the Deceptively Fast Car — Stealth, horsepower, what's not to love? *(CT498)*

Ed 'Big Daddy' Roth — Paperback reprint of a classic best seller. *(CT500)*

Car Spy: Secret Cars Exposed by the Industry's Most Notorious Photographer — Cool behind-the-scenes stories spanning 40 years. *(CT502)*

CarTech®, Inc. 39966 Grand Ave., North Branch, MN 55056. Ph: 800-551-4754 or 651-277-1200 • Fax: 651-277-1203
Brooklands Books Ltd., PO Box 146 Cobham, Surrey KT11 1LG, England. Ph: 01932 865051 • Fax 01932 868803
Brooklands Books Aus., 3/37-39 Green Street, Banksmeadow, NSW 2019, Australia. Ph: 2 9695 7055 • Fax 2 9695 7355

Visit us online at www.cartechbooks.com for more info!

More Information for Your Project ...

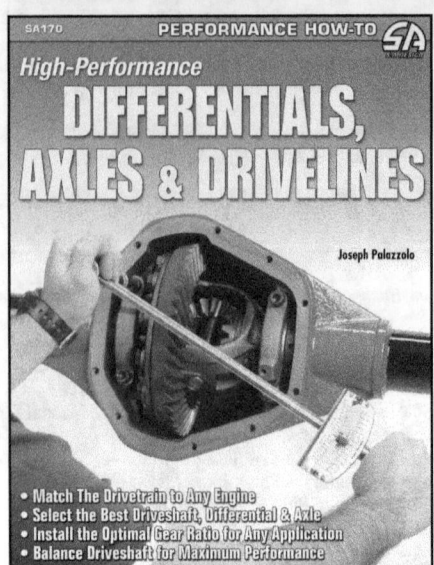

HIGH-PERFORMANCE DIFFERENTIALS, AXELS & DRIVELINES *by Joseph Palazzolo* This book covers everything you need to know about selecting the most desirable gear ratio, rebuilding differentials and other driveline components, and matching driveline components to engine power output. Learn how to set up a limited-slip differential, install high-performance axle shafts, swap out differential gears, and select products for the driveline. This book explains rear differential basics, rear differential housings, rebuilding open rear differentials, limited-slip differentials, and factory differentials. Ring and pinion gears, axle housings, axle shafts, driveshafts, and U-joints are also covered. Softbound, 8-1/2 x 11 inches, 144 pages, approx. 400 color photos. **Item #SA170**

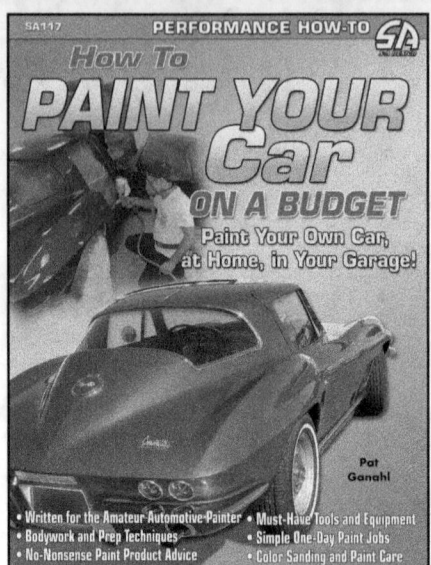

HOW TO PAINT YOUR CAR ON A BUDGET *by Pat Ganahl* If your car needs new paint, or even just a touch-up, the cost involved in getting a professional job can be more than you bargained for. In this book, author Pat Ganahl unveils dozens of secrets that will help anyone paint their own car. From simple scuff-and-squirt jobs to full-on, door-jambs-and-everything paint jobs, Ganahl covers everything you need to know to get a great-looking coat of paint on your car and save lots of money in the process. Covers painting equipment, the ins and outs of prep, masking, painting and sanding products and techniques, and real-world advice on how to budget wisely when painting your own car. Softbound, 8-1/2 x 11 inches, 128 pages, approx. 400 color photos. **Item #SA117**

THE STEP-BY-STEP GUIDE TO ENGINE BLUEPRINTING *by Rick Voegelin* this book is simply the best book available on basic engine preparation for street or racing. Rick Voegelin's writing and wrenching skills put this book in a class by itself. Includes pro's secrets of using tools, selecting and preparing blocks, cranks, rods, pistons, cylinder heads, selecting cams and valvetrain components, balancing and assembly tips, plus worksheets for your engine projects, and much more! Softbound, 8-1/2 x 11 inches, 128 pages, over 400 b/w photos. **Item #SA21**

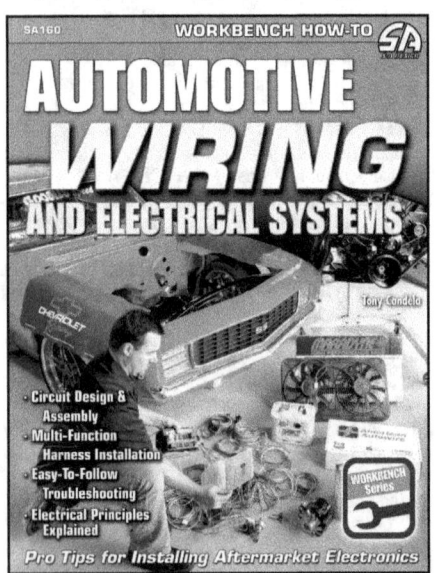

AUTOMOTIVE WIRING AND ELECTRICAL SYSTEMS *by Tony Candela* This book is the perfect book to unshroud the mysteries of automotive electrics and electronic systems. The basics of electrical principles, including voltage, amperage, resistance, and Ohm's law, are revealed in clear and concise detail, so the enthusiast understands what these mean in the construction and repair of automotive electrical circuits. Softbound, 8-1/2 x 11 inches, 144 pages, approx. 350 color photos. **Item #SA160**

AUTOMOTIVE BODYWORK AND RUST REPAIR *by Matt Joseph* This book shows you the ins and out of tackling both simple and difficult rust and metalwork projects. This book teaches you how to select the proper tools for the job, common-sense approaches to the task ahead of you, preparing and cleaning sheet metal, section fabrications and repair patches, welding options such as gas and electric, forming, fitting and smoothing, cutting metal, final metal finishing including filling and sanding, the secrets of lead filling, making panels fit properly, and more. Softbound, 8-1/2 x 11 inches, 160 pages, 400 color photos. **Item #SA166**

PERFORMANCE AUTOMOTIVE ENGINE MATH *by John Baechtel* When designing or building an automotive engine for improved performance, it's all about the math. From measuring the engine's internal capacities to determine compression ratio to developing the optimal camshaft lift, duration, and overlap specifications, the use of proven math is the only way to design an effective high performance automotive powerplant. This book walks readers through the wide range of dimensions to be measured and formulas used to design and develop powerful engines. Includes reviews the proper tools and measurement techniques, and carefully defines the procedures and equations used in engineering high efficiency and high rpm engines. Softbound, 8.5 x 11 inches, 160 pages, 350 photos. **Item #SA204**

www.cartechbooks.com or 1-800-551-4754